OUT OF
MY LEAGUE

OUT OF MY LEAGUE

A ROOKIE'S SURVIVAL IN THE BIGS

DIRK HAYHURST

CITADEL PRESS
Kensington Publishing Corp.
www.kensingtonbooks.com

CITADEL PRESS BOOKS are published by

Kensington Publishing Corp.
119 West 40th Street
New York, NY 10018

Copyright © 2012 Dirk Hayhurst

All Kensington titles, imprints, and distributed lines are available at special quantity discounts for bulk purchases for sales promotions, premiums, fund-raising, educational, or institutional use.

Special book excerpts or customized printings can also be created to fit specific needs. For details, write or phone the office of the Kensington special sales manager: Kensington Publishing Corp., 119 West 40th Street, New York, NY 10018, attn: Special Sales Department; phone 1-800-221-2647.

CITADEL PRESS and the Citadel logo are
Reg. U.S. Pat. & TM Off.

First printing: March 2012

10 9 8 7 6 5 4 3 2 1

Printed in the United States of America

CIP data is available.

ISBN-13: 978-0-8065-3485-5
ISBN-10: 0-8065-3485-0

With love,
I dedicate this book to my mother and father,
for showing me the right path to walk in life.

And to my dearest Bonnie,
for agreeing to walk the rest of it with me.

A NOTE FROM THE AUTHOR

Of all the memories I have from my playing career, the day I told my teammates I was writing a book shall forever be one of the most vivid. This should come as no surprise since people often remember near-death experiences with uncanny accuracy. When I made it public I was authoring a book about life inside the game, I didn't expect anyone to throw a party for me, but I also didn't expect to be told it would cost me my career or, as some players promised me should they end up in the book, my life.

As the pages of *The Bullpen Gospels* came together, my world got a lot quieter. Lively conversations stopped instantly when I came into the room. Friends prefaced chats with, "This doesn't go in the book, okay?" Management monitored me with a paranoid eye, choosing criticisms more delicately for fear that harsh words might get them referenced in an unflattering way. Despite how many times I promised them I wasn't out to get anyone, it never seemed to compute. As far as they were concerned, *The Bullpen Gospels* was going to be another exposé diatribe fueled by destroyed reputations in its race to make a buck.

I'm pleased to report I'm still alive and, obviously, still writing. This is so only because I kept my promise: I didn't hurt my teammates. This promise I shall keep once again.

Let it be known that this book's purpose is to entertain, not to name names; pull the cover off the bare ass of drug use; show cheaters, adulterers, or tax dodgers; or do any other whistle-blowing. If you are looking for someone's dirty laundry, you won't find it here. Names have been changed at the request of some players and at my discretion, to give them more of a character feel as well as to protect identity. Some characters within are composites blended together for ease of reading. While everything in this work is based on actual occurrences, I have attempted to conceal identities for the benefit of those who don't want to deal with any extra drama this book may bring their way. Mind you, I was a teammate before I tried my hand at writing, and I hope to be one long after this book is published.

However, if there is one thing I've learned since my first book, it's that sometimes the things we think matter most in this world turn out to be rather expendable and disappointing, while sometimes the things we take for granted are absolutely priceless, and that is what this story is all about.

ACKNOWLEDGMENTS

I've always believed that a wise man makes friends with people smarter than himself. With that in mind, I would like to extend a special thank-you to four very gracious, patient, and incredibly intelligent gentlemen, without whose help I would not have been able to do any of this writerly stuff.

Steve, Keith, Richard, and Jason: Thank you for putting up with me long enough for me to be able to claim importance by association.

Chapter One

"It's dead, Dirk," she said, without even so much as a concerned look from the wheel as we drove. "You're just going to have to deal with it."

I dealt with her tactfully delivered news by letting my head fall into the passenger side window glass with a disparaging *thunk*. What the hell was I going to do for transportation now?

"Cars do that, honey, they just die," she added.

"Remind me to never leave you with a puppy," I said.

"Oh, for Christ's sake, it's a car. There are others out there."

"That car and I had memories!"

"I don't know what you want me tell you." She accelerated our currently living car onto the freeway as she spoke, heading south from the Akron-Canton Airport. "Your dad thought it was the fuel injectors or something. I think it just rusted through and croaked. Either way it would have cost more than what you paid for it to fix. Your dad sold it for scrap already."

"You sold my car!"

"It was dead! And your grandma said she could smell leaking gas. She demanded we remove it from her house, called every day until we did. Said it was going to blow up and kill her."

"Was it leaking gas?" I could envision my deranged grandmother crawling beneath my car punching holes in the gas tank to spite me. She doubled as my landlord during the off-season and used some Gestapo-style tactics to get me to do her bidding, threatening me with everything from eviction to prosecution. I wouldn't put it past her to practice sabotage.

"I don't know, that's what she said. We didn't check," said my mother.

"How could you not check?" I threw my hands up at the injustice.

"It doesn't matter! It's gone now. Dad got $150, since the tires were still good."

"My poor car . . ." I imagined it being obediently led to a dark scrap yard someplace, getting patted on the hood one last time, then rolled into a vicious crushing machine while a fat man with a cigar laughed and counted out a wad of money with my grandma. "You let it die," I said to my mother. "I asked you to keep it safe for me and you got it killed. You're a car *murderer!*"

Mom, taking her eyes from the road to look at me for the first time in our conversation, simply said, "I'm glad you're home, sweetheart. Now shut up."

When I got off the plane that brought me home from the 2007 Double A championship season, it was as if the whole thing never happened. There was no ticker-tape parade. No flashbulbs or requests for autographs. No screaming fans, endorsement deals, or bonus paychecks. The big leagues didn't call and request my immediate promotion, and I wasn't mentioned on ESPN. There was just Mom, waiting impatiently for me in her car so she could taxi me home before she was late for work.

One may wonder how the elation that comes with jumping onto a pile of screaming teammates and uncorking fountains of Champagne to celebrate ultimate victory can fade away so quickly. That's because minor league championships are great, but they are still minor league. Once all the champagne is sprayed, the pictures are taken, and everyone's had a chance to make out with the trophy, it doesn't mean much. I was part of an event I could always be proud of, and Lord knows, winning feels a whole lot better than losing, but in the grand scheme of the minor league economy, my name in a record book was just that. I was still going to be living the next six months on my grandma's floor, looking for another source of income, getting ready for a new season while wondering what being a Double A champion really meant.

Such is the lot of a career minor league baseball player, because, even at its best, minor league baseball struggles to translate into a better quality of real-world life. Sure, there are wonderful moments like winning, the thrill of competition, and the joy of watching teammates twenty beers deep get really emotional about how much they love you at a championship party. You get to put on the jersey, lace up the spikes, and listen to John Fogerty croon out "Centerfield" all summer long. But the season always ends, for better or for worse, and that's when you find yourself face-to-face with a reality that tells you your car is pushing up daisies and your dad only got $150 for its tires.

Life seems so blissful when all you have to do is focus on the next pitch—assuming that next pitch doesn't get hit over the fence. When you are on field, living in the moment, it's easy to think all that matters is the here and now. Yet, when the pitching is done, the truth is revealed: league title or total defeat, the clock is always ticking, waiting for you to break into the big time or settle up the debt you made trying to get there. I had showered three times since my San Antonio Missions brethren and I celebrated our championship by soaking one another in cheap Champagne, but nothing got me clean like the cold, sobering splash of reality my mom gave me on the car ride home from the airport.

"So, do you think you're guaranteed a place on the team for next year?"

"I don't know, Mom." There was no way to know that.

"You don't think the championship made you more important to the club?"

"I don't know." Or that.

"Didn't they tell you what their plans are for you?"

"No." Or that.

"Did they tell you they couldn't have done it without you?"

"No."

"Well, what did they tell you?"

"Good job, we're proud of you. See you next year."

My mom paused in her onslaught of prying questions for a moment and then declared, "Well, that sucks."

"I thought it was all pretty cool until we started talking about it, actually."

"Oh. My. God. You are so depressing. You'd think you'd be happier after winning a championship. "

I caught myself before I could object to my mom's logic. Telling her she was doing that thing she does where she inadvertently sucks the pride from a situation wasn't going to work now since it hadn't worked during any of the other years I tried explaining it to her, so I said, "I'm just telling you what I know, Mom."

"This is why I read the Internet sites, you know. You never tell me anything."

"Whatever." I rolled my eyes.

"Fine, let's talk about something else then." My mom took a highway exit for the area of Canton where my grandma's house was located. "What are you going to do for a job?"

"I just got off the plane, Mom." And I was beginning to wonder if I could get back on it.

"I know, but you'll need a job if you want to get a car."

"I realize that."

"I suppose you can borrow your grandmother's car until you get one."

I deflated with a long, exasperated exhale at the thought of patrolling the streets in my grandmother's ark-like car-asaurous. It was a monster of steel and chrome that devoured economy parking like Tic Tacs and swilled down fuel like minor leaguers on cheap booze.

"Who do you have to impress? No one knows you're back," said my mom, noting my disgust.

"I have a date tomorrow."

"A girl!" she squealed. Meddling in the events of my baseball life was only secondary pleasure to the joy she took from meddling in my love life. "How is that even possible?"

"Thank you for being so confident in your son."

"I mean, how did you meet one from around here during the season? You've been gone all year."

"On eHarmony," I said.

"Oh, a technological romance." She nodded her head as if she thought this was what all the kids were doing these days. "What's her name?"

"Bonnie."

"Does she know you're a baseball player?"

"Yes."

"Did you tell her you sleep at your grandmother's yet?" My mom giggled.

"No, Mom."

"What do you think she'll say when you do?"

"I don't know."

"Is she a nice girl, I mean, not a stalker or something?"

"No, Mom, she's not a stalker."

"Where are you taking her out to?"

"I don't know yet."

"Well, if you need my advice, I'm always here." She smiled at me to let me know my questions were always welcome, though I knew I never had to ask her any to get her answers. "You can ask anything, honey, you know that. Even sex-related questions. I know you say you aren't having it, but you can still ask me if you're curious."

"Okay, Mom. That's enough."

"I think it would really help you relax if you did. You are so high-strung. Does Bonnie know how high-strung you are?"

"That's enough, now." I started humming something to tune her out.

"Has she had sex, or is she a religious type like you?"

"Okay, Mom, time for another subject change. How's Dad doing?"

My mom shut up at this. The glee of sucking details from me like some social vampire dissipated. "Don't ask," she said, looking back to the road.

"Why? What's wrong? I thought things were going well at home."

She said nothing.

Concerned, I turned to her, "Brak isn't drinking again, is he?"

"No, your brother kept his promise," said my mom. She looked like me trying to answer her questions.

"Then what is it?"

"We're here," she said, and spun the wheel.

My mom pulled the car into the driveway of my grandma's house and parked under the canopy of trees close to the garage. The leaves were turning in the autumn weather and had littered the driveway with reds and yellows. My grandma was vainly raking them up with a metal-fingered rake that scratched across the pavement of the drive. When we exited the car, I made my way over to my grandma and offered to hug her, which she accepted. It was a nice moment—maybe I was wrong to suspect her of punching holes in my deceased car's gas tank after all? When we finished our embrace, however, she thrust her rake at me and said, "Finish gathering up these leaves. When you're done, those stupid neighbors' dogs shit in my backyard again. The shovel is in the shed." Then she walked into the house.

"Well," said my mom. "Welcome home."

"Thanks." I said, holding the rake, which smelled faintly like gas.

"It's a place to live," said my mom with a shrug. "If you need anything, call me."

"I need a lot of things," I mumbled.

I unloaded my luggage, told my mom I loved her, then watched her pull out of the drive and make for work. I was home, if you could call it that, and I had a lot to figure out. I needed a job, transportation, a place to train, the name of a nice restaurant, and the courage to ask my grandmother if I could borrow her car. Yet, before all that could happen, I needed to finish raking the leaves from the driveway, then go shovel some dog shit.

Chapter Two

Women are the best way to ruin a perfectly good career, or so the baseball lifers are fond of saying. Women have a way of changing your priorities, pulling your mind from the field of play and placing it into confusion. After a woman enters the equation, they say, the next thing a player knows he's quit the game to hold her purse and fetch her lattes—or, in my case, clean lattes off his pants.

Though Bonnie would say her most vivid memory of our first date was when she saw me for the first time after months of chatting via an eHarmony matchup, mine was when she spilled hot coffee on my lap. Aside from forgetting how to grip cups, she was so nervous to meet me she nearly forgot who she was. She kept shoveling gum in her mouth for fear of bad breath and forgot where she parked. She was a train wreck, which ironically, I found incredibly attractive. I made her nervous, she confessed, because I was handsome. This flattering sincerity made the clumsiness easy to forget. That, and she was left-handed, which for the sake of any possible future baseball-playing Hayhurst progeny deserved at least one more chance.

The second date was much better than the first. That was when we discovered our chemistry. The real Bonnie came out, and she was a sweet and genuine woman with energy and charisma and all the other things I never would have suspected from a girl who couldn't remember where her car was in a lot that held only twenty. And she was beautiful. I don't know why I wasn't stunned by this on the first date, maybe it was because I was preoccupied with collateral damage, but I couldn't miss it the second time around. She wore a yellow sundress with beads and bangles and sandals. Her brown hair was still light from the summer sun, and her face had the slightest hint of freckles around soft brown eyes. She brought a guitar with her and taught me how to play a few chords, interlacing her fingers with my own across the fret board.

With everything we did, she had fun, like a child who treated life as an adventure. Being with her was addictive, and when she left me that night, I was sad to see her go.

In time, we were meeting nearly every night we could see each other. She lived in Cleveland and I in Canton, which presented logistical bridges that only love could cross. Love and a crap job working at a local Circuit City, that is. I couldn't drive my grandma's car forever, not with the way it swilled fuel. The dating economy demanded I make some investments if I wanted to keep up the relationship. I took the little minor league savings I had accrued, bought a used Corolla, and committed myself to working at Circuit City for the holiday season. It wasn't the most common thing to see a pro athlete do, but it was the only way I could keep the car gassed up, and dates paid for.

Ironically, of all the things that Bonnie liked about me, baseball wasn't one of them. It was a bonus, she said, like icing on a six-foot-two, dark-haired, blue-eyed, likes-long-walks-on-the-beach cake. We shared the same faith, which was big because she was worried about getting matched with an Internet-spawned psychopathic killing machine. I told her that, historically speaking, there have been several psychos who believed in Jesus, but she told me if I gave her any trouble she'd kick me in the crotch and run—she told me it was what Jesus would do.

Though not the key pillar of our relationship at first, whenever the question came up of how things would get paid for, or why I never invited Bonnie over to my residence, or why I worked at

Circuit City, the line always traced back to the same point: baseball. As things got more serious, the role baseball played in my life became more apparent to her, and to me. Everything I did, I did with the game in mind. It was my first love and it was a commitment I had to honor, hoping that Bonnie would understand. She did, or at least she did her best to look the part. She supported me and encouraged me, but people have a much easier time understanding stuff when you're right next to them explaining it. In two months' time I'd be gone, out chasing the dream of playing in the big leagues while Bonnie would still be here waiting on me. If it wasn't for the fact that it was so wonderful, I'd say it was unfortunate that Bonnie and I liked each other so much because no matter how good things were right now, there was no way she was going to avoid pain by being my girlfriend, or I by being her boyfriend.

Dating a baseball player is much more complicated than dating your average Joe, and dating me was more complicated still. I had baggage in the shape of a crazy old woman and a family with a past history of violence and alcohol abuse. Bonnie hadn't met any of them yet, but that was what today was supposed to be about: lunch with Grandma and coffee with my parents. I had resisted the idea of her meeting my family for as long as I could, but I knew, even from the short time we were with each other, that Bonnie and I would be heading toward bigger decisions. We didn't have a lot of time together, so she deserved to know what was ahead of her before committing to a year of holding her breath on her dreams while I chased mine.

The first major obstacle in front of any kind of relationship Bonnie and I might have was currently passed out in her recliner, head lolling sideways, dentures roaming freely about her gaping mouth while she sucked air. This was Bonnie's first official encounter with the eldest woman in my family, the same woman I called landlord, and it started to the soothing sound of a ninety-year-old with sleep apnea gasping for air, only to find it, then fart.

The television next to my grandma was tuned to Judge Judy with the volume cranked into the upper ranges. Still, Grandma snored away. There are only two types of show my grandma watches: programs that document stupid young people, and news about stupid young people being shot. To emphasize this point, in Grandma's hands lay a newspaper open to the obituary section. She enjoys seeing whom she's outlasted, crossing their name off a death list she keeps next to the framed family portrait, wherein some of her "less desirables" have been cut from the scene. Most days she watches Jerry Springer while reading her collection of Bible walk-throughs concerning the Apocalypse. She doesn't make it through the Bible or the programming before she falls asleep. For her, there is something irresistibly relaxing about watching sinners fight over trailer park politics while she reads God's comforting promises of roasting them in hell—her own variation on the modern bedtime story.

My grandma practices her "you hope I'm dead, but dead people don't fart in their sleep" impression pretty regularly these days, ever since I started dating Bonnie, actually. I used to think Grandma was tired because she went out late at night to feed, but I later discovered it was because Grandma liked to stay up and eavesdrop on my conversations with Bonnie.

Though they've never met, my grandma doesn't like Bonnie and she tells me so every time I leave the house with a smile on my face. According to my grandma's twisted algorithm of what makes a woman proper and respectable, Bonnie just doesn't add up. Grandma says a woman should never date a boy she met on the Internet; that makes her a stalker. She says a woman should never drive hours to see a boy; that makes her desperate. A woman should never talk to a boy after midnight; that makes her a whore. And above all, says my grandmother, a woman should never date a boy who doesn't make any money; that makes her stupid.

I firmly believed that if my grandma met Bonnie in person, she'd change her opinion. However, considering my grandma was also fond of listening to the counsel of imaginary people when rendering judgment, I decided her napping might not be a bad thing.

"Should we wake her?" asked Bonnie.

"No," I said.

"Are you sure?"

"Absolutely. If she's asleep every time you come over, I'll be perfectly fine with that," I said with a beaming smile of hope.

"I feel weird. I mean, look at her."

Grandma was drooling now.

"Don't feel bad," I said. "She'll wake up soon and then we'll do a quick, painless lunch. If she wonders what happened, I'll act like she was awake the whole time and just can't remember. I've done it before. Let's put these groceries on ice and make the most of our good luck."

Bonnie had brought the meal with her. A picnic in December, she called it. She even brought a bottle of wine to put the meal over the top. We put the picnic on hold, stuffing it into my grandmother's cemetery of a refrigerator to await its time. Then I playfully herded Bonnie toward my bedroom with tickle prods.

Aptly named, my bedroom was almost entirely occupied by the air mattress parked there. Since there was no room for chairs, Bonnie and I took a seat on the bed, which, being a giant inner tube of sorts, groaned and squealed like a pool toy when we plopped on it.

"Do you ever feel embarrassed by the fact that you are dating a guy who lives with his grandma?" I asked, looking around the room at the suitcase that served as my dresser and my travel companion, the card table I used as a desk, and the four feet of open space not occupied by a collection of my grandmother's antiquated heirlooms.

"No. And don't ever think it does," Bonnie said. "Besides, I still live with my parents."

I thought about her answer for a second. We were both stuck in that age of sacrificing independence for a chance to get a foothold in our dreams. Giving up some pride was par for the course. Bonnie had an amazing job as a music therapist working with people with special needs as well as with Alzheimer's patients, and was living at home so she could save money before moving out to start her own therapy practice. I was trying to survive long enough in baseball to wash up on the golden shore of the big leagues. Dream chasing; it made sense when you took time to explain it, yet when my eyes fell upon a picture of a little girl getting into a bathtub with her bare butt showing, which my grandmother had hung on one of the floral-papered walls a century ago, my determination waned.

"Nope," I said, "there is definitely something wrong with a guy who lives with his grandma at age twenty-seven. Besides, your parents are cool, and you're a girl. It's different for you. A man needs to be out on his own, it's a pride thing. Why do you think I always resisted the idea of you coming over here?"

"I love my parents and it's a good situation, but I'm twenty-eight, for crying out loud. I'd like to have my own life too."

"I know. I'm sorry," I said.

"It's okay." She looked up at the picture with me. "Though that *is* a little awkward. But, look, we'll have our own lives eventually. It's not like we're not successful in our work, right?"

"I'm so glad you don't know much about baseball," I said.

"Why is that?"

"So I don't have to explain how much of my life is 'what have you done for me lately?' "

"I think you're making this into a bigger deal than you need to."

I lay back on my bed with a sigh. "Maybe."

"For sure," said Bonnie. She didn't wait for me to counter her argument as she leapt on me. Soon we were giggling and tickling and smooching. We rolled around on my squeaky inner tube of a mattress, and when we came to a stop we were staring into each other's eyes in that special way that ensures girls love romantic comedies while men barf.

In that moment, I wanted to say something I'd been feeling since we started dating, like how I could see my future in her eyes, staring back at me like a promise in a life so full of fog and questions. I wanted to tell her I had big plans and I knew how they would all come together. I wanted to tell her so many things, but when I opened my mouth the door of my bedroom swung open and slammed into the wall with a loud bang—there she stood, risen from her slumber, the other woman in my life in all her terrible fury.

Chapter Three

Bonnie and I were lying on each other on my bed, completely clothed, including our shoes. Bonnie was so startled and embarrassed by the intrusion she rolled violently into the wall. I just covered my face with both hands and said, "Haven't you ever heard of knocking?"

"What's going on in here?" demanded my grandma in her raspy, undead voice.

"I'm sorry, I don't believe we've met, I'm—" Bonnie tried to introduce herself as she smoothed the excess embarrassment out of her clothes, but was cut off.

"Why is there wine in my house?" continued the inquisition. Grandma took no heed of Bonnie, but kept her eyes trained exclusively on me. It would be like her to investigate any changes in her kitchen before inquiring upon houseguests.

"Jesus gave it to me," I said, sitting up.

"Dirk!" Bonnie scolded me. Then, looking toward my grandmother, Bonnie continued, "I brought the wine, Mrs. Hayhurst. We were going to have it with this great meal I planned—"

"You're a drunk!" Grandma wailed, trampling right over Bonnie's confession. "Just another good-for-nothing Hayhurst drunk!" The way she locked on to me, you'd have thought she'd found a kilo of cocaine in the house, not a bottle of dessert wine.

"I've never been drunk in my life. Hell, I don't even like wine," I said.

Bonnie frowned at my response, I tried to stammer out an explanation about my developing a taste for finer beverages, but Grandma was back on me.

"That's what all the drunks say! All of the Hayhursts are drunks and liars. Just like your grandfather, the biggest liar of them all," she said, referencing the saintly and long-dead Mr. Hayhurst.

"What did Grandpa ever lie to you about?"

"He was having an affair on me!"

"Oh, for the love of God. Here we go again with the cheating stories!"

Bonnie looked back and forth between Grandma and me with a lost expression.

"He cheated on me all the time. That's how he got the gonorrhea."

"What? He never had gonorrhea."

"Oh yes, he did, he got it from the woman who sold food at the bowling alley."

"Ah, yes." I looked at Bonnie with a smirk. "The seductress of the bowling alley, singing her siren song between serving decaf and disinfecting shoes. Well, with charms like that you can hardly blame the man, right?"

Grandma burned me down with her eyes. "You're gonna get it too! You need to get back into church doing the things you're doing."

"And what things would those be?" I raised a cocky eyebrow.

"All this drinking and sex having. Booze and gonorrhea! I heard you two in here fooling around on that mattress. I saw what you were doing. I knew you were a liar about being a virgin. I've heard your phone calls. Ever since you two commenced to dating, you're always trying to get alone. Now you're in my house fulfilling your lusts! Well, I'm not going to allow it."

Bonnie's face became a sunset of embarrassment. I was just

stunned by it all. "You mean, you were faking sleep just so you could listen through my door?" I stammered at my grandmother. "You have, haven't you? You've been acting it up just to listen at my door."

"Fornicators!" she howled. Then, for the first time, she looked at Bonnie. "You should be ashamed of yourself. What kind of girl acts the way you do?"

"Okay, that's enough. Come on, Bonnie," I said, "we're leaving, mealtime at the asylum is cancelled." I took Bonnie by the hand and commanded my grandmother to dislodge herself from our path. We went into the kitchen and collected our things, including our bottle of Satan's Kool-Aid, all the while Grandma monitoring us as if we might steal from her. Then, as my hand hit the door handle to exit, Grandma said her good-byes like this: "What's the matter, have to take your whore someplace else to have sex with her?"

I froze. Maybe this person who read me bedtime stories, took me shopping for school clothes, and made me milkshakes as a boy did not say what I swore I heard, but Bonnie's eyes, wide as they were with shock, told the truth.

This was a test, I thought. I had a choice to make. Aside from her normal batch of insanity, Grandma was probably jealous that another woman had moved in on her man. She was cracking the whip over me, showing me who was the boss around here. She had the upper hand because if I blew up, she'd take away my "home," and she knew I knew it. If I lost my cool, I'd probably lose Bonnie too. I had to stay calm, be mature, let it go. I took a breath and turned the door handle. Everything would be all right. This was only a test.

"You need to take that whore back to the street corner you found her on!"

And this was a test I was going to fail.

"Bonnie, wait in the car," I said, as I directed my shell-shocked girlfriend out of the house and shut the door after her. When I turned to face my grandmother, she was wielding a broomstick with a queer smirk derived from finally getting control of her man. In turn, I held the wine bottle tightly and envisioned smashing it over the kitchen table and dueling Grandma with the jagged remainder. We stared each other down like gunfighters in an old Western, if old Westerns were rooms with linoleum floors and flower wallpapering.

"You planning to make your getaway on that?" I said, pointing at the broomstick.

"Oh, you shut up. You're no grandson of mine."

I strode before her, towering over her hunched, blue head. "Listen, you old battle-axe, I don't care about the crap you say about me because I know you live in a fantasy land and aren't to be taken seriously. But when you spew your poison on people I care about, you've crossed the line. Bonnie is a saint, and the first time you speak to her you call her a whore? What's wrong with you?"

"She's got a voice like a whining dog," mocked my grandmother, and then she began barking at me. I could only shake my head in disbelief as she yelped in imitation with her hands up like paws.

I raised my wine bottle like a club, indicating I'd like to knock the dentures out of her mouth.

"Go ahead, I'll have you put in jail!" promised Grandma.

"Really?" A beautiful thought came into my mind. "I don't think you've thought this through. If the police show up at this house, I'll be forced to explain that I live here to help you get around, because you are senile and incontinent and delusional." She choked up on her broom. "The family didn't want to see dear old granny go to a home, so I volunteered to look out for you. But now that you're violent, things have changed. I'll tell them how you routinely burst into my room to accuse dead relatives of having affairs."

"Bah," she snorted and waved me off like I was bluffing.

"Think about it. You think your testimony is going to convince the police?" I let the question hang over her head for a second. "It's my word against yours and the only other witness, a woman clinically trained to work with seniors who suffer from Alzheimer's and dementia, you just called a whore. So go ahead, Grandma, make my day."

"You can't talk to me that way, this is my house! I want you out, get out!"

Satisfied I'd made my point, I consented. Grandma wouldn't be insulting Bonnie anymore, not unless she wanted a visit from some gentlemen in white coats. I turned my back on her and headed for the exit.

My victory was short-lived, however, as I didn't make it two steps before I felt the rod of her broomstick crack me over the head.

"Have you lost your mind?" I said, turning to the old bag while rubbing my lumped skull.

"Someone needed to knock some sense into you!"

I fought the urge to club her over the head like a mole in a carnival game. She pulled her broom up and swung at me again, but I caught it. Holding on to the stick, I said, "I want you to know that one of these days I won't be at your mercy anymore. One of these days I won't need your sewing room floor just so I can chase baseball. One of these days I'll break free of here, and then what are you gonna do?"

"I'm better off without you!" she bellowed as she swung her broomstick free. She chased me from the house like she was a tribal warrior in a kitchen apron, waving her broom like a spear. I dove into Bonnie's car and we sped away, leaving Grandma to cut my face out of all the family pictures.

Chapter Four

At a four-way stop a few blocks down the street from my grandmother's house, I put the car into PARK. It was Bonnie's car, and considering what just happened, I wasn't sure if she wanted me to continue driving her someplace far away, or if she wanted me to get out and never speak to her again. I tightened my hands on the steering wheel and slowly looked over to her in the passenger's seat for my answer.

Bonnie looked at me and smiled. Then she started laughing.

"I hate to say I told you so, but I told you so," I said with a return smile. The car was in motion again as I drove us across town to my parents' place.

"I know. I know you did." Bonnie laughed. "I just expected her to be more cantankerous and less, uh—"

"Calling you a whore-ish?"

"Exactly."

"Don't take it personally. Hateful slurs are her love language."

"She must *really* like me, then."

"Oh, you noticed it, too?"

"What did you talk about when I left?"

"She said you had a voice like a whiny dog."

"She what?"

"Again, a compliment. She's a huge Lassie fan."

"You like my voice, right?"

"I love your voice. I love knowing that if I ever fall down a well, I can rely on you."

"What did you tell her?"

"I just put her in a headlock and told her what I'd do to her if she acted up again."

"No seriously, what did you say?"

"I told her she was out of line, that she should be ashamed, and that I won't be around to act as her punching bag forever."

"How did she take that?"

"She hit me."

"She hit you?" Bonnie put her hand over her mouth.

"Yeah, but, you know, I'm a man, I can take it." I rubbed my head. This was done by design as it instantly had Bonnie rubbing my head and kissing my cheek for defending her honor.

"Look, about my parents," I said, changing subjects. "Are you still up for this?"

"Of course," she said, massaging.

"Well, they'll probably love you. Probably. But keep in mind, they're not my grandmother. They're pretty raw and they won't apologize for it. They've been through a lot. Actually, they're still going through a lot."

"I know, honey. You told me. Don't bring up your brother's drinking and don't be offended if your dad is distant or depressed. And don't get annoyed by your mother's million questions."

"Yeah, I know, but the language and environment is not like your family's place at all," I said, thinking of how Bonnie's parents were normal, functioning members of society. They had a nice place, with no holes punched in the walls from fights. They had two successful kids: Bonnie and her brother, who was nobly serving his country in the military. They were members of a local church, with a well-kept lawn, living in a town that wasn't shrinking ever since the steel industry left.

"I'll be alright. Just try not to get hit again," Bonnie said smiling.

I did not smile back, however. I looked at her quite seriously. "I can't promise you that."

I needed this meeting to go well, though I knew better than to expect my parents to act like foreign dignitaries. There was no covering up the rough edges in this family; however, my dad could have at least put on pants.

Bonnie stood next to me in the kitchen of my parents' place. My mom was nearly on top of us, practically bubbling over with enthusiasm the way mothers do when they smell even the slightest hint of possible grandchildren. One of the house's four cats swished around our feet impatient for attention. We ignored it though, as we were too busy navigating the awkwardness centered around my dad's perforated pair of tighty-whities.

Bonnie was the first to speak, cheerily saying, "So, you're a Hanes man, huh?"

My dad glanced up at Bonnie from the kitchen table where he resided. "I'm a whatever's-in-the-drawer-when-I-wake-up man. Sometimes there's nothing. Count yourself lucky." He took another pull on his cigarette but offered a sly hint of a smile.

I nudged Bonnie and gave her a *he likes you*–type of nod.

"Uh, my dad loves to lounge in his underwear, too." She continued, "Sometimes he does yard work that way. It's your house, wear what you want, right?" Bonnie looked back to my dad.

"Hmm," said my dad.

"So, I hear Grandma wasn't exactly glad to meet you," my mom began.

"She called Bonnie a whore," I said.

"Well," my mom said, clapping her hands together, "in that case, you two are meant to be! When I first met Grandma, she called me a bitch!"

I slapped my hand to my head. When I first met Bonnie's parents, her mother served a roast while wearing an embroidered apron she'd cross-stitched herself. Then she asked me if I would say grace for everyone as we held hands around the table. My folks can't make it five minutes before they're pantless and swearing.

"Did you tell her she was a miserable old dinosaur?" asked my mom.

"No," said Bonnie. "It doesn't bother me. I'm used to dealing with, um, 'inappropriate elderly' from my nursing home days. I've heard worse."

"You're used to it? Well, that's a good thing because we've got a lot of 'em in this family, isn't that right, Sam?" My mom gestured to my dad while laughing at her own wittiness. My dad merely offered a cigarette smoke–leaking grunt of affirmation.

"So, do you like baseball?" asked my mom.

"I've never really paid much attention, but I will now!" Bonnie took my arm.

"Have you seen him play yet?" asked Mom.

"No, but I'm excited about it."

"It's nerve-racking. I've watched him since he was little, and I can't tell you how many cigarettes I smoked to make it through his games." Mom laughed in that *you know what I mean* kind of way after she said it, like chain-smoking menthols while you watched your son pitch between the cracks of your fingers was something everyone could relate to. "I think this year is his year, though," continued my mom, implying that this year I would make it to the big leagues. "But watching you on television is going to give me a heart attack! What do you think, Dirk?"

"Do I think it'll kill you? Maybe, if you don't cut back on the cigarettes," I said.

"Do you think this is the year?" said my mom, and with her question all eyes turned to me for an answer.

With Bonnie sitting next to me, there was nothing I wanted to say more than "Absolutely." In fact, I wanted to say this was the year it would all change: Grandma's floor, crap jobs, being broke, and being single. I wanted to say I'd make it to the Show this year and live happily ever after with money in the bank and a sports drink contract. But I couldn't. As the pitcher's mantra goes, once the baseball leaves your hand, the rest is out of your control. I knew what would happen this year about as well as a gambler knew what would happen before he let the dice go.

I did have a good year last year, but that didn't guarantee me anything. A lot of other guys had good years, too, guys on my team and on teams all over the game. Guys I didn't even know existed but whom I would be competing against after Padres scouts went out and grabbed them from other clubs in an effort to have the best talent available come spring training. At the higher levels—levels I was competing for—it wasn't uncommon to lose a roster spot to a player you'd never heard of who got a good review by a scout you'd never seen. There is a whole economy taking place behind the scenes of the playing field, and behind the backs of the players. This is because when it's time to consider who gets promoted to the Bigs, money, recommendations, trades, age, scouting reports, and arbitration eligibility all play a role as large as strikeouts and ERA. What players do on the field is only half the battle.

At my age, I needed to be on the Triple A roster when the dust settled at the end of spring training. That would be tough since I wasn't rated as a true prospect. The deck was stacked against an average right-handed reliever like me, coming off one above-average year. It was more likely I'd get sent back to Double A, where I'd have to prove I could excel again and that last season wasn't a fluke. In which case, this forthcoming year would be just another audition for a real chance next year. Of course, no one sitting around the kitchen table wanted to hear such a logical and depressing answer, including me. So I simply said the portion everyone wanted to hear: "I got the best shot I've ever had, that's for sure."

"Have the Padres talked to you about it any?" asked Mom.

"No, Mom, they don't talk to us about that stuff during the off-season."

"He never tells me anything good," said my mom to Bonnie.

"I tell her everything I know and it's never enough," I pleaded.

"You never tell me what I want to hear!"

"Sorry, Mom, I'm going to the big leagues. They're sending a limo right now."

"Don't be a smart-ass."

"Stop telling me I never tell you anything."

The phone rang and interrupted us. My mom answered, then immediately rolled her eyes. "It's your grandmother, again," she mouthed at us. "It'll be at least ten minutes before I can get her to shut up." Mom got up and snuck into the other room, leaving us to sit with my dad.

"So, I understand you're into music," Bonnie said to my dad, changing the subject.

My dad looked at Bonnie.

"What's your favorite stuff? I'll bet I've played it before."

"Dylan. The Stones. A few others," said my dad in a disinterested tone. There were days back before my dad's depression when he'd play records for hours on end, filling the house with everything from Alice Cooper to ZZ Top. He used to work in the garage, fix the car, and even spank us kids to music.

"You know, you'd like my dad," said Bonnie. "He's into all the old music, too, but he never plays it anymore."

"Why is that?" asked my dad.

"My mom won't let him."

"She won't?" My dad furrowed his brow and snuffed out his cigarette, but he was now more into a conversation than I'd seen him in years.

"Mildred, she's a nice girl, you can't call her names like that and not expect Dirk to get angry with you." My mom's voice overlapped our conversation as she paced past the door of the adjoining room.

"No," continued Bonnie. "It's tragic because I'll bet he knows every band you listen to."

"Bet I got a few he's never heard of," said my dad with a hint of pride.

"They are not having sex, Mildred. For God's sake, I don't think the boy even knows how to use it." I dropped my forehead on the table.

"Dirk said you had a big collection."

"Organized it alphabetically," said my dad.

"I'd love to hear some of it," said Bonnie.

I looked at Bonnie. I couldn't believe what she was coaxing my dad into doing. Was it part of her therapy method, or just the idea of a cute young woman taking interest in my half-naked father that got him out of his chair? He threw his shoulders back like some romance novel cover model with ketchup stains on his shirt and holes in his underwear, and headed for the stereo.

"I'll let you pick," said Bonnie. "I'm just curious if you'll pick something my dad likes without me telling you."

Dad pulled out a tape and put on the Kinks, "Sunny Afternoon."

"Oh, this is one of his favorites," said Bonnie.

"No, Mildred, we're not having a party. Sam put on some music. Yes, Sam. Yes, he still listens to that *hippie crap*," said Mom.

"You know, my parents used to sit around when they were first married and smoke joints and listen to this while watching a light board plugged into the stereo," said Bonnie.

"Your parents?" I was stunned.

"Oh, that's nothing," said my mom, who was now tuning my grandmother out completely in favor of us. "Sam and I had a whole room of fish tanks and we used to get high and pretend we were under the sea." My mom made a swimming motion, and said, "No, Mildred, no one's getting high."

"Those were the good days," said my dad. "Didn't have to worry about dirty diapers and little boys who would cry without their binkies." My dad nodded at me. "You know, when Dirk was a boy, he had a whole set of pacifiers. If you tried to take 'em away from him, he'd cry bloody murder. I think he finally stopped sucking on them last year."

"That's interesting," said Bonnie, turning to me with a coy smile.

"I tend to disagree," I said.

"Yeah," continued my dad, tapping his finger to the beat now. "He was allergic to everything, too. Couldn't drink regular milk. He had colic so bad he used to poop his diapers like a toxic waste spill. Had to feed him goat's milk." My dad leaned into Bonnie with one hand over his mouth and whispered, "We think he's part goat."

Bonnie laughed as my dad got up to change the tape. Then she leaned over to me and said, "Your dad is cute, and so are you, my little goat boy."

I went to steal a kiss, but the sound of my brother's voice split us apart.

"Mom!" yelled the rough and expectant voice of my brother. He called to her from upstairs, yelling down the stairwell. My brother worked the night shift and was now starting to stir for the day; no doubt we had awakened him.

"Mom!" It came again, this time more demanding. My mom tensed, and my dad's fingers stopped tapping. Like a dark cloud on the horizon, bad weather was coming.

Chapter Five

Something about the voice made Dad's countenance change. My mom set the phone down, ignoring my grandmother, who was still harping through the receiver. Obediently, she went upstairs to answer my brother.

My dad stopped talking. The music played on in the background, but the notes seemed sour to him now. The voices of my mother and brother above us spiked like thunder, sending a few strong, angry syllables echoing down the stairwell and into the living room where they seemed to strike my father. He lit a fresh cigarette and pressed one hand firmly against his head, as if he needed to support someplace inside he could not reach. "Jesus Christ, Brak, just deal with it. You'll live!" cut my mother's voice.

"I ain't going to work until I see the fucking doctor. If I get fired, it's your fault."

My father twisted and squirmed at the table, as if he were fighting inside himself. I clutched Bonnie's hand and started gesturing toward the exit. I knew she couldn't feel the ground shaking, but I could. I could feel it coming, like it had so many times before, the approach of the darker side of my life. It was only a matter of seconds before it arrived. Bonnie, smiling sweetly, didn't know what was ahead, couldn't read the signs. I stood up and motioned for her to do the same.

My mother marched downstairs and pushed in front of us to a shelf that contained a small wicker basket of medicine bottles. Within were all manner of drugs, from painkillers and antidepressants for my dad to unfinished bottles of antibiotics the family had hoarded.

"What's the matter with him now?" asked my agitated father.

"He says he's not going to work because he's got a sinus infection."

When my mom said that, whatever it was that was fighting to get out of Dad broke free. "Awwgaaawwwd . . ." my dad sickly groaned. He clenched his fists and pressed them against his forehead like something had stabbed him in the mind. Then, just like the flick of a switch, the scene came undone.

Abruptly, Dad struck the table, throwing all its contents to the floor. Then he began shaking. Bonnie jolted upright at the sight of it, and I backed her out of the room as the scene continued. Over and over, my dad's fists came down. In a mix of agony and anger, he bawled, "God dammit! God fucking dammit!" A great inhale then a great rupture of contempt poured out.

Drawn to the anger, my brother started down the steps to confront his rival. Shorter than me but stocky, with thick forearms and a neck like a bull, my brother was ready to charge into my father. He took Dad's angry outburst as another personal attack of rejection. He'd settle it the only way he knew how, in a fight that would surely leave the house wrecked. That was how the hole in the wall was made, how the lamps got busted and why the doors didn't shut right.

Mom was quick to cut him off. "Stay up there, Brak, just stay up there. I'll handle this." She held up pill bottles like a sacrifice, in hopes to appease, or at the very least, to distract the bull. "I've got another refill on this bottle of decongestants. I'm going to call it in right now. You can take them along with some of my leftover antibiotics—it's what the doctor would give you anyway. Then you can go to work, right?"

"That's not going to help me today."

"Oh, would you just work with me on this, please?" begged my mom.

"No, goddammit, no!" roared the monster my dad had mutated into. "He's gotta learn. No more fucking excuses! If he thinks he's so fucking great, he can stop making excuses!" Laboring for air, he started up from his seat. Unable to spring upright, he flipped a chair over and lumbered to the foot of the stairs like some shambling creature. My mom stayed in the way as an intercessor between the bull and the monster.

My brother fired first. "What the hell do you want me to do, just not be sick?"

"I want you to act like a man for once, Mr. Alcoholics Anonymous."

"A man? You mean like you, sitting around all day feeling sorry for yourself and being useless?" The cavalier, almost mocking way the words were delivered drove the insult in deep.

"Brak, shut up! Go upstairs and shut up," Mom pleaded.

It was too late. It wasn't that my father's fuse was short; it was that there was no fuse at all. "Fuck you! You hear me," Dad screamed. "Fuck you, you worthless son of a bitch, I should have shot your drunk ass when I had the chance. You worthless, you—" He couldn't hold it together long enough to speak anymore.

"Sam, calm down," my mom pleaded. "I can handle this."

"You should have shot yourself, you mean," grandstanded my brother.

Dad burst into a maelstrom of incoherent cussing and threats. He wanted to attack my brother, nearly foaming at the mouth to kill him. Then, when he couldn't negotiate the steps with his poor balance, the other side came; the pain and the frustration of being crippled and powerless hit and he wanted to kill himself. He screamed it all out, then fell down gulping for breath as though he might have a heart attack. My mom tried to help him up, but he lashed out at her with "Get away from me, you enabling bitch!" Then he grabbed his head and sobbed like a man destroyed.

I felt like I was dying inside. Like everything I hoped for, had

worked so hard to keep balanced this off-season—my whole career in fact—was now burning down around me, and all I could
do was sit and wait for the flames to take me with them. My eyes
had collected tears but I didn't notice until Bonnie squeezed me,
pulling me back from the nightmare. I was instantly horrified
that I'd kept her here to witness this. I wiped a hand across my
face and escorted her out the door.

Trudging through the snow to Bonnie's car, I had no words. All
I could do was stare into her face, embarrassed and remorseful
that this was my home.

"I'm sorry," I said.

"It's okay. It's not your fault."

But it was, and I knew it. It was my family, and Bonnie's forgiveness was nullified by that undeniable fact. I shook my head.
"I'm so sorry," I said again, almost robotically.

"It's okay," she repeated, wrapping her arms around my waist.
"I want you to be okay."

"How are you still here right now? How are you not running
for your life?"

"Why would I run?"

"Because I can't think of one single good reason for you to
stay."

"How about because I want to be here with you?" she said, and
let me go to look at me, to make sure I could see that promise in
her eyes again.

My mother flung the house door open and marched into the
snow, pill bottles in one hand and a wad of bills in the other. Behind her came my father. He heaved with the same loss of control
he showed in the house, his face flushed and wet. He still had no
shoes or pants on. The nerve damage he'd received from his tumble off the roof so many years back rendered his feet numb to the
cold. Even so, going the way he was, it was unlikely he would have
noticed.

"You should go," I said to Bonnie.

"You want me to leave you here?"

"I'll be alright." I kissed Bonnie good-bye, tucked her into her car, and shut the door. She backed out and drove off slowly down the road. I stayed, turning to face my parents.

"We ain't got the money, Pat!" my father continued as my mother cleaned snow off her car.

"It's always about the money, Sam. Money, money, money! There's never going to be enough of it, so get used to it!"

"There would be if you'd stop being such a goddamn idiot with it."

At this my mom threw her hands up as if she were appealing to an invisible jury, as if she were saying she'd done all she could but it was no use, Your Honor.

"How dare you, you hypocritical bastard? You spend whatever you want on tools and comic books to make yourself feel good and I don't say a word, and when I go to get Brak some pills to keep him employed, to make sure he's out of the house at least eight hours a day, you throw this tantrum. He's right, you have lost your mind. If you're so concerned about this, then take it, I'm leaving." On that, she threw the wad of bills at Dad, got into her car, and backed out past me, over the same tire tracks Bonnie had just made.

My dad hobbled desperately after the bills before the wind could blow them away. He ended up falling to his knees trying to bend over. Then, on all fours, he crawled after the money, oblivious to the cold and the wife who'd left him.

Chapter Six

After years of battling with alcohol addiction, my brother sobered up last season. My winning the championship with the San Antonio Missions was great, but his was the real victory, or so we thought. It was supposed to mark the start of something new and wonderful for our family, but it soon became apparent that things were more complicated than we thought.

The attention my brother's redemption garnered made him self-righteous. Since he'd solved his own problem, he thought he could solve all the rest of the family's problems too. He began with pronouncing judgment over my dad, a man crippled with physical and mental ailments stemming from a horrific fall. My brother demanded my Dad pick up his cross and follow in his footsteps. Anything less, said my brother, was weakness.

This didn't go over well with my dad. To him, my brother was a tone-deaf thirty-year-old going on thirteen. His sobriety did not change the fact that he didn't pay rent, he made messes, he wasted utilities, and he had to be supported, reminded, and motivated to keep jobs. Now my brother, the prodigal son, was forcing answers to things he didn't comprehend down my father's throat when every day my dad suffered more than the previous for reasons he could not articulate or control. He was explosive at the drop of a hat, weeping in grocery stores, melting down in restaurants; it was like the fall had infected him with something, and as the days passed, more of my father disappeared into the darkness spreading through him. My brother's cure was an accelerant. All my dad wanted was for the firstborn to grow up, act his age, and leave him alone as the seconds of his own life ticked away.

Their frustration with each other grew, and soon the house became a war zone as the pair traded what they hated most about each other, screaming horrible things that made you wonder how anyone could ever call the four of us kindred. As it turned out, my brother was not as perfect as he thought, and without the guise of intoxication to hide behind, there was no doubt all his harsh and cutting words were intentional. Dad, on the other hand, didn't care about his own life, let alone how the words he screamed would affect the lives of others.

Mom remained stuck in the middle, trying to hold the pieces together. The normally placid nature she maintained while handling the household drama was ebbing away, and just a few weeks ago she called to tell me she wanted out. She was sick of being the ocean that caught the molten overflow. She was sick of catching love like some food drop for refugees in hostile territory.

This was my family now, and I remained ever the outsider. I tried my best to distance myself through baseball, but this was always mine, waiting behind the lights of the game for me to return to it. After six years of beating-around-the-bush leagues, I now knew my biggest challenges weren't in the game of baseball, but what happened in the off-season.

When my dad finished picking up the money, he retreated to the house. I didn't follow. I had no place to go and no car to get there, but any place was better than being in my home. I walked aimlessly to the backyard, to a stretch of open acres that rolled out against farmland and a forgotten wooden wall that stood there.

In my youth, my dad had erected a makeshift pitching target in the center of the backyard using scavenged lumber from my old clubhouse. He painted it with a white square to mark a strike zone. Sixty feet away, staring down at the target, Dad built a pitcher's mound: a lumpy pile of shoveled earth formed into a grassy hill with a cinder block for a rubber. I scored many muddy ruts into that mound as I practiced, pretending I was striking out hall of famers. On and on I'd go until I had won the World Series, and the family's bucket of baseballs had turned into ragged dog toys.

It had been years since my last innings on Hayhurst Field. I scaled the snow-covered mound once more, kicking off enough powder to find the brick rubber beneath. I scooped a handful of snow, packed it into a ball, and came set. I knew what to do next, the familiar routine of winding and delivering, but I couldn't move. I just stood there frozen by a memory. For all the grand victories I'd won on that mound, it was the greatest defeat I thought of most.

Nearly a decade ago, the local newspaper said I was the best chance my high school, Canton South, had of beating the unstoppable powerhouse that was Central Catholic High. In fact, I could remember reading about myself on the day of the game, how the paper said I was a major college prospect and that Central, a private Catholic school known for its shameless recruiting of area studs, would struggle against the publicly educated mighty-righty. All the players on Central's varsity squad were groomed for college scholarships, and a few were getting interest from pro scouts. It would be the biggest game I'd ever pitch in and the first time I'd ever know the compounding effects of media hype.

Central beat me like a drum. I felt naked on the mound as run after run scored. The Central kids read the paper, too, and for Catholic school kids they sure talked a lot of shit. They taunted and mocked me, using lines from the newspaper as I struggled to make it through innings. Then their parents, who showed up in luxury cars and dressed in luxury clothes, screamed at me from the stands that I had no business being out there, that I was a waste of their kids' time. It stung and infuriated me, but the worst part was when the voices of my own teammates started to turn from encouragement to complaint. I can't remember how long the innings lasted, but it didn't matter; it's always too long when your own team is embarrassed by you. Even my dad left before the game was over.

I hated Central, I hated my teammates, I hated the newspaper, and I hated myself. I didn't live up to anyone's expectations, especially my own, and the anger I felt at the people who pronounced judgment over me boiled in my stomach until I could spit fire.

I came home that evening and went straight to the practice mound and wooden target determined to make things right. Those were the glorious days of youth when I could throw and throw and not have to worry about arm problems. Fixing my issues was as simple as lathering up in a sweat and leaving it all on the mound. But that night, I couldn't. My arm was fine, but the mound was occupied by another thrower.

It was my dad who stood on that homemade pile of lumpy earth. I hadn't seen him there in years, but there he was with the family bucket beside him, a ball in his right hand. He wore no glove; it would have been too hard for him to grip a baseball with his left hand ensnared in a mitt, if he could even get a mitt on. As it was, he had to work the ball into his gnarled fingers. After his accident, his hands wouldn't work right anymore. The nerve damage had not only deadened their sensitivity, but also caused them to contract and shrivel like wilted flower petals. Still, he persisted, and once he had a hold on the ball, he rocked, took an unsteady step down the mound toward the target, and tossed. The tattered ball popped free, hung in the air for an awkward second, then crashed to the earth below.

My dad looked upon the ball for a moment, watching it lie lifeless only a few steps from him, then grabbed his fingers and began stretching them, coercing them to function better. He reached back into the bucket, took a new ball, mashed it into his stretched fingers, and repeated the motion. The ball tumbled through the air, crossing the thick grass that swallowed my dad's Velcro-fastened shoes, and landed with a soft thud a few feet from the target. Over and over he did this, each throw landing in an unpredictable nature until, finally, one ball flew from his hand, crossed the landscape, and thudded into white paint. Nature stopped around my dad. He stood motionless, crooked from the damage to his body yet sturdy like some statue of marble and majesty.

I didn't realize it at the time, but I'd just witnessed a truly beautiful moment. My dad, robbed of a childhood joy because of a harrowing accident, had just reclaimed a lost piece of himself, a part thought dead when it was he who had tumbled through the air and landed on the ground, not in a soft thud but in a cacophonous blast that accompanied the destruction of life as he knew it. He stared at the target from high atop his throne of sod and dirt, then looked at his own still capable hands. He took the emptied bucket and made his way around the yard, laboriously plucking baseballs from the grass like Easter eggs. After he'd shepherded them home, he once again threaded the bucket handle into the contorted digits and made his return trip to the mound.

That was when he saw me.

My dad, standing in his overalls, forehead glistening, froze at the sight of me. He looked surprised to see me standing there, ashamed even. He dropped the bucket and asked, "You need on here?"

I needed to go into the house and avoid my homework, play video games, call girls, be a teenager. I needed to ask my father if he wanted me to catch him, or collect the stray balls, or if I could simply remain and observe. But I was young, and I was angry.

"Ya, I want the mound."

"Alright then," said my dad. He stepped off.

I emptied that bucket of balls time and time again, pounding the white square until the sun set and I could no longer make out the target. My dad stayed to watch. He had left after I was pulled from the day's game, but he stayed then, watching my frustration pour out as I tried to knock the target down. I didn't get any better, I didn't fix anything, I just threw wildly in the fog of my defeat.

"I was horrible today," I declared to my dad. "Just a huge embarrassment. The paper said I was supposed to be great, but I fell apart and everybody thinks I suck."

"That stuff don't mean anything," he said. "It happens."

"It means everything, Dad! You don't understand. There were scouts there. I had my chance to get noticed and I blew it. I'm never going to get drafted now!" I rifled another ball into the painted wall. It ricocheted off into dark grass.

My dad said nothing and his silence angered me. I stared him down from the mound and expected him to give an answer that would fix it all. When it didn't come, I turned away, utterly dissatisfied with him.

"I keep reading how good Maddux is," I said. "I try to be like him but I'm not. He makes it look so easy. All those guys do. If I was as good as them, I'd have whipped Central today."

"You think Maddux never struggled?"

"Not like me."

"You're not Maddux. You're you," said my dad.

"I know. I'm terrible. Thanks a lot, Dad. I'm just saying I wish I could be like great pitchers. They never screw up. Haven't you ever wanted to be like someone great before?"

"I have," he confirmed. "Today I was trying to be like you."

"Whatever," I said, batting the sincerity aside. "No one wants to be like me, I'm awful." On that, I picked up the ball bucket and walked away, leaving my dad there in the dark.

I dropped my snowball; it didn't have any answers, nor did this mound or this broken home. I no longer wanted to pitch in a fantasy World Series, and I didn't want to strike out the side. I didn't want to be some glorious hero coming back in victory. I wanted to go back in time and change things. I wanted to be on the roof so many years ago. I wanted to stop my brother from drinking. Then I found myself wanting the house to burn down, praying the ground would open and swallow it all. Make all the pain vanish without a trace, but nothing happened. Nothing ever seemed to change.

In my moment of contempt, I tried to think of one sure thing I had in my life, and all I could be sure of was that, Double A champion or World Series champion, if I came home to this, it wasn't worth it. I was tired of my life being nothing but a title and a jersey, and it was time I did something to change it.

Chapter Seven

Days later, I found myself pacing around the kitchen of my grandma's house with my cell phone pressed to my head and the dulcet tones of my agent tickling my ear. "We could get you down there for the second half," he strummed. "There's usually a big turnover rate around the holidays, and they're always looking for fresh arms. I could get a guy like you there easy because you can do every role."

"I don't know, Adam," I mumbled. I sat down and flipped aimlessly through a newspaper circular as he spoke, looking at ads for televisions and their bold slogans of savings and holiday joy. "I just don't feel comfortable with it."

"Look, they'll put you up someplace nice," he insisted. "Sometimes it's even a resort. Think about that, Shizzle, a resort in the middle of winter! And don't worry about the crime stories; the team owners give you an armed escort for the big games. As long as you don't go into some dark alley, travel alone, or piss off the natives, you shouldn't lose any limbs."

"Why doesn't that make me feel confident?"

"I'm your agent. I have to tell you all the risks, no matter how small."

"So you consider making sure I stay with the people who have guns indicative of a small risk? I understand you have to sacrifice for this game, but a player has to draw the line somewhere."

"Guys go down there all the time and they come back just fine. You're smart. You'll make it out in one piece. Besides, I'm more worried about them blowing your arm out than blowing your head off. That's the *real* danger of Winter Ball."

I had called my agent asking for a way out of the mess that my off-season was turning into and he gave me one, though going all the way to South America wasn't exactly what I had in mind. He was my baseball agent, however, and this was his best solution. I'd already spent half my year riding buses through the backwoods of America, so the last thing I wanted was to take another bus through what many players referred to as "The Jungle" during the "rejuvenating" months of my off time.

Players may joke about the remote feel of some of the smaller burgs that host minor league teams, but in The Jungle, you really do travel through areas where natives live in huts and livestock must be cleared from dirt roads for the team bus to advance. Winter Ball takes you to a part of the world that is less developed than the United States, but this doesn't mean it's not without its own unique charms—like paying you upwards of ten grand for a month of service. Fact is, unless you're a big leaguer, you can't beat the money down there, and ten grand feels like a hundred grand when you're a minor leaguer used to living off paychecks that make a shoe shine boy snicker.

The cash incentive makes competition for jobs fierce, and the demand for results even fiercer. The rivalries are so fierce that the turnover on pitching is like a miniature stock exchange. If you want to make it in The Jungle, you have to win, period. Go down and suck, and you'll get sent home with no second chances. Even if you come back to the States and roll up an all-star season the following year in American ball, The Jungle doesn't forget. It wants people who can win on its turf, and it will pay top dollar to get them. It's not uncommon for teams in Winter Ball to pay proven winners obscene amounts just to pitch in one game. On the other hand, it's not uncommon for Winter Ball teams to send players packing after one bad outing.

Some players say this is a more pure form of baseball, that it's survival of the fittest and thus the only way to play. Others say it's a mockery of the sport and that it turns players into hired mercenaries with no loyalty. Most don't care about the ramifications and just want to see the money and where to sign. I would fall into that category, and Adam knew it, especially since I just called begging him to get me out of my grandmother's house, or at least help me find a legal way of getting her committed. But, as quick a fix as Winter Ball could be, I was reticent to pull the trigger.

I had my reasons. First, the money, as good as it is, doesn't always show up. There have been cases of guys not getting paid what their contracts stipulated, or not getting paid at all. Did I really want to give up my off-season just to run the risk of getting stiffed? Then, there is always the rumor mill of guys experiencing everything from theft to abduction in some of the more volatile cities. I couldn't verify how much of that was truth or just locker room tales gone wild, but when your agent is telling you to take comfort in the fact that your driver is strapped and a very good shot, you at least have to think it over. Finally, there are things a player values doing during his off-season that can't be bought away, and that was the part really holding me back. I just didn't want to admit it to Adam.

"I'm sorry, Adam. I don't think it's for me this year," I said.

"You're telling me you'd rather work at a television store than make ten grand playing baseball?"

When he said it like that, I wanted to lash myself as a penance for my stupid emotions. I remained committed. "Yeah, I just don't think I want to risk it."

"There's no risk. They love Americans!"

"You're right, I'm sure those stories about fingers mailed to parents in exchange for ransom payable to local drug lords are greatly exaggerated."

Adam groaned in the background, and I realized this great debate regarding me as a pitching gladiator in The Jungle would continue unless I came up with something more respectable than fear.

"Look, I believe you, Adam," I said. "I'm sure it's safe as long as you can run faster than the bad guys, but I'm talking about the safety of my arm, here. I put a lot of mileage on it this year. You know how I insist on throwing so many touch-up bullpens between outings? Those add up! I may not have had a huge amount of recorded innings like a starter, but my stats don't include all my warm-ups and shutdowns in the pen. Do you really want me to go play for a team that wants to win so bad they don't care if I break? Is ten grand really worth a busted arm to you? I have to keep the big prize in mind."

Adam paused to assess my new evidence. Self-preservation sounds a lot like investment preservation if you say it right.

"You have a point there," said Adam. "That's what I like about working with you, Hayhurst. You're smarter than the average minor league misfit."

"One of us has to look out for me," I said.

"Hey! I'm always looking out for you. Most guys I have to talk into staying home and resting. I'm just trying to get you down there because I know you wanna get off your grandma's floor. You called me, remember."

"I appreciate you thinking of my economic circumstances," I said, "but you know how baseball players are about their superstitions. If I want to have another good year, I have to stay here and fight with grandma. It's like Rocky and Apollo Creed."

"Alright, Shizzle, have it your way. I just want you to know you've pitched yourself into a better situation and you have options." He paused, anticipating I might say something. I didn't. "Well, go give Grandma hugs and kisses for me, and if you change your mind, you know where to call me."

"Will do. Thanks again for the offer and have a merry Christmas."

Adam cut me loose. I closed my phone, set it on the table, and continued flipping through the circulars as I tried to rationalize what I'd just done. Instead of taking a first-class flight to tropical sunshine, I'd be working through holiday madness at Circuit City.

My stomach turned at the thought of lost wages. I could just see myself, Winter Ball check in hand, cartwheeling into the bank to cash it. I could see myself in a resort, slurping drinks from coconut husks, smoking cigars with a drug lord who promised to "solve" all my grandma problems if I just kept winning. Then I looked at my reflection in the windows of my grandmother's kitchen and realized I was going nowhere except work in about twelve hours. There was no beach, no cigars, no tropical drinks. I was a prisoner in a cell of shag carpeting and plastic-covered furniture. My agent had just tried to spring me and I volunteered to stay behind. What the hell was I thinking?

My phone buzzed. The vibration sent it scooting across the table where I snared it and answered, "Hello?"

"Hi, honey, how are you?" It was Bonnie.

"I'm good, you?"

"I'm fine. Just wanted to call and hear your voice before I started work."

I smiled and plopped my head on my hand. "I'm glad you did," I said.

"Did you talk to Adam?"

"Yes. We just finished."

"And?" She hung on my response.

Bonnie was the reason I was staying around. The only reason. If I had tried to explain that to Adam, he would have slapped me through the phone, and rightly so. I was turning down the first life-changing chunk of cash I'd ever been offered for a girl I met on an Internet dating website four months ago. For God's sake, where did I think this was going to go?

But there it was, whispering in the back of my head, that voice, that silly, irrational, not-to-be-listened-to voice that knew Bonnie would say yes if I asked her to marry me right now. The thought had bounded through my head almost every waking moment these last few months, tempting me with ideas about futures and happiness and smashing cake into faces. It brought me dreams of a life not lived on Grandma's floor, where words like *virginity* were no longer cause for my mom to pry or my teammates to laugh. It even controlled my hand to unconsciously take hold of *Cosmopolitan* magazine when the words "How to Know You've Met 'The One'?" were plastered across the top. Lately, that little voice had been screaming at me, every time I looked into my grandma's irritated face, every time Mom explained she was going to come back because my dad promised to get help. Every time I looked into Bonnie's soft brown eyes. Maybe Bonnie was a chance to build a refuge? Or maybe it was just another soon-to-be-killed baseball romance? I had to know.

"I said no."

There was a silent stretch while Bonnie considered what it meant. "That means I get to keep you for a few more weeks! Oh honey, that makes my day."

She didn't know it, but her reaction just made mine too.

"Bonnie, I'd like to talk with you about something I've been thinking about lately. I was wondering what you thought—"

"Hello, Miss Abigail. You look beautiful! Is that what you're going to wear on the big day?" said Bonnie, extra cheery. Then, returning to me, she said, "I'm sorry. My client is here. Can we talk more tonight?"

"I have to be in early tomorrow because of extended holiday sales hours."

"I'll be setting up for the Share Day event all day tomorrow. Can we talk after?"

"I have to pitch against the Walsh team."

"You're still coming, though, right? We're still going out afterward, right?"

"I wouldn't miss it," I reassured her.

"Can it wait till then?"

"Sure, I guess."

"Great, I'll talk to you tomorrow."

We said our good-byes. Tomorrow was a long way away, affording plenty of time for me to lose my nerve.

Chapter Eight

In my line of work, there is always someone with a bat standing between me and my goal. So it should come as no surprise that the person keeping me from reaching Bonnie's concert on time was sixty feet way, with a chunk of lumber in hand.

If you want to get to the top in this game, you've got to be a flexible opportunist. It's a competitive industry, and no one has any sympathy for why another player gets chosen over you; not because you don't want to go play ball in The Jungle; not because you've got a date with your girl; and especially not because you couldn't find a place to throw during the off-season. When I have the opportunity to throw to a catcher on an angle in the winter, I have to take it. But, as is usually the case, there were a few strings attached. Winter facilities are hard to find, and tonight's use of a catcher came along with a complement of college hitters from local Walsh University who wanted to test their bats against a pro guy's fastball the same evening as Bonnie's concert.

I was just bringing my arm out of off-season hibernation, so it wouldn't be much of a test. As a matter of fact, I came into it purely to get my body used to throwing off a mound again. I failed to take into account the ego factor of young male competitors, and soon, what was meant to be a friendly, knock-the-rust-off practice session turned into all-out testosterone warfare.

Now batting, the Walsh University baseball team captain. He was a husky dude with a buzzed head, bulging arms, and blunt skull. He got into his stance at the plate like a power lifter, taking practice swings that could topple a bull elephant. Pine tar was slathered all over his bat and caked onto his helmet. Wrists taped, fingers taped, bat taped, he rolled up his sleeves to show how dedicated he was to bicep curls, not to mention the art of shaving his forearms. Finally, he adjusted his crotch while scowling at me, as if I'd done something to make him uncomfortable down there.

Hitters are stupid. If they weren't, they'd be pitchers. No one in their right mind would pick the side of the game that considers three out of ten good unless they're slightly unhinged. I would bet if it were a real game, this guy would have on enough eye black to make him look like a member of KISS. I would bet he has a tattoo on him someplace, like an iron cross or a band of barbwire, or a mystical Chinese symbol meaning "strength" that really means "jackass" because no one who gets a Chinese tattoo knows how to read Chinese. I'll bet he definitely fake tans, Nairs his package in the desperate imitation of his favorite porn star, and spends Saturdays stacking emptied Natural Light beer cans into silver pyramids on the coffee table.

In his last at bat, Captain Curls here may have gotten a hit off me. He may have earned the high fives and butt slaps of his teammates, but I doubt it. Of course, it's hard to tell what's earned when you're pitching in a batting cage in a modified storage barn in the winter—everything that comes off the bat flies into the netting with what seems like home run force.

I toed the facility's bike ramp turned pitching mound and went into the stretch position. Our catcher, a teammate of Curls, was also acting as our umpire. So caught up was he in the fear of who to side with in this matchup—the pro guy or the team captain— he simply ran through signs like a slot machine until I nodded.

After I picked which finger I wanted to throw, I came set, kicked, and stuck a winter speed fastball on the corner. Curls fouled it back for strike one with a massive uppercut that would have sent the bat bursting through the ceiling and into a plane if he let go of it.

Moans of "Oh, he just missed it," echoed through his entourage.

"Almost got you there," said Curls, grinning at me.

Did he really just say that? What a douche bag, I thought. I said nothing, of course, but reloaded on the mound, kicking and firing my response with a high and tight fastball, sending Curls spinning out of the box with a little chin music.

"Almost got you there," I said.

Curls enjoyed this, the trash talk and the competitive anteing; you could tell by the way it seemed to charge him up. It was as if these little boasts were micro tests of manhood and winning them justified all the extra trips he made to the tanning bed.

Watching him thrive reminded me of what it was like to be young and full of naïve stupidity. Poor bastard; if only Curls knew what was out there ahead of him, waiting to tell him to pick up dog turds. I almost felt sorry for him as I let a changeup tumble in for a called strike two.

Curls leered at his supposed teammate umpire/catcher. "Whose team are you on, anyway, dickhead? That was six inches off the plate!"

"What? He put it right in the spot!"

"Your mom puts it right in the spot."

The ball was returned. I reloaded and fired again, another fastball fouled. Next came a change for a ball. Then a fastball for the kill that just missed. Then a change spit on. Soon we were in a full count and the adrenaline had reached its peak.

"You're not going to walk me," said the suddenly confident captain.

"I have no intention of it," I shot back.

"I'm staying in here till I get you or you get me."

"Right, because that would happen in a real game."

"You scared?"

"Am I scared?" No, but I was aware of the situation. I knew if he got a hit off me now, after all this buildup, I'd never hear the end of it. Bested by a douche bag with a tattoo that read "egg roll," inconceivable! My only option for clear-cut victory was to punch him out. The problem was, it was too early in the winter to take my curveball or slider off the shelf. I could roll a big sloppy hook in there for ball four, or a slider that doesn't slide and catches that long, ogre swing. I needed something else from my bag of tricks. Something he hadn't seen yet, maybe ever.

"Okay, big dog. My best versus your best," I said.

"Best fastball?" He salivated.

"Best fastball. I'm putting it right down the middle," I said, charging him up. "All you have do is hit it."

"Alright then, let's do this!" he said, finishing our exchange of action movie dialogue. Curls offered a toothy grin, knuckled up on his bat, and dug in.

I reset on the bicycle ramp and put my best weapon to work: my brain.

Baseball players are funny, predictable creatures, especially when they're young. When the pressure is on and intensity is turned up, it's natural to try to do too much—a classic shortcoming that's plagued the breed for years. When that big payoff moment arrives, pitchers rear back and try to throw their arms off, only to miss the spot by four feet or get clubbed off the wall. Hitters swing like berserk Vikings only to whiff or watch their bats explode in a shower of splinters. Sometimes intensity is the enemy. Sometimes less is more. Sometimes a player needs to slow down and realize that by adding to the drama, you're just playing into the other guy's adrenaline high.

For the payoff pitch, instead of my normal, methodical delivery of coming set and kicking, I came set, held, then stepped instantly home in a sharp, abbreviated motion, almost like I was picking off to the plate. I knew I wasn't going to throw that hard this way, but what I lost in velocity I made up with the element of surprise.

Captain Curls stood loaded at the plate, timing me in anticipation of a juicy heater. Instead, a 70 mph batting practice heater lazily lumbered right down the middle to a confused hitter who watched it float by.

Remorsefully, his catcher and teammate, the dickhead, called him out.

Instantly Curls's minions turned on him. "Dude, how do you not swing at that? It was right there!"

"Shut the hell up!" protested Curls. "That's not even a legal pitch, right? That's not a legal pitch, is it?" he said, glaring at his catcher. "He can't do what he just did!"

"I, I don't know, dude," sputtered the catcher.

Curls dropped his bat and stared at me. "What the hell was that crap?"

"You striking out. Perfectly legal," I said, stepping out of the cage. To be honest, I wasn't sure if it would work. I never had enough guts to do something like that in a real game. Coaches always talk about how effective a little timing variation is at screwing up a hitter, but it can also screw up a pitcher. I decided I'd have to hold on to that little trick.

"That wasn't your best fastball," continued the captain.

"Best is such an arbitrary term," I said, changing my shoes and stuffing my glove into a gym bag.

"You're done? You can't leave us on that."

"Sorry, gentlemen, I have to. I got a date tonight and you're out of time."

"You got a date? You're blowing us off for a girl?" Like a group of seventh-graders, they all oohed over my admission.

"Easy, princess. Don't be mad at me because things didn't work out in there the way you wanted."

"I ain't mad. You beat me with an illegal pitch." Curls stepped from the cage, his teammates filling in around him.

"No, I beat you with something you've never seen before. Spend as much time as I have in the minors and you find new ways to get things done," I said, throwing my bag over my shoulder.

"Yeah, but now you're walking away from getting better for a girl. That's crazy. You're a pro player, man. You can get a girl anytime you want. You only got a little while to get better before spring training."

Curls took a dry cut with his bat while he waited for me to respond, to confirm his belief that life was centered around the ease at which things came to those with a professional baseball title. As I looked back at him, I felt like I was looking at a younger version of myself, a Dirk who believed that baseball had all the answers. I was never as cocky or well tanned as Curls, but I was just as naïve, just as convinced that baseball would always love me as long as I dedicated myself to it. But that was years ago, as far away from me now as Curls was from hitting my last fastball. I would never be able to explain it to him. He knew what he needed to know for where he was, and where he hoped to go—but not for where I hoped to go.

"It's not what you think it is," I said.

"That's because you haven't made it to the Bigs yet," said Curls. "You make it to the Bigs, you can get all the girls you want, right?"

I sighed, thinking about baseball's Promised Land. "Maybe."

"Then what's more important: girls now, or girls in the Bigs?"

"I don't know," I said. The words must have sounded like heresy as the troupe exchanged shocked faces.

"You aren't going to make it with an attitude like that," said Curls. But it wasn't his voice I heard; it was my own that had been saying the same thing for a while now.

"Easy, bro," I cautioned him, "I don't think you know what you're talking about."

"I'm just saying it sounds like you can't keep your priorities straight."

"What do you know about priorities?" I came on Curls, angrily. "What do you know about life? I've been through shit you can't imagine to keep this game a priority. I think you better learn your station before you shoot your mouth off." I slung my pack off my shoulder and reached for the door handle. "Besides, I'm not ducking out on a chance to improve. I struck you out nine times tonight on winter fastballs and horseshit changeups. Facing you isn't going to make me any better. Hell, it might make me worse." We stared at each other in silence for a moment. "Now, I gotta go see about a girl. Don't let the tee strike you out while I'm gone," I said, nodding to a bucket of balls and a batting tee sitting in the corner. Then I opened the door and walked out. Bonnie's concert was starting soon, and I was already running behind.

Chapter Nine

The extra arguing—and stopping to get flowers—made me late for the start of Bonnie's Share Day concert. I had to sneak in to the event, sitting just before the first act finished. Ironically, after all that effort to arrive on time, the music turned out to be terrible. The rhythm was rarely kept and the melody was almost nonexistent. The drummer banged off tempo while some of the other performers couldn't play their instruments at all. Vocalists frequently lost harmony; in fact, some of them forgot the lyrics to songs altogether. And yet, all things considered, it was easily the most moving, most beautiful musical performance I had ever seen.

The audience was composed of parents dressed as if their children were performing live at Carnegie Hall, not some local church stage. Some held cameras, some flowers, some the hands of other children to keep them from wandering off to create commotions of their own.

"Abigail," called Bonnie, standing center stage, "it's your turn to share."

All the performers were spectators in the audience when they weren't themselves performing. Abigail, a teenage firecracker with frizzy dark hair, did not spectate well. She talked through most of the performances, shouting out what she saw or felt. As rude as it was, it did not bother anyone in the audience; in fact, in its own way it was charming. Abigail was autistic, as were almost all of the performers in attendance.

Bonnie was a music therapist. I could try explaining it but I wouldn't do it justice. Some say she's a music teacher, some say she's a special needs assistant, and some say she's a miracle worker. As the show went along, parent after parent of these special children broke down in tears of awe as their sons and daughters went onstage to try singing, playing instruments, and dancing. When most of these kids came to Bonnie, they could barely speak or articulate feelings of any kind.

Abigail was escorted by her mother to the steps of the stage where Bonnie met them. Bonnie took Abigail's hand and brought her onstage asking, "Are you excited?" though the answer was quite obvious. Abigail flapped and flailed her hands like she was pleasantly on fire with emotion; then she nodded over and over and stomped her feet.

"Tell everyone what you are going to be performing tonight, Abigail."

Abigail strangled the mic, pressing it up to her face until you could hear her breathing through the assembly hall speakers. *"High School Musical,"* she said. The audience laughed at this. Abigail might be autistic, but she was still a teenage girl.

Bonnie played the score of Abigail's song on the piano and accompanied on vocals, but Abigail, as was the case with the rest of the children, was the star of the show. Abigail wore a radiant dress, which swished like a streamer as she twirled in the excitement of being a star. Sometimes she twirled so hard she flashed the audience with the tights she wore underneath, an event that left Abigail's mother with her hands on her head. When the music finished, Abigail clapped for herself then bowed so sharply the headband that corralled her wild mop of hair flew off, allowing the brown, frizzy mane to engulf her face. Within seconds Abigail was met with a standing ovation.

While Abigail and the rest of Bonnie's clients bowed, Bonnie bowed out, never trying to steal a hint of fanfare for herself. I noticed this, if only because it seemed so counterintuitive to me. All my life I'd been chasing a job that would give me attention, fame, and glory. Yet here was Bonnie, spending her life to give the attention to others, people who couldn't champion their own causes.

I loved her; I loved her world. There was no trash talking here. No competitive anteing. No crushing the other person so you could stand out as the best. This was a place where everyone had a chance to shine. Bonnie was selfless and caring and openhearted. Her tenderness drew me to her. She afforded me an opportunity to drop the guard that living in a world of testosterone stats, broken family relationships, and long-shot odds forced me to construct. Being around her reminded me of the Dirk I was before professional baseball caught me between its hammer and anvil, and before alcoholism and anger left its scars in my personal life. She made me feel creative and capable. She made me feel safe, and keeping that feeling was easily worth ten thousand dollars of lost wages. In fact, as I watched her onstage, I believed it was worth whatever price, even if I moved baseball permanently out of my number-one priority spot.

After dinner, we sat in Bonnie's car, a beautiful new Audi, parked next to my car, a crappy, rusted-out Corolla, in the parking lot of the value-based Italian restaurant where I had taken her to dinner. Bonnie was curled up with my arm around her, both of us gazing at the winter sky through the unfrosted portions of the windshield. The radio was on some oldies station playing music you could still make out the lyrics to. This was our only alone time now. Privacy was at a premium for us; our dates consisted of fleeting hours meeting after work, staying at coffee shops or bookstores or restaurants until they closed, and then lingering in their parking lots.

Though I was in Bonnie's neck of the woods tonight, she wasn't comfortable with me hanging out at her house too late. Bonnie still lived at home with her parents, and Bonnie's mom had a tendency to "sleepwalk" if she suspected a boy was in the house doing anything more than G-rated behavior with her daughter—though her daughter was twenty-eight. Unlike my family, Bonnie's had good relationships, good jobs, and a nice house. Bonnie's folks loved having their daughter around and even encouraged it, as they considered it good Christian parenting to keep an eye on her until a suitable gentleman came calling. This conservative, chaste imprinting was also one of the reasons Bonnie and I had only shared kisses and snuggles and not much else. That and we both drove compacts.

"You know, I've been thinking about ways you could brand your business when you go solo," I said. "I was thinking you could have a mascot, like the minor leagues have, you know, to distinguish yourself."

"A mascot?" repeated Bonnie, skeptically.

"Yeah, something special and unique, like the kids you work with."

"And what would this mascot be?"

"Well, I was thinking it could be the combination of two animals to make one special one, that could be a symbol of specialness, you know?"

"And this special animal would be called . . . ?"

"A Garfoose," I said. "You know, half giraffe and half moose? It could have purple spots and big moosey antlers. He would love children and breathe fire when you tickle him, and—"

"You want me to brand my business based on a fire-breathing giraffe with antlers," Bonnie rephrased.

"When you tickle him, yes," I said.

"Hmmm, well, as good as that idea is"—she took a thoughtful pause—"I'm not sure it's best that I brand myself with something so, uh, flammable."

"Think about it for me, okay? Who knows, the Garfoose might grow on you."

"Who knows," she repeated, smiling as sincerely as she could muster before leaning her head back on me and settling back into the solace of the evening.

I took a deep breath. I needed to tell her what was really on my heart.

"I'm leaving in two months," I said, breaking the mood, "but I want you to know that I don't want to leave you."

"I know. I don't want you to go, either, but I understand why you have to."

"I know you do." I offered a melancholy smile and hooked her hair over her ears. "I quit my job at Circuit City today," I said.

"Really, why?"

"It just wasn't worth it. I was making next to nothing to be there and it was more of a distraction than an asset. I've got enough saved now to get through the rest of the off-season and I have baseball lessons that pay well. There are other things I want to focus on now." I looked at Bonnie, who seemed to be following along as best she could.

"That makes sense, I guess," said Bonnie.

"You know how much Adam said I could make in Winter Ball?"

"No, you didn't tell me."

"Ten thousand dollars."

"Wow, really?" Then, like a chill took hold of her, she was suddenly aware of where this conversation was going. "So, you're going to go after all?"

I looked away, trying to find some hidden strength to lift the words I had on my mind. "No. No, I'm not."

"But if it's such a good opportunity, why wouldn't you?"

"I love playing baseball, but it's not giving me the quality of life I thought it would. I'm not sure if the money would do that, either. I'm sure it would help, but . . ." I wasn't sure if my rationale was accurate or not since I'd never had money before, but I said it anyway. "Honestly, I don't know if getting to the big leagues is going to justify all the crap I've gone through to get there. I've seen what life is like when all you have is baseball.

"Can I ask you something?" I continued.

"Sure."

"Something big?"

"Of course." She inched back to take me in.

"Something really big?"

"Yes." She chuckled. "You can ask me anything."

"I think I want to marry you."

Bonnie started blinking as the words hit warp speed in her head. A smile bloomed on her quickly blushing face. "That's not a question," she objected.

"Bonnie, I love you. I love you for all the right reasons. When I'm with you I feel better about who I am and where I'm going. It's like I know that even if everything else goes wrong, at least I got you right. As long as I'm in this line of work I know that I have to give up half of my year to my job, and for the first time in my entire career I'm more worried about what I'll lose during that half year than what I might gain. I don't want to lose you."

"You're not going to," she promised.

"You say that now."

"You're not," she insisted. Her face was like a dam ready to burst with emotion. Then she sat up on her knees and looked me in the face. "But you still haven't asked me anything."

"I know, and I'm kind of afraid to, even though I think I know what you'll say." Her face was practically sending out the invitations. "I'm afraid because I want to do this right. I don't want circumstances to dictate how this will work. I don't have any money for a ring and I don't even know when we could do it, but I need to know. I need to know the reasons I'm acting on aren't unfounded. Instead, let's say if I were to ask you *that* question, what do you think you would say, considering a few—"

"I'd say yes," she blurted.

"That's, well, that's wonderful! Believe me, I am *so* happy you said that, but I wouldn't feel right if I didn't tell you everything I was thinking." Bonnie sat back as I explained all the details concerning marrying a baseball player, the distance issues, the money issues, and the timing issues.

"I've been thinking about it a lot lately. Baseball kills relationships. I don't want this one to die. That's why I want you to know that"—I took a breath—"if you want me to quit baseball in order to help you put all this together, I will."

Bonnie started shaking her head at me, slowly at first, but then distinctly in disagreement. "No," she said, "absolutely not. I don't want you to do this with any regrets."

"I wouldn't be regretting anything," I said. "I've gotten to play longer than most people ever do. I've played at every level besides the Bigs, and even if I get there"—these words were particularly hard to hear myself utter—"there is no guarantee it will make up for all I've given, and would give, to do it. I'm ready for a life beyond baseball, and you're a wonderful reason to move on."

"You don't have to move on. We'll make this work. Dirk, I love you. I love you for the man you are and the way you treat me. I love you because you make me feel free, even though you insist you're not going anywhere. I want to be with you and I wouldn't have said yes if I didn't think we could do it. I think getting married after the season is a wonderful idea and it's not going to get in the way. We'll figure it all out and it will be incredible, because the people involved are incredible, right?"

I started to smile, but her positive attitude could not defeat the unresolved details and failure-to-launch experiences I had in my mind. Bonnie deduced this and said, "Don't worry about all the details. I've only been waiting my *entire life* to plan them—I got it covered!"

"Okay then," I consented.

"Okay? Okay! This is great! We're going to get married!" Bonnie opened the car door and ran out into the snow.

I followed her out of the car. "So you're not disappointed that I asked you instead of just proposing? I didn't ruin some momentous, once-in-a-lifetime girl experience for you?"

"I'm glad you asked me if you could ask me."

"That doesn't sound very romantic, though."

"No, but it's smart, and I know you'll come up with a real romantic official proposal. I trust you."

"Oh, well, no pressure. You know, if I get sent back to Double A, it could be a while before I can gather up enough to get you a ring. Of course, if I get sent back to Double A after the year, I think that would be baseball's way of telling me I should move on."

"Then you have two great reasons to make the Triple A roster. Now stop trying to kill my buzz!" Bonnie wadded up a snowball and threw it at me—it missed by six feet.

"No wife of mine is allowed to miss a spot that bad." I made a snowball and drilled her in the back. Soon we were snowball fighting, then wrestling, then sitting on the hood of the car kissing.

"I hope I can give you a wonderful proposal experience."

"You worry too much. I don't care if you propose with a doughnut, I'll say yes."

"Do you have any particular flavor doughnut you'd like?"

She kissed me. "I love you, Dirk Hayhurst." Then she jerked away from my lips and said, "Oh my gosh, you know what we have to do?" I braced myself for the onslaught of wedding ideas that were about to pour forth. I had just given her the power to shackle me to every single nauseating decoration idea, dress choice, and color scheme obsession.

"We should call your grandmother and tell her we're getting married, and that we plan on living in her basement."

I smiled. "You are going to make a fantastic Hayhurst."

Chapter Ten

Two months later, Bonnie walked with me through the airport lobby to the security checks. We both stopped and came to terms with what the next few steps would mean. The off-season had run its course, and it was time for me to board a plane that would take me away from her and back to the game.

"I'm not a big fan of good-byes," I said.

"Me neither," said Bonnie.

"I feel like I'm doing something wrong, like I shouldn't get on the plane." I searched Bonnie's face. "Should I get on this plane?"

"You're doing the right thing. This is your big chance and you're going for it."

"It feels different this time."

"I wouldn't know. This is my first time sending you off to base-ball."

"You're not going to cry, are you? You're allowed to, but I'll just feel bad."

"I'm not a crier," said Bonnie. "If I do, it will be when I'm back in my car." Then, as if on cue, she started to cry anyway.

There was no way around it: the next few months were going to be rough. I had prepped, coached, and encouraged Bonnie as much as I could. I helped narrow down dates and ticket prices to overlapping rendezvous cities for all the possible team schedules I had the chance to play on. I even upgraded my text-message plan so I could spam Bonnie with "I love you"s at all hours of the day. Yet, even with the combined force of all that preparation, there was no way of taking the sting out of what was ahead of us. If it's not the distance baseball creates between you and your lady, it's the lack of resources it gives you to bridge the gap. We would see each other a grand total of twenty days this season, if that—circumstances that are hard to overcome for any new relationship, let alone one vowing marriage.

Speaking of which, we still had a wedding to plan. Venues, caterers, décor, and all the other stuff that make a Big Day big. Bonnie and I split up responsibilities accordingly. All the accoutrements that would make the day one to remember were left in Bonnie's capable hands. Meanwhile, I was left with the responsibility of earning ring money so I could make the engagement official by Western civilization's standards, and asking her parents for their blessing.

Like the proposal, things seemed to be functioning out of order. Whether it was the fact that Bonnie's parents were powerless against their daughter's enthusiasm, or that they were simply incredible at understanding the unorthodox circumstances of my baseball career, they told me that when I was ready to ask for their blessing, they'd be ready to give it and, in the meantime, they would reinforce our pocketbook "within reason" when it came to planning the Big Day. I told them I'd gladly take their money, but held off on the blessing since I figured I should at least have the ring first.

While Bonnie's parents were understanding, mine were not. My parents thought the entire occasion was a catastrophe waiting to happen. When I told my parents about Bonnie and me, my mom told me she'd heard this kind of talk out of my mouth before, and then, *poof,* I was single again. She told me I could talk myself into, or out of anything, and after a healthy, screaming Hayhurst debate on the subject, she told me she would believe it only when it happened. My dad, on the other hand, told me point-blank that Bonnie wasn't the one.

"She's cute, as far as that goes, but she ain't it," he said.

"How would you know?"

"She just ain't. I know you. She's a distraction, but you'll get tired of her. You did all the others."

"I don't think you know me as well as you think you do," I said, angrily.

"Don't I? I don't think you know you, is more like it."

"How can you say that? The most you talk to me is when you're yelling."

"You don't know shit about marriage. You just met this girl. You're just gonna piss all you've worked for away 'cause you got some girl waiting? That's just stupid, Dirk."

"I'm not gonna piss it away."

"Well, I don't see you pulling this off doing baseball."

"Then I'll have to quit baseball."

"Ah, Jesus, you see, that's what I . . ." He threw his hands in the air. "Just stupid. Just fucking stupid. Whatever," he said. "It's your life. I don't give a shit what you do."

It wasn't the reception I was hoping for.

My dad was right about one thing: it was my life and I would prove my parents wrong when I worked things out in my favor. I'd make this relationship work and do fine in baseball, too. I didn't have the best example of just how to make a marriage function, but I did have every example of how not to.

But as Bonnie dampened my shirt with her tears, I realized what a precarious position I was truly in. Was it confidence or arrogance that made me think I had this under control? This year would be like a tug-of-war, with Bonnie on one side, baseball on the other, and me in the middle trying to hold it all together. Could I really do it?

Rocking her gently, I said, "We'll call when we can, video-chat every chance we get, and be creative during the times in between.

Before you know it, you'll be out to visit me. The first two weeks are the toughest because of the routine change, but if you stay busy, the time will fly by. We're going to do this—we are. I promise you." And secretly, I promised myself as well.

"I know, I know," said Bonnie. "It's actually good I'll have all this extra time to work on wedding details." She offered me a melancholy smile.

"There you go. Focus on the prize. Speaking of the wedding," I said, taking a gravely serious tone, "I think the most important thing is how we can fleece as many of our guests for as much money as possible. You know how they have jars you have to stick wads of cash into to make us kiss and stuff? We need more ideas like that. I want this wedding to be so profitable, we will consider doing it a couple of times."

"Don't worry," said Bonnie. "I've been to so many other peoples' weddings, I know all the tricks to use for my own."

I kissed her on the forehead. "You're the perfect woman."

She pulled away from my embrace and looked me in the eyes. "In case you were planning it"—Bonnie patted me forcefully on the chest to make sure I got her point—"don't even *think* of proposing to me on a baseball field."

"I thought you said I could do it anywhere?"

"Anywhere but there."

"Great, well, if you think of anyplace else I'm not allowed to do it, let me know."

"I just don't want to be on the big screen in front of a million people."

"Big screen? Million people? You haven't been to a lot of minor league ballparks, have you?"

"No baseball proposal," she said firmly.

"Fine, no baseball proposal. Got it." Bonnie went back to resting her head on my chest while I looked out the window to planes in motion on the tarmac. It was almost time for me to go.

"I just want you to know," I said, "no matter what happens from here, this is the biggest year of my life. I always thought making it to the big leagues would mark my biggest year, but it turns out it was you."

"This is the biggest year of *our* lives, babe. We're going to have to start thinking plural now."

"Weird," I said.

"I think it's great," said Bonnie.

"Yeah, I guess I think it's great, too."

"You're going to do awesome this season."

"If I do, you're the reason."

"Whatever," she said, tearing up again. "Listen, you do this, okay? You focus on this and don't ever let me be the reason you didn't try your best."

"I won't, honey. I'm a professional, remember?"

"Promise?"

"I promise. I love you," I said.

"I love you, too," said Bonnie.

She kissed me, squeezed my hand, then turned and walked away.

She did not look back.

Chapter Eleven

It took about seven hours to reach the Phoenix airport, if you count the layovers. Strolling down the concourse with my carry-on over my shoulder, I turned on my cell. There were oodles of messages waiting for me. Bonnie mostly. I didn't reply to any of them; there would be time for that later when I was in my hotel and accounted for. Right now, it was important to get my mind right. There would be very little alone time now that I was once again bought property, and it was important to get focused on what I was trying to do here.

This was my sixth spring with the Padres. That's a long time in baseball years. The first time I flew in to train with them, I dressed up: slacks, suit jacket, shoes, the whole production. I didn't know who was going to meet me on the concourse, but I wanted to make a good impression. In fact, I thought it might help me get to the big leagues faster if my new employers thought I was a snappy dresser. What if Kevin Towers, the Padres' general manager himself, was at the airport waiting to give me an extra-warm welcome only to discover I looked like a slob? The results could be disastrous. I didn't sign a contract with enough guaranteed money to afford missing any first impression opportunities.

As it turned out, the guy who picked me up was a three-hundred-pound Samoan clubhouse attendant who had been collecting other confused, overdressed rookies all day. He didn't know who I was and he didn't care. To him, I was just another jock to wash and he wanted me to get in the van because he had to get back to the spring training complex in time to change the laundry over. Thus began a long series of revelatory moments in professional baseball, many of which were not as euphoric as the childhood fantasies I'd always held on to.

The first player I shook hands with told me he knew my college of origin, Kent State, and that he remembered playing against us during a regional matchup. He said he suspected our conference to be fairly weak since we didn't seem very good. I informed him that I started that particular game and he asked if I knew someone in the Padres organization, because he didn't understand how I got drafted. I started to wonder that myself after one of the higher-ranking player development figures, a man we would later come to call Wyatt Earp because of his obsession with the radar gun, watched me throw a bullpen less than twenty-four hours into my career and said, "Eighth rounder? I expected better."

My first roommate was a Mormon guy who staunchly avoided tea and chew. However, he did not avoid regularly bringing girls back to the room and sleeping with them, with me in the room. The next day, I found out my prudish Christian scruples on kissing and telling, and exactly what can be kissed and told about on a woman's body, were not shared by the bulk of my new coworkers.

But the worst discovery of my young career, and the one that would haunt me for years to come, was learning just how hard life can be for those players who profess baseball ignorance. My first spring training locker was not too far away from a gentleman named Valenzuela Jr. The person who occupied that locker was not very athletic-looking. He was short, stubby, and rather rounded when compared to the other tall, sculpted Adonises who made the professional ranks. I thought he might have actually been one of the favor drafts I was accused of being just a day earlier. If it was true, then, considering my own experiences with the title's implication, I thought this round young man might need a friend. I introduced myself, then asked what I thought would be a harmless small-talk question: "Junior, eh? Did your dad play too?" When he told me I was a fucking idiot, I honestly had no idea why.

People get pretty offended when you don't know the history of their greatness, and everyone who becomes pro thinks they're great, at least for a little while. Stuff they did in college, stuff they did in high school, stuff their parents did. They all know someone who knows someone; they all have a friend a couple of levels higher up in the system; they all think they know something you don't, some inside track on how they will soon be great themselves.

The bitter irony of it all, which coaches point out at the start of every camp, is that most of us, no matter what our pedigree, won't make it to the big leagues. Of those who do, almost none will have careers long enough to retire from. Our life in this game is short, though none of us chooses to accept this when we're young and dreaming of playing for decades. For a rookie, signing a minor league contract means the world is your oyster and the future is as bright as the lights atop a big league stadium. If it doesn't work out, we feel we've got nothing to lose since we'll always be able to say, "At least I made it pro," and how many other people can say that?

After a few years of grinding in the game, that statement isn't good enough. Even though we realize what we're playing for is nothing greater or less than a simple window of time, that moment becomes the center of our universe, a moment where we're on top of the heap, a moment in which we can actually make our history worth remembering. We lose sight of the fact that baseball, for all its high drama and patriotism, is a lottery ticket job with few winners and lots of losers.

Once the game is in your veins, it's hard to kick the habit. It keeps you hooked through hope, and strung out on chances. It makes you believe that just a few days in the big leagues will justify all the years you traded trying to get them. A rational man would walk away from the whole thing once he figured out what was happening to him, but baseball is not a rational place. There a very few careers that offer you such a life-changing opportunity mixed with the fulfillment of victory. The trouble is, you're not buying that opportunity with dollars, but with years of your life you can't have back once spent.

Now I was betting years of Bonnie's life alongside my own. I knew Bonnie would let me chase my window of time as long as I wanted, even beyond the point of lying to myself about the window of time that I had. At present, I honestly believed I still had a chance and, like I said in the kitchen at my parents' house, it was the best one I'd ever had. But that could all change in the blink of an eye, and if it did, I had to be willing to change with it.

I never wanted our life together to become one of scraping by with crossed fingers, taking handouts from our parents like mine still did from theirs. For me, this was a make-or-break year. If I went backward, if things went south, I needed to be the rational man and walk away. I didn't want it to come to that, but I was no longer playing for some loose ideal of greatness or an opportunity to make some trite statement about how close I came. I would never be a twenty-year veteran with hall of fame numbers. I would never be a franchise icon. I would never have my jersey retired. If I was going to marry Bonnie, the only way I could rationalize remaining in the game was if I was going to use it to meet the needs of an adult player, not to fulfill the dreams of a child.

If I was going to keep pushing, I needed my best opportunity to become a reality, and I needed it to happen this year.

Chapter Twelve

Slappy stood next to Maddog in the middle of the complex's minor league clubhouse with a smile painted across his face, head
bobbing up and down in appreciation of the pure genius in their
new business plan. At their feet were several open shoe boxes, and
in those boxes were porn DVDs, dozens and dozens of them.

"Only four dollars, guys. Don't be scared. Step right up and get
your four-dollar porn," said Slappy like some carnival caller.

"Get 'em here for four dollars or pay fifteen dollars back at the
hotel on pay-per-view. You know you're going to do it later, so you
might as well save!" echoed Maddog.

Today was the official report day for minor league pitchers and
catchers. The morning was dedicated to getting medical issues in
order so we could be cleared to play. Various testing stations were
set up around the complex to collect medical data, things like
urine and blood, and if you had any lumps on your testicles. There
were enough tests that if all the guys in camp evenly distributed
themselves, the event would run smoothly. However, since everyone wanted to do the same tests first, namely the blood and urine,
lines formed in front of those stations that wrapped around the
complex.

The reason you give blood first is because you can't eat until
you do. The reason peeing first is so desirable is because it's noto-

riously hard to go wee-wee with some doctor staring at your package. Since most guys have to pee first thing when they wake up, players hold their morning waterworks for the test, which means by the time they show up at the park, they're all ready to burst. Attend enough spring trainings and you learn to show up early to beat the lines. Beyond that, there is really nothing else a player can do except endure the day. Or, so I thought—Slappy and Maddog found a way to make a profit on it.

Aside from getting us into season-worthy shape, spring training was also seven weeks' worth of guys seeing nothing but other guys. Guys on the field, in the weight room, out to lunch, in the hotel, and in the shower. It's absolute penis overload. In fact, if everything goes according to tradition, within the first twenty-four hours of spring training, management will make certain we know that if we're caught bringing women back to the hotel room, we'll pay a hefty price. Fines can get up into the two-hundred-dollar range, roughly two weeks' worth of meal money, giving credence to a commonly heard spring training phrase: "Make sure you get your money's worth."

For some players, being chaste for a month and a half in order to avoid debt is a minor annoyance. For others, it's a fate worse than death. Asking these extremely hormone-driven individuals to keep their pants on is like asking them to hold their breath for six weeks. Fortunately, bringing back an X-rated film to the room is not a fineable offense. While it may not be the real thing, it is a lot cheaper and also explains why there are guys on every minor league baseball team who can play entire rounds of *Jeopardy* based solely on clues concerning Jenna Jameson. Some may call those players perverts, but for Maddog, who was now passing out business cards for *Four-Dollar Porn,* those players were big money.

All things considered, Maddog's four-dollar dynasty was not only cheap, but practical, and many of the guys occupying the expanse of the clubhouse came over to at least investigate what kind of product was being brought to the market.

Rosco, a reliever from last year's High A team, the Lake Elsinore Storm, plucked out a DVD and looked it over. *"Ravenous Asian Sluts, Volume Seventeen,"* he read. "Seventeen? There are seventeen volumes' worth of *Ravenous Asian Sluts?"*

"No," said Maddog. "There's at least twenty-one. The rest are in another box."

"What's a matter, Rosco? You don't like Asians?" asked Slappy.

"Not these ones. Haven't they ever heard of razors?"

"What do you expect for four dollars?"

"Why would I spend four dollars on this stuff when the Internet is free?" asked Rosco, holding two DVDs next to each other, doing a bit of comparison shopping.

"Because the Internet has viruses, especially *those* sites, and I know the ones you're going to because we've roomed together. And, because Net access is like ten dollars a day at most hotels," said Slappy.

"Shit, I don't need a day's worth. Most of the time I only need about a preview's worth to get the job done," said another player named Dalton, fumbling through the selection.

"Yeah, only perverts actually watch a whole porn movie, start to finish," added another player nicknamed Blade, rooting through Dalton's discards.

"You two are bad for business," said Slappy.

"Yeah, where would America be with that attitude?" said Maddog.

"Besides, this stuff is good for your career. You can't play all plugged up," said Slappy.

"You may have a point there," said Dalton.

Dalton was a regular wild man, and last year he immortalized himself as such by dangling from a bus's luggage rack naked and tea-bagging other players as they walked from the bus lavatory—aka "spidermanning" them. Blade was another reliever from last year's championship team. Unlike Dalton, who made himself famous for creative uses of nudity, Blade's forte was his needling sarcasm. On the other hand, Slappy and Maddog, like Rosco, were relievers from last year's High A Lake Elsinore team. That team was a madhouse compared to the Double A bunch, with the maturity bar set so low it made Dalton look like a high school principal. Slappy was the spark plug of the group, an easily excited lefty who seemed to function without any hint of a moral conscience. Maddog, a cool, near stoned-looking righty, never went looking for trouble, but he sure liked to hang around those who did, which was why he never seemed far way from Slappy. Rosco was the group's balance, if you could call him that. He was the voice of wisdom who, every so often, would say something insightful like, "If you do that, you're a complete dumb ass."

Since I split time on both teams last year, I made friends with both sets of relievers. Watching them together reminded me just how many different personalities there are in the baseball community. It also reminded me how fast they can overcome those differences when they share a topic of common interest, like porn. This was what player interaction was like in spring training: a constantly moving mass of personalities that bumped into one another like blind tadpoles wearing the same jersey. Most players will stick with the groups and teams they've spent the most time with because we'll never all spend enough time together to become best friends unless we're placed on a team, or in a hotel room together, or have a good reason to branch out, like Asian sluts.

"I never pay full price for porn because I ain't gonna make it through more than five minutes' worth," continued Dalton.

"Think about it like this," said Slappy, sliding next to Dalton. "There's like eight scenes on every disk; that's at least eight preview trailers. Eight trailers for four dollars is fifty cents a trailer. It's still a bargain." Dalton stopped to consider Slappy's logic against the glossy, unshaven pictures on the DVD cases.

My locker was about ten feet from the clubhouse's new and growing red light district. I had peed and bled already, and was taking a break from the rest of my tests, checking my issued uniform pants to see how the fit was. After coming to the Padres, Grady Fuson, the director of player development, had instituted a "must show sock" rule for which all the minor league players would be held accountable, starting today. Funny, you could get fined hundreds of dollars if you had your sister in your hotel room or didn't show enough sock when in uniform, but there was no charge for vending pornography in the locker room.

Drawn to this spectacle, more players came to investigate the Four-Dollar Porn Company. Most of them picked up a volume of something with nurses or librarians, chuckled to themselves, threw it back in the box, and went back to their lines. Everyone in baseball has seen porn, even me, Mr. Goody Two-Shoes Hayhurst, who refused to drink for five professional years and was still waiting for marriage. I made this confession to the boys last year in an attempt to show unity when they started to wonder if I was gay for not being sexually active. Instead of debating porn's objectification of women and desensitizing of the male psyche, I just told them I was religious, which was also why I sounded like a judgmental prick. They accepted this, and now that I was casually drinking, it was almost like I was a regular baseball player.

"So," said the voice of a player not affiliated with either of the teams I played on last year, "when you talk to your girl tonight, what are you going to tell her happened in the locker room today?"

"Good question," I said. One of the guys at the porn kiosk was now demo-ing a particular position he learned from a video referred to as "oil derricking." "I think I will opt out of discussing this morning's activity."

"It starts already," said my new friend, lacing his hands behind his head as if philosophizing. "Lying to protect your woman."

I didn't particularly like the sound of that. Probably because, in all my concern for how we would pull off a wedding while 3,000 miles apart, I forgot that baseball was infested with perpetual slimebag teenagers thinking under the full influence of their penises. I wanted my relationship with Bonnie to always be honest, and never based on omission. But how do you discuss things like affairs, cleat chasers, slump busters, and the locker room red light district with the woman who longs to be your wife because you're supposedly a pure, noble gentleman who would never associate with such behavior?

After six years, I was desensitized to it all. But Bonnie was, for lack of a better term, a rookie. Sharing any of the details that happened in the world of baseball day-to-day could get our relationship in deep trouble. Then again, so could lying like none of it ever happened, setting Bonnie up to find out the ungodly truth behind the title when some veteran wife spilled the beans. Baseball has so much dirty laundry in it a player is practically guilty by simple association, and that was something I would have to own up to.

"You know, I think I will tell her," I said. "I'm sure she knows groups of guys can be crude. This stuff shouldn't shock her. I'll just need to impress upon her that I wasn't participating. You'll be my witness, right?"

"How much is my testimony worth to you?"

"How much is me actually throwing the fingers you put down worth to you?"

"A fair point."

My friend's name was Aden, and he was a catcher. He was also my newest roommate back at the team's spring training hotel. At about five years younger than me, he left me scratching my head as to how he managed a hotel suite since this was only his second spring training. When I was going into my second year, there was no way in hell I would have landed a suite.

"I wonder where they get their supply from?" I said, nodding to the porn.

"Asia, obviously," said Aden.

"Is it just me, or does baseball seem more sexually deviant this year?"

"Feels like the same place it was last year to me," said Aden. "Minus the, you know, porn salesmen in the clubhouse."

"Yeah, it's probably just because I'm seeing all this through the eyes of a man about to be married."

"Probably."

"Hey, Diggler." Rosco was talking to me. *Diggler,* another Dirk-spawned nickname, was not an ironic choice considering the current situation. "Didn't you say last year that you liked the librarian-style, shy girl porn? Well, I just found the perfect twenty-DVD set for you."

"That's alright, I'm good," I said.

"Yeah, Digs is getting married," said Maddog.

"Oh shit! Really? In that case, you'll need something a little crazier than librarians. You don't want to disappoint your girl on your first night."

"Yeah!" said Slappy. "Let me show you the Oil Derrick."

"Shut up, Slap. You don't do that to your wife. Marriage is sacred," said Rosco.

"If you can't do it to your wife, who can you do it to?" said Slappy.

I laughed at it all. Baseball season was definitely here again. "Thanks for your concern, fellas, but my wife-to-be isn't a librarian."

"But is she Asian?"

Chapter Thirteen

When I showed up at spring training last year, the Padres' head minor league weight coach told me I was fat during the body mass examination. This distressed me greatly. For one, I disagreed. I knew what fat was because I had many role models in my family I could cite as references, and it was easy to tell the difference between them and myself. Second, there was a strong amount of hypocrisy involved in that statement because the person calling me fat looked like he'd made too many trips to the Twinkie box himself. Not only that, but this so-called expert in fat spotting told me players who want to make it to the big leagues can't afford to be fatties. I found that statement offensive and ignorant, especially since David Wells was a member of our big league roster at the time.

To find out exactly where the fat was hiding, this overweight weight coach used special calipers to pinch and tug on the flab in my skin. The results were uncontestable: I was fat, and science was the one pointing the finger at my paunch and laughing. This sounds worse than it was because it's not like I needed a motorized cart to get me around Walmart. If you placed me next to a group of non-athletes, it was easy to tell I was in good shape. However, when you placed me next to some of the best athletes on the planet, I became the ugly girl at the dance.

At first, I blamed this fat condemnation on my grandmother. Her cooking was chock-full of extra calories that she referred to as "flavoring." Things like bacon fat, Crisco, and straight-up lard often accounted for the asterisks in her recipes. However, after the head weight coach gave a mandatory meeting detailing what players should and should not eat during the season, I realized the reason I kept my weight on was not so much Grandma as it was the minor league diet and lifestyle.

In every clubhouse, peanut butter and jelly is the main food staple. It is the lifeblood of minor league athletes. Unfortunately, peanut butter is fat, jelly is simply purple or red sugar, and both get spread on worthless white, bleached bread. Some clubhouses may have a fruit or a vegetable tray present on a daily basis, but these things are more garnish than meal, as the bulk of player nourishment will still come from what is pressed between Styrofoam breading and Jiffy. Sometimes you are served a bag of mangled, processed lunch meat that has more in common with hooves and eyeballs than meat. Sometimes it's a collection of concession stand items like burgers and hot dogs. Occasionally, milk makes an appearance or a booster has pastries delivered. Whatever it is, it's never organic salmon with fresh spinach, figs, and olives.

The weight coach gave a lecture on this minor league eating style, dubbing it bad and to be avoided. He showed us slides of guys eating fresh greens, lean fish, and special fruits, and correlated them to ripped abs, big muscles, and victory. What he failed to connect were big price tags and empty wallets. It takes time and resources to eat well, not something in abundance when you're a minor leaguer living out of a hotel room. Furthermore, night games mean we eat heavy before sleep. Hard travel equals value menu feasting, and the formula for team chemistry always involves at least one part heavily fermented carb. Come the off-season, we're unemployed, but we still have to eat.

I wondered what the hell this guy was thinking by telling us not to eat what we really had no choice eating. Was our athlete's metabolism supposed to take care of it? Well, obviously, mine couldn't, not like the Dominican kid with the metabolism of a jet engine, or the genetic freak who could mix a six-pack with pizza grease and still look like he was carved from wood. I was normal, and when normal people eat crap for extended periods of time, the fat doesn't come off no matter how hard the calipers pull it.

I voiced my complaint about the minor league food system being broken, and for my trouble I was labeled a whiner—a fat whiner—who had a poor work ethic. Since permanently changing my eating habits was economically and logistically out of the question, I had to do the best I could with what I had, which simply meant I was going to have to eat less and work harder to burn off what my trainers thought my slothful reputation was putting on.

That was just what I did this off-season. I busted my ass, lifting weights and pride off the floor, over and over again. Bonnie might have been my largest motivation to get in shape, however, as getting trim for some bastard with a conditioning degree wasn't nearly as motivating as enticing my girl to put her hands on me. Being a better athlete might have factored in somewhere, but it was just icing on a cake I wasn't allowed to eat.

I thought about the weight testers when I got off the plane, when the Padres' shuttle van picked me up at the airport, when I fought to make sure my seniority garnered me a suite at the spring training hotel. I thought about it all night because I knew that if I had a poor showing, the number of my body fat would be displayed in a prominent place in the locker room for everyone to see and, like last year, cause other players to start calling me "Double-Stuffed Dirk."

The weight coaches were polishing the calipers when I walked in the weight room for testing. You can always spot a weight coach because he's the guy wearing a conditioning-sloganed T-shirt that relays some line from a corny eighties power ballad lyric like, "In the hunt," or "Hungry for victory," or "Rock you like a hurricane." Their shirts are typically tucked into mesh shorts, and their standard issue of equipment is a bale of rubber stretch bands and a handful of agility cones. Save the head coach, they don't get paid much and most are interns, but that doesn't stop them from yelling at you like veteran drill sergeants.

"Take your shirt off, Hayhurst," said the boss meathead.

"You could at least buy me a drink first."

The coach did not smile, but motioned with his pen to shut up and strip.

I started taking my shirt off. "You guys have no sense of humor."

"Shorts, too," said the coach.

It's always this way. All the tests are about as tactfully delivered as a prison cavity search. A player feels more like a piece of meat on days like this than any other. As my shirt came off, my glorious pelt of chest hair was revealed. Upon sight of said chest, a few of the players who'd followed me into the testing room yodeled at me like a Wookie.

"Oh, you're one to talk," I shot back at them.

More Wookiing.

"Jesus, Hayhurst, mix in some manscaping," said one of the ever body-conscious weight coaches.

"Now I know why you're a virgin," came a comment from the peanut gallery.

"Are we here to test hair or fat?" I asked.

The answer to that question became obvious when the cold steel tongs came out. First, my dimensions were measured with a tape measure: hips, chest, and height. Then I was placed on a scale to check my weight. Then it was pinching time.

Head Meat pulled my loose arm skin, then back skin, then chest skin.

"Stop flexing," he said.

"I'm not." I totally was.

"If you keep flexing it just hurts more."

The coach continued pinching while reading the numbers as he went. When he got to my waistline, I cringed. This would be the deal breaker. The coach didn't read the number off, but opted to punch it into the computer himself. Finished, they totaled all the data into their fat kid diagnosis machine. I held my breath until the coaches declared I had 16 percent body fat.

"Not bad, Hay, that's a pretty good meltdown since the last time you were here."

"Well, you guys really inspired me to get better," I said.

"Whatever it was, it's a good thing because the last time you were in here you had laid down some serious body fat. What was it the guys called you, 'Double-Stuffed'?"

I stared at the boss meathead, a guy named Stan, thinking of what it would feel like to pinch those calipers around his neck.

"Well, that was before I had you guys here to teach me," I said. "A lot of players don't realize that you're not just here to lay out cones, carry stretch bands, and click stopwatches. I mean, the Padres hired you to help us make our bodies better and that's what I tried to do, take your wisdom and apply it."

"Well, to be honest, it's about time you applied something. You're one of the older guys in this system and we shouldn't have to tell you to be in shape at this point."

"Thank you for being such a *positive* role model," I said through gritted teeth.

"That's my job. Yours is running in group one's conditioning circuit. Now get off my scale, hair ball."

Chapter Fourteen

"I can't believe you're making us do this stuff after we gave blood. Isn't that dangerous?" Slappy asked Stan as our fitness test group marched across the landscaping of the Padres complex to field four.

"You didn't give enough to make a difference," said Stan.

"When's the last time I had to run a ball to home plate?" asked Rosco, objecting to the amount of shuttles we had to run. The relevancy of the spring training fitness test has always been a hot debate among players on the verge of running it.

"It happens. Pitchers have to cover home," said Stan.

"Yeah, but do they stop and run back to the mound, then repeat it twelve more times?" continued Rosco.

"Maybe."

"No, no, no. They don't. They never do that," Slappy persisted.

"You never know," said Stan. You could tell he was enjoying the absoluteness of his power. This was the time of year when weight coaches reign supreme. Come the start of the season, when they can't punish us with "fat camp" or extra running, they try to make friends again. But here, their word is law, and some enjoy it a little too much.

"Pitchers don't do rundowns between home and the mound!" Slappy protested.

"This is the National League. You can get in one on the bases," Stan replied.

"Well, I'm feeling pretty dizzy right now," said Slappy. "I think they took more blood than they should have."

"Besides, Slappy has all kinds of STDs, so he needs all the extra blood he can get," said Maddog.

Stan smirked oh so slightly, marching onward, winding and unwinding the cord of his stopwatch around his finger as he strode.

I walked next to Dalton as the first fitness test group filed along. Dalton was one of the only guys, aside from myself, from last year's championship squad who didn't get invited to big league camp. However, as recompense, we were granted the "privilege" of running the spring training fitness in the first group. Since years of arguing the matter had already taught us there was no way of getting out of this test, Dalton and I turned our attention to bigger issues.

"They brought in the whole fucking island this year," said Dalton, referring to the large amount of Dominican players who were invited to big league camp. "And they brought in everyone else on the Missions team, too. Frenchy, Ox, Macias, Hundo, Headley, Ek, Moreno, even Marique. Everyone. Well, everyone but us."

"Reek?" I asked. "Even him? Wow." Manrique, or Reek, as we called him since he perpetually dispensed burrito-flavored farts, was the name of one of the Mexican relievers on the team from last season. He struggled with the Missions club last season, so it was surprising to hear that he went to camp with the big club. Especially since Dalton and I looked better than him on paper.

"Germ is back, too, and Bentley. Hell, they even brought Dallas over."

"Dallas? *Dallas?* After the year he had?" I sighed heavily; that name really hit a nerve. I had the best year of my life last year and I couldn't even get a sniff from the big league club, but Dallas, a guy who practically self-destructed in Triple A, got yet another invite to camp? What the heck?

"Reek getting invited is surprising, but Dallas . . . fuck," I grumbled.

"They like him. He's one of their top prospects," said Dalton.

"Oh, what does that even mean, 'top prospect'?" I sneered. "Just some stupid *Baseball America* list."

"In this organization, it means you get paid a lot of money to sign and if you don't pan out, someone is gonna get fired."

"I guess."

"For sure. Also, if you wanna be a top prospect around here, you need to get into a bar fight, have two or three kids with different women, develop a drinking problem, a pot problem, or get popped for roids." Dalton looked at me and smiled. "So far, I've got the drinking thing down."

"Good for you, dude. You're never too old to learn a new tool in this game."

"Fuck no, you ain't."

We got to the field where the fitness test was being run and started stretching out. Dalton sat down next to me and worked his hamstrings. "Well," he said, "don't be bitter. Dallas needs to make that team if he's going to keep living like a top prospect off the field. He's got like two kids with two different chicks in one year. Pretty tough pace to keep—guy can't keep it in his pants."

"Yeah, he's his own worst enemy," I said. "But still . . ."

Every team has at least one guy that rubs you so hard the wrong way you can't help but cross your fingers that he'll fail. I'm talking about a guy who butts into your conversation and then hijacks it with stories about himself. A guy who always makes sure you know how impressive he is, yet always has an excuse for why he failed. A guy with no filter, who's never afraid to tell you that you didn't do it the way he would have. A guy who, despite all his shortcomings, is so goddamn good on the field he can get away with being a total ass off it. Ever since I've been in pro ball, Dallas Preston has been that player.

Dallas and I got drafted together and played our first year on the same team. Back then, when we were all new to the game, we didn't have much with which to gauge each other, so our interactions broke down into bragging contests about college pedigrees, signing bonuses, and booze capacity. Dallas had high marks in all of those categories, going along with his plus arm and oversize personality. In a league like rookie ball, where everyone is fresh from a life of being the alpha male in their school programs, big bonuses and power arms barked loud. That, and Dallas wasn't afraid to bite. He was reckless with his drinking, his mouth, and, occasionally, his fists. He once punched me in the mouth for waking him up the night before a start. I did it on purpose, I admit, but only to get even with him for waking me up by climbing onto the hotel roof and throwing beer cans at my window at five in the morning in a drunken stupor. I thought turnabout was fair play, but when I got done washing the blood out of my mouth I consented that Dallas wanted to be top dog more than I did. I thought the other players would take my side in this issue, but Dallas was the best, and in the sports world, those who perform best have a way of making the law bend to their will.

I hated Dallas, not because he hit me—though I certainly didn't want him to hit me again. No, I hated him because of the way he lived. It wasn't fair that a guy could have so much talent and yet live so senselessly. It frustrated me no end to watch his 96 mph heater burn hitters up, then watch him get plastered drunk and cheat on his girlfriends while the Padres cut him checks for more money than my family had made in the last six years combined. Every year, he'd get himself in deeper and deeper, and every year he'd shine on the field in a way that made it all disappear. God, what I could do with just one of his gifts! I was jealous of him, pure and simple.

"Well, whatever," I said. "Good for him. Fan-fucking-tastic."

"It's just an audition. He's not going to make the club," said Dalton.

"I know. But wish I knew I had a chance. A real one, not this 'as long as you have a uniform on your back' jargon they feed us to keep us chasing long odds. One like those guys over there do." I looked over to the big league side of camp.

"I just want the fucking meal money," said Dalton. "It's like a grand a week over there."

"Yeah, that would be nice too, huh?" I said, thinking of the hundred-twenty bucks' worth of meal money the minor league campers got for the same week of service. "I hope Ox shares his with us when he gets back."

Ox was older than both of us and a longtime teammate. He was a hard-throwing, square-chinned, Type A male cut from the same mold as oiled-up action movie stars and professional wrestlers. Rock music, big boobs, and red meat—that was his idea of heaven. We were pulling for him to make the team, but also excited to have him back, and not just for the meal money.

"Yeah right, Ox's probably spent it all on dumb shit like jerky or lap dances."

"He's probably beating Reek's meal money out of him right now."

"Group one, on the line for your test!" bellowed Stan, cutting into our conversation.

A collective groan came out of the group.

"Remember when Danny was the strength coach here and the test was a twenty-minute run?" Dalton asked, walking to the line beside me.

"Yeah, those were the days when we actually did stuff that translated into baseball. God, I miss that guy," I said.

"Hey, Stan," said Rosco, almost perfectly on cue. "When are we going to run these shuttles again?"

"You're not, it's just this once."

"So why don't we just get tested on stuff we'll actually do during the season?"

"You use this kind of stopping and going during the season."

"So you're saying it is relevant to our careers?" asked Slappy.

"Yes."

"Then where are all the coaches at? Where is Grady, or Erp, or Towers? Don't they want to see who can run these the fastest?" asked Rosco.

"I'm the conditioning coach, that's why I'm here."

"Oh, right. So you're turning in a report on our shuttle-running abilities?" asked Slappy.

"I'm telling the organization who is in good baseball shape."

"Based on what your stopwatch says, right?" Rosco asked.

"Yes."

"How many years did you play baseball again?" Rosco continued.

"I didn't." Stan did not look happy.

"So, let me get this straight." Rosco was ready for his finale. "You never played baseball, we're never going to do this drill again, the player development personnel aren't here, and the big league GM doesn't give a fuck." Rosco looked at the rest of us and lifted an eyebrow before looking back to Coach Stan. "How many years did you go to school to learn how to run that stopwatch, again?"

Chapter Fifteen

"It went well," I said to Bonnie on the phone that evening. "Standard first day of camp. I passed all my tests, although, I will say, pissing off your strength coach is not a good way to enter into a conditioning test. I never ran so hard in my life."

"What did you do?"

"Oh, nothing. We just talked about the value of higher learning and one of the coaches got upset over it. You know how meatheads are when you make jokes at their expense. They can dish it out but can't take it. Anyway, I need to talk with you about something."

"Sure. What's up?"

"Let me first preface this conversation with the fact that I love you."

"Is this going to be a bad talk?"

"No, no, not at all. Why would you ask me that?"

"Because you told me you loved me first, which leads me to believe that you are going to say something unloving."

"It's not unloving. It's just that it covers the type of thing that doesn't lend itself to the ladies. It's guy stuff, even though . . ."

"Even though what?"

"Women are the centerpiece"—I couldn't resist—"or, should I say, centerfold?"

"Porn? You've been looking at porn!"

"No. I haven't been looking at it, per se, but I have been around it today." I paused, then sheepishly added, "And most of my baseball career."

"I don't understand," said Bonnie, like I had just told her I'd finally broken off my other relationship for the sake of our engagement.

"Remember how I told you there are things about baseball that you can't possibly understand from sitting in the stands? Well, this is one of those things."

"You guys look at porn together? How could I possibly understand that no matter what job you did?"

"Just let me explain."

"You do. Oh my God."

"No, we don't. You're jumping to conclusions. Well, we do, but . . . Just let me explain."

"Start explaining, then!" she demanded.

"Young guys chase girls, you can understand that concept, right?"

"I have a brother. I know what you're capable of."

"Baseball is a very testosterone-driven environment. Guys being guys, guy talk, guy interests, guy stuff. Except it's . . ." I searched for the words.

"It's what?"

"It's a lot more concentrated. You know all that evil stuff you've been preached to about avoiding since you were a little girl in all the Christian schools you went to?"

"Yes?"

"We're that. Aside from the killing."

"Oh dear God."

"But it's not all of us," I shot in quickly. "It's just the predominant environment. It's the culture of baseball, and as a player you can go with it or against it. I know this is hard to understand, but what I want you to get from this is that I'm not like that. I'm not perfect either, but I'm not perusing this stuff."

"So why are you telling me you looked at it today?"

"I didn't *look* look. Porn just happened to show today, and I wanted to be open with you about what I saw . . . er . . . I mean, witnessed—the events around the porn, not the actual porn itself." I exhaled. "Look, I need you to trust me. I won't be able to play if you don't. Do you trust me?"

There was a pause in the conversation while Bonnie collected herself. "Of course I trust you, honey. But I'm not happy about the fact you're around that stuff."

"I didn't expect you to be."

"So what happened?" Some levity came into her tone. "Were some guys looking at a porn magazine and you just walked away?" She said this hopefully, like she could capture all the chaos in a small bottle if she painted it casually enough.

"They were selling multi-DVD sets in the locker room today."

The levity left. "Who was selling them? The Padres sell you porn?"

"No, not the Padres, the other guys on the team were."

"What guys? That's outrageous!" she protested.

"Yeah, it was pretty funny." I chuckled to myself.

"It's not funny!"

"I'm sorry, you're right, it's not funny."

"It's disgusting!"

"Yes, it is."

"It's terrible."

"Absolutely."

"Those guys are perverts!"

"I know. I know. But the bottom line is, I'm not a pervert, dear."

"Do they sell porn on a regular basis?"

"No, that's new, actually. Most of the time it's free."

"Oh my God."

"Wait, just listen."

"I am, but this just keeps getting worse! When are you going to tell me something I want to hear?"

"I said that I loved you."

Bonnie did not reply.

"Have you ever listened to your dad tell stories about what goes on at his work?"

"Yes, and they don't sell porno boxed sets at his work."

"Well, they don't do that here, either. Most of the time, that is. Today was way out there, an anomaly; you have to believe I was shocked by it too. That's why I'm telling you. Bonnie, I'm sharing my life with you; that's what you wanted, right? Well, these environmental factors are part of it."

Bonnie didn't answer to the use of her own logic against her. I walked over to the window of the hotel room and gazed out into the distance, thinking about what my future was going to be like if my wife-to-be always operated under the assumption that every day at the park was like punching my time card in the Devil's workshop.

"I understand," came her steady voice. "I understand. I trust you. But your teammates are perverts."

"Yes, some are," I said. "In fact, I get made fun of for not being even normally sexually active."

"I value that about you, though," Bonnie said.

"I know you do, but the world of baseball has its own value system."

"I guess so."

"It does, and that's why when I tell you stuff like this, it's really me getting you prepared for the world you are about to become a part of."

"What does that mean?"

"Here's the deal: What happens in baseball is supposed to stay in baseball. It's like a creed shared by thieves. It's twisted, and it's wrong, but it's not our place to judge. Even if guys are doing really bad things, like cheating on their wives, I can't just lie to you and tell you it doesn't happen, because it does. But what you do with that information is the important part. It's not our place to tell the people who don't know, like, say, the other players' wives or families. That's why you can't judge them; it will make turning a blind eye so much harder. It's like—I don't know why this came to my mind—it's like your client privacy laws or something."

"My clients are individuals with special needs. Your teammates are fully functional adult perverts. There is no comparison here."

"You really should meet Slappy before you dismiss the 'special needs' option."

"It's not the same!"

"Fine, but if I tell you something about what goes on in the locker room, you can't tell anyone."

"I don't know anyone to tell." She gave a dubious laugh, probably from the serious way I was conveying it all to her in the face of her perceived irrelevance, since she didn't yet know anyone inside the baseball circle except me.

"We keep our mouths shut because we care about each other," I said.

"More like because you *don't* care about each other. Gosh, boys arc stupid sometimes."

"Hey," I said, offended, "you'll know people to talk with soon enough. When you come to visit me during the season, you'll be put in the wives section, and you'll meet the other wives. You'll get to know them through some of the most awkward, pretentious dialogue you've ever experienced because they all know stuff about each other that they're not allowed to talk about. Then you'll start forming opinions of each other and complaining to us. I'm trying to spare you that. If you think we're stupid, it's only because we know how stupid girls can be."

"Are you calling me stupid for wanting husbands to be faithful?"

"No, no. Gosh no. I'm just saying that we shouldn't become the way other people find out."

"What would you like to do then, since you seem to be the expert in pervert relations here?" Bonnie asked.

"I don't want to lie to you by not telling you what happens in my life."

"You're not lying to me if you refrain from telling me things about other people that don't pertain to me. You're lying to me if you refrain from telling me things about you that pertain to me."

"That's what I just did. That's what this whole conversation was, me being honest with you! Look how well it's going!"

Chapter Sixteen

Aside from a surplus of pornography in the locker room, the first week of camp passed in routine fashion. I threw my scheduled pens, fielded an excessive amount of comebackers, and gave Bonnie the abridged version of the more provocative happenings among the boys. At the start of the second week, the position players arrived. To greet them, the pitching staff was asked to announce their pitches during our first live batting practice matchup, a gesture we resented more than the use of the cumbersome L-screen we were mandated to pitch behind.

During batting practice of any kind, pitchers are sprinkled around the outfield, charged with picking up all balls struck in and out of play. We try to make games out of it—shagging for points or style—but more often than not, the tediousness of the job leads us to congregate into clumps and let the balls roll past while we bullshit about everything from nightlife exploits to our latest pitching failures.

"Sorry we got you into trouble, Digs," said Rosco.

"It's not your fault. I should have known better than to bring the crazy shit you guys do up with my fiancée. A subject like that is just toxic no matter how you handle it. We've agreed to discuss only the crucial stuff, and spare her the disgusting stuff."

"Compromise is the key to any relationship," said Rosco.

"That stupid fucking screen!" fumed Slappy, breaking into our conversation. "I never feel the same behind it." He had just finished his turn announcing pitches on the mound, a particularly bad outing, and was stomping out to the rock pile of Maddog, Rosco and me in left centerfield.

"When's the last time you pitched a game with an L-screen?" he wailed. Before anyone could answer, he continued, "Never, that's when. Not fucking ever. It's stupid."

"Quit whining, Slap. You're just mad because Chang took you deep."

"No, no, no. I'm not mad about that. Hitters are supposed to hit you when you tell them it's coming."

"Well, he crushed it," said Rosco.

"Crushed," emphasized Maddog.

"Probably the longest bomb of all time," said Rosco.

"Of all time," echoed Maddog.

"Screw you guys," said Slappy.

"You said you weren't mad, Slap," Rosco volleyed back.

"Not about Chang. I'm mad because you're my friends. I felt I could express myself in an environment of trust and support. Apparently I was wrong."

"I'm sorry, Slap." Rosco threw a hand on Slappy's shoulder. "How inconsiderate of me. I'm sorry the L-screen made you give up the longest bomb in the history of baseball to a guy who hit a buck-ninety last year."

"He knew it was coming!" pleaded Slappy, throwing Rosco's arm from his shoulder. "He should have hit all of them out!"

"They knew it was coming when I pitched and no one hit my fastball off the moon," said Rosco.

"Was Earp standing behind the backstop when you were throwing?" Slappy asked Rosco.

"I don't know, Slap. I focus on the hitter when I pitch. You should try that."

"Whatever. I hope you get your tits lit up this year."

"Whoa!" everyone gasped in unison. A batted ball rolled past the group. No one made any effort to get it.

"Gosh, Slap. My tits? That's cold-blooded." Rosco grabbed his nipples to make sure they weren't damaged by the harsh words.

"You can't cold-blood me for that. I come out here looking for some encouragement and you guys put a dagger in my back." Slappy took his hat off; he was really getting into the debate now. "You know Earp loves guys that throw hard, and guess what?"

"I dunno. What?" asked Maddog.

"I don't throw hard."

"Well, you better start."

"Yeah, exactly. With Earp back there, that's what I was trying to do. I wound up, threw as hard as I could and"—Slappy made a bat-smacking noise with his tongue—" 'See ya, ball.' "

"So that's why he hit it so far," said Maddog. "You did all the work."

"Thank you, Maddog. I did do all the work. All for Earp! That home run is Earp's."

"You can't let that guy throw your game," needled Rosco. "You make batters feel sorry for you so they groundout out of sympathy. That's your strength."

"Doesn't matter," Slap said defiantly. "In this game, you gotta show the brass what they want, which is fucked up because they all want something different."

"You have to pitch your game, Slap, rule number one," said Rosco, raising his hands as if delivering commandments.

"Ya, but you also gotta pitch *their* game. Ask Hayhurst, he's been around, he'll tell you."

The group turned their eyes to me for an official ruling on the matter. I was the oldest of the bunch, which somehow made me an authority. I stared back, mouth open, wondering how I'd been turned from harmless spectator to batting practice arbiter. "Uh, well . . ."

There was truth to both arguments. To be successful in baseball, a pitcher has to know what he can and cannot do. Often, pitchers get into trouble when they pitch away from their strengths, like Slappy did. However, the guy who rises to the top of the heap in pro baseball isn't always the one doing the best job of sticking to his game. The job of the brass is to promote guys who'll translate successfully into the big leagues. This means that even if a player does well in the minors, if the brass—guys like Earp and Grady—don't think said player will get the job done in the Show, they won't put their seal on him. Or they'll get rid of him. Thus, while it's true a pitcher's best chance for success against a hitter comes from sticking to his strengths, his best chance for advancement means showing the brass what they want to see.

This paradox exists in every professional system, and because of it, players have learned to reverse scout those individuals scouting them. You won't read it in *Baseball America,* but players work just as hard at learning what certain coaches and brass members like, which tools they favor, and which aspects of the game they prioritize, as they do at honing their on-field skills.

As a matter of fact, Earp wasn't the only coach with scouting reports filed on him. While Earp was renowned for his obsession with power arms and radar gun readings, hence his nickname, it was generally accepted that Grady was all about pitch efficiency and guys with good changeups. When Earp was around, guys put a little more effort into lighting up the radar gun. When Grady dropped in, the percentage of changeups thrown seemed to increase substantially. There were other folks in the evaluation system, but none seemed to have as much pull as those two.

As polarizing as their views were, having two distinct scales for what constituted a successful pitcher in the eyes of the brass was actually a good thing. The soft strike throwers did their best to suck up to Grady whenever possible, earning them the nickname "Grady's Boys" for their trouble. In turn, guys who threw flames buttered up to Earp, and were dubbed "Earp's Boys." True or not, there is nothing shameful about surviving, even if it means being accused of kissing ass. When the life and death of a career comes down to the opinion of a coach who sees you play once or twice in a season, holding on to a job can be as critical, and ridiculous, as a popularity contest.

"I'm going to have to side with Slappy here. Sometimes you have to show 'em what they want to see, fellas."

"Bah." The detractors waved me off. Not because I was telling them something they didn't know, but because I was allowing Slappy an exit from their bullying.

"See! See! Thank you, Hayhurst. I've always liked you," said Slappy.

"You're welcome, Slap. But remember, giving up a six-hun-dred-foot bomb is way more impressive than turning your 87 mph heater into 89 mph. Sacrificing what you do best when you have to tell the guy at the plate what's coming might not be the best time to accommodate the whims of some jackass with a radar gun."

"Amen!" said Rosco. "Pick your battles: rule number two." His hand went up again.

"Whatever. With friends like you, I hope I get released," said Slap.

"Keep pitching like you did today and you'll get your wish."

"I'm just telling you what I know, Slap," I said.

"Whose boy are you?" Rosco asked me. "Earp's or Grady's?"

"Anybody who'll have me," I said. "Rule number three: kiss all asses more powerful than your own."

Chapter Seventeen

"Alright, bring it in here, ya mutants," said Earp, stepping off the golf cart that shepherded him around the fields. On his cue, the hoard of minor league campers broke from their sewing circles and assembled for another morning meeting on the left side of field four.

The Padres spring training complex holds six fields in total, all divided up like slices of a pie with each slice acting as home base for a minor league team level. Morning meetings are always held on field four. Once the morning meetings are over, the horde breaks to their respective fields for stretch. Following stretch, the teams rotate clockwise as each field also plays home to a specific training drill. Today, bunt defenses were on the High A field, pick-offs on the Low A field, comebackers on the Double A diamond, and the tiresome covering first routine was located on field four—Triple A's home turf. That's only four rotations for six fields, but the other two fields wouldn't factor in until later in camp, when cuts got made.

In the early stages of spring training, everyone gets to entertain the thought of playing a few levels higher. I, for example, was working out with the Triple A group, though I wasn't letting myself get too comfortable. The first cuts would soon be made at the big league level, which would put into motion a domino effect throughout the organization. The big league amputees would get grafted onto the Triple A group, and force out the borderline players currently there. In turn, those players would fall to Double A, forcing Double A fringe players to High A, and so on. The cycle repeats all the way to the bottom of the system, rolling along like a snowball, gathering more and more players as it goes. Finally, when combined with fresh draftees, there would be enough rookies and castaways to form two full short season teams.

Earp stood in the center of our semicircle of players, holding a clipboard full of names, locations, and times. We were three weeks into camp now and games had just started. Every afternoon, groups of players were leaving the complex to take on another club someplace else in Arizona, while, in turn, that opposing club sent a pack of their boys to take on us. Earp, when not evaluating talent, coordinated who went where, including who crossed the line and went over to big league camp as a backup.

"Double A, Triple A guys, you're staying home today, which means High and Low A is on the road. Kick their asses, boys, the vans leave at noon, make sure you're on 'em." He flipped a piece of paper on his clipboard. "Guys going to the pros today." He cleared his throat and started reading off who would serve as backups to the big league side, also known as JiCs, or *just in case* players—though we players just call them "jicks"—who would serve as indentured servants to whatever the big league club had planned for the day.

"Why does he always say 'the pros' when he means the Bigs? We're all pros," I whispered to Aden, who was standing next to me in the circle.

"Because he's a fucking retard," said Aden.

"Didn't he sign you?"

"Yeah, but he can still be a fucking retard."

"You won't say that to his face."

"Nope. I'll tell him he's Jesus Christ if that's what gets me to the Bigs."

"Amen, brother. Amen."

Earp read through the list. When he got to the *H*s I held my breath, thinking he might name me, but he didn't.

"We're minor leaguers for another day," I said to Aden.

"Living the dream," said Aden.

Going over to the big league side of camp on JiC duty is a great opportunity, but one that comes at a healthy price. First off, you go into it knowing you're not supposed to play. That's the whole point of a *just in case* player: everything needs to go wrong for you to get in the game, and I mean everything. The big leagues provide their own backups and failsafe players, so there is a whole wall of guys standing in front of you for a chance at pitching in the presence of big league coaches.

It gets worse. Since you're at a lower rank than those who actually belong in big league camp, you get stuck with all the busywork. Things like fetching foul balls, carrying equipment, and manning the ball bucket during batting practice. The big league club plays at night, so a minor league JiC who gets the call will often attend a full day of minor league practice, pull ball bucket duty for the big league club that night, sit isolated through a big league exhibition game, then give the uniform back with a thankful smile about "experiencing a taste" of the dream. Any player who's accrued any significant amount of time in this game hates being a JiC, including me. But here's the rub, if it all does go wrong and the opportunity comes, you have a chance to leave a mark.

Even so, the opportunity to leave a mark was not what dominated my mind when I thought of going over to the big league side. It was fear, actually.

I had an ugly track record of embarrassing myself around big leaguers. The first time I ever JiCed was during a preseason exhibition game wherein the Padres came to Lake Elsinore in 2005 to beat the snot out of the Storm. I was playing for the Storm at the time, but I was told to go to the other side of the field and play for the Padres because they didn't bring enough pitching to finish the game. I was told to borrow a Padres uniform so I could look like a big leaguer, but the Padres didn't have any extras. I had no other recourse but to sit in the big league dugout wearing the uniform of a minor league team, silent as a church mouse, trying not to get in anyone's way.

When the Padres came off the field to hit, I got off the bench to make sure I didn't take anyone's seat. I moved down to the water cooler and hovered next to it, even going so far as to pour cups of Gatorade for some of the players, hoping to be seen as respectful.

Everything was going fine until Jeff Blum, the Padres veteran utility man, shouted out, "Hey, batboy."

I, not being the batboy, paid no attention to this.

"Hey, batboy!" the shout came again. I remained still.

"Jesus, hey, batboy, what are you, deaf?"

I started looking for this batboy who was either too deaf or dumb to heed the call of a big leaguer when I realized that everyone in the dugout was looking at me. In fact, just as I turned, Blum tossed a handful of sunflower seeds on me to get my attention. I obediently came over to him, wiping seeds from my shoulders, eager to clear up our case of mistaken identity. I actually thought he may have just been joking—some prankish put-down of younger players—but when Blum asked me to spin around and model my uniform so he could see the full logo, making the comment, "Wow, that's a real jersey; nobody on the team wanted number 22?" I realized this was no joke. He dismissed me back to the water cooler when he was finished. I went as told, stupefied and snickered at by a few other big leaguers who understood exactly what had happened. In no time the story found its way back to the minor league side, and I spent the rest of the year being called the batboy just because some big leaguer, a god in our profession, mistook me for one.

It would be different if this were an isolated event, but last year I embarrassed myself so badly in front of Trevor Hoffman it brought a team meeting to an abrupt close when I asked him how he "inculcated" himself. Then, there was that time I was given the JiC busywork job of warming up the right fielder, only to send him chasing my overthrows to the wall so many times they had to call in a reliever for me.

"It's alright," I said to Aden. "Probably wouldn't play anyway. Huge waste of time."

"Totally," said Aden.

"Guys going to tomorrow's road series in Tuscon." Earp flipped to another page on his clipboard. "Players traveling need to take the early van to the park tomorrow morning." He put his finger on a list and started reading from it. "Abignail, Crakhower, Hayhurst, Johnson, Richardson . . ."

"Ah crap," I said.

"Try not to inculcate anyone," said Aden.

Chapter Eighteen

Before the buses left for Tucson, they let us JiCs inside the big league portion of the spring training facility where snacks and goodies were set out for those going on the road. The big league side of camp was a thing of beauty. Every locker had a large, leather rolling office chair parked in front of it. There were refrigerators filled with sports drinks and tables covered with snacks. Clubhouse personnel zipped around wearing latex gloves to pick up the clothes the big leaguers wantonly cast on the floor. Most of the guys in the place wouldn't be on the team when the spring ended—they were expendable—and yet they were still treated like kings. Seeing it all made me feel stupid for ever being awestruck by the minor league side of the operation where I once thought it was cool that each stool had the Padres logo painted on the part where your butt goes.

There were two buses taking us to Tucson, and both were virtually unoccupied. I was told that the big-name players got out of traveling altogether, and the few who didn't usually drove by themselves in their own cars. This boggled my minor league mind. We plebeians were forbidden to drive to any games, spring training or otherwise. We always had to travel with the club and, if we brought our cars to spring training, we weren't allowed to drive them to the city we played in unless it was Lake Elsinore.

I also learned big leaguers always got two buses for travel whenever they didn't go by plane—part of their union agreement or something. I didn't understand the particulars; I just knew it was awesome. Something about riding on a barely occupied tour bus after years of being stuffed like cattle into a trailer made me giddy. The bus, the snacks, the lack of player congestion, these little niceties were paltry compared to some of the stories I'd heard about what it was like to actually be a big leaguer, but I relished them nonetheless.

Just before we pulled out of the gate, a few other JiCs boarded, including two players from big league camp: Manrique and Dallas. Manrique sat near me while Dallas, who was screaming on his cell phone, was oblivious to me, consumed by the fight he was having on the phone.

"That money isn't for you to buy goddamn Gucci purses with. That's for my daughter," shouted Dallas. Though no one on the bus was looking at Dallas directly, they weren't talking to one another either, indicating they were listening in on the drama. Dallas's face scrunched tighter and tighter as whoever was on the other line spoke. Then, he blasted, "Goddammit, Mandy, I am being a part of her fucking life, quit throwing all this shit on me!"

Dallas made his way to the back of the bus, went into the lavatory compartment, and shut the door. There was a long series of pounding and muffled shouts. Everyone on the bus looked at one another, wondering if we were all seeing the same scandal.

"Reek. What's up with Dallas?" I whispered to Manrique.

Manrique shook his head. "That guy, all the time fighting with his girl. I don't know why, but they"—he banged his fist together—"all the time."

Discretion was not Dallas's strong suit. Going to the back of the bus so he could scream was about as undercover as he got. When something went wrong in his life, you knew it because he'd talk to anyone about anything at anytime. His mouth had no filter, one of the reasons everyone around camp knew his circumstances. Generally, it's nice to have some wild man around because wildness usually makes for good entertainment during a long season. Dallas knew this role well and enjoyed playing it, doing his best to soak up the attention that living like a rock star won him. However, as players got older and more and more of Dallas's shenanigans caught up with him off the field, his need for attention became more pathetic than iconic.

Dallas kicked his way out of the bus lavatory and came back to a seat near Manrique and me. Manrique hustled to put on some headphones and look occupied, but I made eye contact with Dallas, which was just as good as saying, "Go ahead and tell me what's on your mind, son."

"Fuck!"—conversations that start this way are never good— "You give a woman money to feed your kid with and you'd think she'd fucking feed your kid, right?"

I looked to Manrique, who pretended I was invisible. "Right," I said, not really knowing what else to say.

"I know." Dallas shook his head and punched the seat back. "God, she can be such a bitch sometimes. Don't get me wrong, I love my daughter, but I hate her mom. I mean, yeah, I know, I got her knocked up, but I'm trying to do right and shit, taking care of my girl. But then her mom takes that money and spends it on purses and goes to parties. I want to know who's taking care of my fucking kid. I should just cut her ass off, that's what I should do."

I opened my mouth to say something, but Dallas spun on me. "But I can't, Dirk. Don't even tell me I can because if I did, the court would be all over my ass. That's what's fucked up about our legal system, ya know. A guy gets bent over for child support but nobody's watching how the girl spends it. It's like if you're a dude, you should just get used to getting screwed over every time you make a mistake, you know." Dallas finished his statement by staring at me, anxiously waiting for me to agree.

I wasn't sure if Dallas was done ranting or not. I didn't want to speak up and then get yelled at for possibly saying something that he wasn't imagining. I chose to stay quiet, which turned out to be a bad choice because it pissed him off.

"Fuck, Dirk. I thought you were a Christian, man. I thought you'd for sure have something encouraging to say to me."

"Well, uh, Jesus loves you."

"Doesn't feel like it right now," he said.

He'd just backed a dump truck of too much information up on me and was asking me to wrap it up with a word from God? I wanted to slap him in the head, but I knew that if I told him something he didn't want to hear, I'd most likely be the one getting blows to the skull.

"The Lord works in mysterious ways." I offered another cliché.

"You know what the worst is? Every time I talk to my wife about this, she gets pissed. It's like she doesn't understand how hard it is for me to deal with all this shit. Like I wanted it to be this way. She doesn't understand the environment we're in."

I tilted my head at Dallas, wondering how he could use the same language I used to talk about baseball with my girl but with a completely different meaning. Then I wondered if he could even hear the words coming out of his mouth. This was probably not a good time to point out that he had cheated on his wife before they were married a full year, which, generally speaking, tends to upset wives.

"What, dude?" he asked, observing my expression.

"Oh, nothing, my neck hurts." I rubbed it. "Sucks when people don't understand what you are going through."

"Hell yeah, it does. And on top of that, I'm here, fighting for my life to make it in the game. Trying to make money to feed them kids. Shit, this can be a real grind sometimes, you know. It's like they don't understand that."

His complete lack of self-awareness disgusted me. He made his money up front, never had to scrounge a day in his professional life if he didn't want to, and now he was complaining about how hard this was because he made stupid choices? I wanted to scream how wrong he was, but he nodded his head at me, indicating what response I was supposed to give him.

"Totally," I said.

"Fucking, you know. You've been beating around longer than I have."

"We got drafted the same year," I said dryly.

"Shit, that's right. I forgot 'cause we're never on the same team very long. Hey, I heard you were getting married?" He changed subjects.

"Yes, I am," I said.

"Oh snap. Well, don't let me ruin it for you. You probably love your girl and shit."

"Yeah, I really do," I said.

"She understands how hard this shit is, right? That's how you know she's a keeper, when she understands how this shit makes you do crazy stuff."

"Yeah, she understands shit," I placated.

Dallas's phone rang. "Hold on," he said to me, then picked up the phone. "What?" A pause was followed by a dramatic increase in volume. "Go ahead and call them! I'm going to tell them you're not spending what you're getting now the way you're supposed to." Another pause. "No. No, you ain't!" Dallas got up and went back to the bathroom. "Do it! Do it and see what happens!" The door slammed.

I turned to face Manrique, my eyes wide as saucers.

"I know, bro. I know. He's *loco*. All the time. It's sad, bro."

"It's something," I said, looking at the back of the bus.

It was a long trip down to Tuscon to be part of a game I didn't play in. There were very few actual big leaguers present. As it turned out, most of the big leaguers were in China. At first I thought it was a joke, but the Padres had actually sent a team's worth of players to China to play in some type of international exhibition series marking the MLB's first games in that country. I could imagine it, Trevor Hoffman standing on the Great Wall of China while I sat in the bullpen at a game I couldn't play in, wishing I could build a great wall between myself and Dallas's never-shutting mouth.

Chapter Nineteen

I got called over to big league camp nearly every other day of the next week, until the players sent to China made it home. Dallas dumped on me whenever he could, and I found myself praying he would pitch just so I wouldn't have to listen to him anymore. My prayers were answered in bittersweet irony as Dallas pitched fairly often while I didn't pitch at all. I did, however, get very good at convincing myself that my constant presence around the big club meant my name was known to them, and that had to count for something.

When first cuts were made at the big league level, things got crowded in the Triple A group. There were more pitchers than available roster spots, which meant the fringe guys, Rosco, Slappy, Dalton, and a few others, were sent down. On the bright side, the San Antonio Championship crew was reassembled. Frenchy, Ox, Moreno, Reek, Anto, and the rest were now back in Triple A with me.

The days got longer too. With more minor leaguers who needed to get work, we played anywhere from ten to fourteen innings so every pitcher who needed to throw could get live mound time. On the big league side of things, rotations were being set and many big league pitchers were coming down to the minor league side of camp to get work in so they could avoid traveling—passing that privilege off on the minor league JiCs. When I was younger, I thought they did this because they wanted extra practice, not because they didn't want to miss their tee time.

Today, Ox, Frenchy, and I stood behind the backstop of field four watching High A intersquad against Low A. Ox had been a friend of mine since my first full season five years ago. He'd more than earned his big league camp invite. Frenchy, however, had just joined the team last year. He was a super prospect with the seal of both Grady and Earp, which was why he was in big league camp in only his second full season of play. He dominated both High and Double A, and was on the fast track to the Bigs courtesy of his Bugs Bunny change and left-handed finesse.

None of us were scheduled to pitch for the day, but we still had to stick around and watch. It's organizational policy that all players have to watch five innings of their fellow players' games before they are allowed to leave minor league camp for the day. This rule, commonly referred to as the "Five and Fly Rule," is the reason why players flock from field to field in search of the game moving the fastest. Today, the crowd was at field four for two reasons. One, it was moving the fastest, which probably had something to do with the second reason: Greg Maddux was pitching for the Low A team.

"I've been watching him since I was a little kid," I said to Ox and Frenchy as we watched the Professor of Pitching himself lob sinkers down and away to hitters who hadn't been alive as long as the guy they were facing had been playing professionally.

"This is completely unfair," said Frenchy. On cue, the umpire called a strike on a pitch that looked to be a foot off the plate. "See what I mean?" Frenchy pointed at the umpire's call as if citing evidence. "First, if you're a hitter, you know you're facing a guy with a reputation for throwing strikes that spans decades, so you have to know you're going to get screwed on anything close. Second, if you're the umpire, you know you have to call anything close a strike because it's Greg Maddux. What are you going to do, tell Maddux he just missed after twenty years of never missing, in a minor league game no less? He could throw shit over the back-stop and they'd call it a strike."

"I wouldn't put it past this guy to throw shit at you just be-cause. That fucking savage." Ox shook his head.

"Who, Maddux?" I asked.

"Yeah," Frenchy and Ox said in unison before sharing a know-ing laugh over the subject.

"What do you mean?" I asked.

"Don't let the professor shtick fool you. Maddux is high king savage," said Ox.

"This guy?" I flipped a thumb at Maddux as he waited for a ball to be tossed back from the infielders. Granted, he didn't look like the Maddux of my youth. More like a guy who played beer league softball on the weekends and attended the occasional cy-cling class in between. But that was part of his legendary character stream. He got you out with his mind and with his sniper-like control. He was the one guy who gave hope to everyone who be-lieved pitching was more than rearing back and throwing as hard as you could, like Captain Curls did back during the off-season. Furthermore, Maddux was a dying breed, a guy who knew how to get bunches of outs in the big leagues but didn't have good enough "stuff" to get drafted in the modern age of baseball. He was testa-ment to the craft of pitching. He was an icon, one of the few in this game whose name was synonymous with pitching mastery. And, maybe most important, he was one of my heroes.

"He peed on me in the shower," Frenchy said.

"What?" I gasped.

"I saw this guy wipe his ass on a shower towel and then put it back in the stack for someone else to dry off with," Ox said.

"I saw him wipe his ass on a sanitary sock, and put it back in the bin," Frenchy volleyed back.

"I heard he wiped his ass with a towel and buried it in some poor bastard's locker so they wouldn't be able to pinpoint the smell until it was too late," said Ox.

"*That's* what that smell was," Frenchy said.

"This guy? Maddux?" I said, pointing out to the field. "Him?"

"Yup," they both said with admiration.

"He's old-school. Guys in his generation really mess with rookies hard," Ox said. "Crapping on other people's stuff. Now that's how you do it."

"Yeah. Think of how many people will ever get to say they got peed on by Greg Maddux," said Frenchy.

I tilted my head at the thought of it. "You're right, that is pretty cool."

Ox slapped Frenchy on the shoulder as if congratulating him on his good fortune. I looked away from them both, slightly jealous. The thought of Bonnie saying, "Boys are so stupid" flashed through my mind.

"Well, I didn't get invited to big league camp but," I said proudly, "I've had a lot of big league backup opportunities this year. I haven't gotten to pitch any, but people know my name, though none of them peed on me."

"That sucks," Frenchy said.

"I'm sure I'll get peed on eventually, if I play my cards right," I said.

"No, the pitching part."

"Yeah," said Ox. "It's a waste of time, especially at this point of camp."

"Why do you say that? I thought JiC'ing was a great opportunity."

"It would be if you weren't trying to make the Triple A squad," said Frenchy. I had to take a moment to digest the fact that Frenchy, who had less than a third of the time in pro ball as I did, was giving me inside information on the value and meaning of camp proceedings. Behold the power of the big league camp invite.

"You're not going to make that team, so helping them out just gets you out of the sight of the people deciding who is going to be on this team," Ox said. "Triple A is your path to the Bigs. You need to be pitching well here. Sitting on the fucking bench on a team you're not going to be a part of doesn't help."

Maddux wheeled-and-dealed an absolute turd of a changeup that splintered the cap of a bat belonging to a youngster who couldn't keep his weight back.

"Jesus, I can't make hitters do that on my heater and he makes 'em do it on his 45 mph diarrhea," said Frenchy.

I suddenly lost interest in all of Maddux's bowel movement incarnations in favor of the direction my career was headed. "So you're telling me all the time I've spent up there has been hurting me?"

"Hard to say," Frenchy said. "I mean, maybe they think you're going to make the Triple A squad for sure, which is why they're comfortable juggling you around. Maybe it means they think you're expendable. Who knows? I wouldn't worry about it, nothing you can do."

"Ya, bud." Ox grabbed my shoulder and gave it a shake. "Who knows what these bastards are thinking, right? Fuck 'em."

"Right," I said weakly.

Maddux finished his inning. Opposing him was a young Latin kid who threw a million miles per hour with zero control. Consequently, the crowd of minor leaguers fled to another field where things moved more swiftly.

I stayed behind. Standing there alone, I thought of dominos, minor league dominos, all of them standing in a row about to be knocked over. No matter how they rationalized why or how they would fall, they were still going to fall, and there was absolutely nothing they could do about it.

Chapter Twenty

A few nights later, back at the hotel, I sat at the kitchenette's mini table, across from a reclined, couch-bound Aden, who was watching some horror movie about zombies, when my cell phone rang. My parents' number flashed on the screen. Picking up the phone, I went into the other room, shutting the door behind me to tune out the sound of people getting mauled by the undead.

"Hello?"

"So, are you still getting married?" asked the voice of my mother.

"Nice to hear from you too, Mother."

I stepped over a pile of dirty clothes that sat at the side of Aden's bed, heading to my bed on the far side of the room in case any screaming on my end proved disruptive to Aden's enjoyment of the screaming on his end.

"I'm just asking you a simple question." Simple, but loaded.

"Yes, I am, Mom. I told you I was and I meant it. Is that all you called for?"

"Just making sure. Gosh. Calm down. I wanted to know because your grandma said you're a no-good son of a bitch and you took her bird figurines—"

"I never touched her bird figurines!" I shouted.

"She can't find the one with the blue jay feeding its babies."

"Did she check behind those camel figurines she—oh, forget it! Why am I even talking to you about this? God, I'm three time zones away and I still can't get away from this crap. It doesn't matter, I'm not going back there, and I don't care about the bird figurines. Why are you calling me, just want to piss me off?"

"I thought you'd want to know what she said. I thought you'd find it funny."

"You're amazing, you know that?" I sat down on my bed, palming my face.

"You know how your dad goes over there every once and a while when you're gone to make sure she's not dead?"

"Yes," I said, thinking of how odd my family's definition of visiting Grandma was compared to others. Grandma had insisted she was going to move out of her house and into a comfortable assisted-living home for the last ten years, but had yet to make any effort. Instead, she'd become an expert in finding reasons why not to move; everything from the terrible food to "too many colored people." The family had come to terms with the fact that she was never going to leave, and consented to performing a weekly "death check" on her.

"Your dad wasn't there five minutes before she started in on your dead grandfather," said Mom.

I let out a long sigh.

"She said Sam can't be your grandpa's son because your grandpa had gonorrhea and couldn't have kids. Your dad asked her who she had an affair with to give birth to him, and she told him to go to hell because a woman of her good graces would never do such a thing. Your father and Jesus"—Mom laughed—"the only two people in history to be immaculately conceived."

I didn't say anything.

"Oh, come on, Dirk. That's funny."

"Whatever."

"Wow, you're in a bad mood, huh?"

"Is it that obvious?"

"Well, let's talk about baseball. Do you know if you're going to make the Triple A club?"

I thought of how hard it would be to explain to her all of the possibilities that could derail a shot at Triple A. I thought of how hard it was explaining it to myself. "Camp is over in two weeks, call then."

"Fine. How's Bonnie?"

"Mom, the last time we talked, you and Dad told me getting married was the same as pissing my life away. Now you want to chitchat like that didn't happen?"

My mom let the receiver go silent for a minute or two. I lay down on my bed and stared at the spackle on the ceiling.

"I don't understand why you are still so upset about that," said Mom.

"How can you not understand that? I'm trying to take my life my own direction right now, and instead of supporting me, you and Dad are both resistant to it. It's like you think I'm fucking up my life by splitting myself into a person who doesn't strictly focus on baseball."

"We're not resistant to you."

"Then what, you don't like Bonnie?"

"She's a wonderful girl, we love Bonnie. We love whoever you love."

"Then why, when Dad told me he didn't think Bonnie was the one, did you not say any of this? Why did you say you'd only believe it when it happened?"

"I don't know," Mom said meekly.

"Bullshit, you do know."

"I didn't feel it was my place."

I grabbed my head. "Not your place? Well, then, whose place is it? You're my mom, you're his wife."

"That's right, I am his wife, Dirk. And for the last couple of years I haven't wanted to be. You have no idea what marriage is like, what it can turn into when things fall apart. Your father is right: you don't know what you're getting into. You're starting a relationship at the expense of things you've wanted your whole life. You've been spending the last how many years of your life doing this job, and now you're okay with not doing it anymore for a girl? The last thing you want to have when you start a life together is regrets."

"I won't have regrets walking away from our family mess, Mom. And if for some reason I do, I wish you'd just support me instead of telling me I'm going to fuck my life up."

"We just want you to be happy."

"Are you happy?"

"No! No, I'm not. I can't remember the last time I've been happy."

The conversation stopped for a long stretch of time. One thing children do well is criticize their parents, and I was so full of criticisms I had no room for sympathy. I knew she was in a bad place. I knew she was unhappy in her relationship with our family, but so was I. I hadn't enjoyed my relationship with my family for the last several years. I too wanted out and was hoping to make my break into something better with Bonnie. I didn't want to be told what dangers I might be headed toward by people I never wanted to be like. I didn't want to listen to anything she had to say. If she wasn't for me, she was against me.

"Your dad is bipolar," Mom said, breaking the silence.

"Did Grandma say that too?"

"No, the doctor did."

"What doctor?" I sat up again.

"Dad came home from your grandma's angry 'cause she went nuts on him. He got into it with me because he couldn't make any headway with her and he needed someone to yell at." The customary casual tone she used for all the stuff she recited to me left her voice in favor of a more serious tone. "I told him everything you probably wanted to. He got the gun out of the closet and ran me from the house with it. I left, and I only came back to make sure he wasn't dead.

"He didn't do it," she continued. "He cried for hours, but he didn't do it. I took him to the hospital when he was calm enough to go. I thought he was going to have to be committed, Dirk, I really did. I thought he'd finally lost it. The doctor who checked him out asked me if he'd ever been treated for bipolar disorder."

Mom went on to explain how, given my dad's extreme mood swings, it was worth trying to treat him for post-traumatic bipolar disorder, since the other options were more severe.

"So, what does this mean?" I asked.

"I don't know. It will take a while to see how the medication works on him. But if it doesn't, Dirk, I . . ." The phone went blank again as I waited for her to finish, but she never did.

"So, what if it doesn't work?" I asked.

"I don't know."

"Would he go to an institution?"

"He would never let that happen."

"What does that mean?"

"This isn't your mess, remember. You just worry about you, okay? You're good at that."

"What the hell does that—"

She hung up.

Chapter Twenty-one

I pulled JiC duty again the next day. Since my conversation with Ox and Frenchy, going over to the big league side of camp no longer felt like a lottery ticket opportunity. Now I felt a lot like one of the red shirts in *Star Trek*: nameless, faceless, and the first to die. Convinced the event was a waste of time, I didn't pay much attention to the major league operation. Instead, I spent most of the day in my head, trying to decide how I should feel about my phone call with Mom.

I knew things were getting worse with my dad, but I wasn't sure if I should care or not. After so many years of watching the family tear itself apart, I'd developed a sort of immunity to it. As much a survival trait as anything else, there are only so many knock-down, drag-out fights a group of loved ones can have before their hearts become callused, and mine was pretty tough these days. I almost wanted there to be casualties now. Thinking in such a way felt cold, even in my hotheaded state, but it might actually solve the problem. My dad didn't want to live anymore; he hadn't wanted to for years. The only activity he seemed to share with the family was fighting. My mom was miserable and wanted out; so did I, and so did my brother.

It was surprisingly easy for me to wash my hands of it all. I was going to be married, I thought, heading off in my own direction.

Maybe my mom, despite her anger, was actually right? Maybe I should worry about myself and let the dead bury the dead? Besides, what could I really do from here anyway?

The big league bullpens always have more goodies than the minor league ones, a fact not lost on a guy who never exited it, like me. I'd gotten good at sifting through all the gum, candy, seeds, and bars available to me during my stints as a blowout counter measure. I had stuffed my pockets full of the choicer-flavored gums and was adding to a wad lodged in my cheek, mulling over the next step I should take with my family, when I spotted the great Trevor Hoffman making his way across the field. He always had such a regal gait, like he was gallivanting his way through some Renaissance-era court, not a baseball field. The bullpen coach, Darrel Akerfelds, accompanied Hoffman, as well as another gentleman dressed in a Padres uniform.

Like Maddux, Hoffman was a hero of mine. I took every opportunity to watch him move on a baseball field. Unfortunately, each time I'd been called to JiC, Hoffman had been MIA. Today, he was here in all his splendor, and yet it was not him I watched but the unidentified person in full Padres dress walking next to him.

Unlike Trevor, this person did not move gracefully, but slowly and methodically. Indeed, he labored for steps as it didn't seem like his legs' natural inclination was to obey him. His right hand was curled up slightly, and his right arm stuck to his side like an injured wing. Even so, he walked along wearing an expression that exuded joy, doing his best to match the pace of Hoffman and Akerfelds, who, in turn, did their best to match his.

When they arrived at the bullpen gate, Hoffman found a chunk of outfield grass to stretch in while Akerfelds tended to bullpen business, hanging charts and rosters near the pen's phone box. The mysterious man stood near the gate, using the solid construction to steady himself while he watched the players loosen. Occasionally, one of our boys would walk by and slap the mystery man on the shoulder and say, "Hey, Stump. How you doing?"

"I'm doing great, buddy. How are you?"

"Good, man. Real good. Looking for a win today."

"You know it," said Stump.

Sometimes the conversations would stretch longer, revealing that Stump had trouble recalling a word or a two, stammering to get them out. Sometimes he would trace the word in the air in front of him with this left hand until it came to him or the person he was talking to did so for him. I marveled at this. Not because I'd never seen a handicapped man before. In fact, this wasn't even the first time I'd seen one on a baseball field. Rather, I stared at Stump with transfixed eyes because he looked remarkably like my dad, except happy.

"Excuse me," I said, looking to one of the players nearest me in the bullpen.

"Heath," said the player, introducing himself and reaching to shake my hand.

"Dirk," I said, taking his offer. "I was wondering, what is the story behind Stump?" I looked back at Stump, who was laughing with someone.

"Oh, Mark?" asked Heath. "Mark Merila? Everyone calls him Stump. He used to be the bullpen catcher for the Padres until he was struck with a brain tumor back in '05. He had a seizure on a subway train to Shea Stadium, that's how they found out." We both looked over at Stump, smiling and talking with the players who stopped to chat with him. "He's a great dude, a medical miracle," said Heath.

"You ready?" Hoffman called at Stump.

"I'm ready, big man," Stump said.

"Then quit jackin' around and let's get to work, man," said Hoffman, pretending to actually be angry, which made Stump as well as everyone else laugh.

Stump ambled to the white foul line parallel to Hoffman's

patch of grass in the outfield. About sixty feet away, Hoffman stood, ball in glove, at the ready. Akerfelds handed Stump a catcher's mitt, which Stump worked on to his left hand before putting it up as a target for Hoffman.

Stump looked so much like my dad it was uncanny. Not only did their faces share similarities, so did the way their afflictions manifested in their bodies and movement. I actually moved toward Stump to make sure he wasn't some supernatural thing, some figment of my imagination. I simply could not believe there was a man on earth with so many similarities to my father, and so merry. However, when Stump lifted that mitt, I realized I *was* watching something supernatural.

Now it was me who needed the gate's support, as what happened next was the single most beautiful thing I'd ever seen on a baseball field. Stump's range was obviously limited given his condition. Even so, no one stopped him or told him what he was about to do was dangerous. They paid him the biggest compliment they could, which is to say, they acted like nothing was out of the ordinary. Of course, the person with the largest role in the execution of this event was Hoffman, who shouldered the responsibility of putting the ball in Stump's mitt, or as close to it as possible. I suppose it should come as no surprise that, of all people in the game, baseball's all-time saves leader was up to the task. This isn't to say Stump didn't make it look easy catching every ball thrown to him.

After receiving each throw, Stump turned his mitt over so Akerfelds could collect the ball and throw it back to Hoffman. The cycle repeated until Hoffman finally confessed, "I'm good, Stump. Thanks a lot."

"Anytime," Mark said.

I didn't want them to stop throwing. When they finished, it was all I could do to not burst from the pen and ask if I could pitch to Mark. But as I stood there, holding on to the gate, I realized I didn't want to pitch to Mark, but to my dad, that I would give anything to see him happy, if it meant we could share a moment like Hoffman had just shared with Stump.

Then I realized that it was only minutes ago I'd convinced myself that my dad killing himself didn't matter.

"Where's the players' bathroom?" I asked Heath.

"Out the gate, second set of double doors." He pointed to the path. "There's two sets, you can use whichever."

I got up and left the bullpen. Walked past fans asking for autographs. Pushed through the double doors and into a bathroom where I turned on the faucet, before collapsing into a corner where I wept.

That night, when I knew my mom was at work and I was sure she wouldn't answer, I called her cell phone. "Hey. It's me," I said when the voice mail picked up. "I was just thinking. When Dad looks like he's feeling down, you should put on some of his music. A little music therapy or something. I think he'd like that. I'll . . . I'll talk to you later."

Chapter Twenty-two

The end of camp had come, and cuts were upon us. It was the hardest camp I'd ever been through as there had never been so much that was unknown. When I did get my chances to pitch, I pitched well, but had I pitched enough? Unfortunately it was too late to do anything about it now. This spring training had run its course, and the bulk of my audition for a Triple A job would ultimately rest on what I did last season.

I took comfort in knowing I had made the most of all my opportunities, including following all the ass-kissing rules off the field: laughing at Grady's jokes and agreeing with Earp's criticisms. I told them what they wanted to hear any time they were willing to hear me tell it. Of course, this didn't stop me from agreeing with the rest of my teammates that the brass were assholes whenever they needed to hear it. In fact, as the locker room ran quiet in reverence for the cut day's fallen, I found myself saying exactly that to guys who'd been let go. I told them that, once they made it to the Bigs with some other team, the bastards who released them would rue the day they got rid of them. It was a bullshit line, the kind you say to keep the tough and macho feeling secure when they want to cry like little children, but it was the least I could do since saying it to them felt way better than having someone say it to me.

I was still on the Triple A roster at the start of the day and, normally, seeing your name on a roster at the start of a cut day is enough for a player to know he's made a team. Not me. Last year, I made the Double A list but, by the time the day was over, I was heading to High A cursing the bastards I spent all spring sucking up to. Things could change in a heartbeat this time of year, and even though I wanted to relax now more than ever, I refused to let my name on a list make me feel comfortable.

I spent the day watching over my shoulder, waiting for some coach to pull me off the field and break the bad news, but it didn't happen. Morning meetings were held. Stretch came and went. Pitchers' fielding practice, batting practice, and the last simulation game of the spring, all passing by like normal.

Then, as we came walking back to the lockers from our final workout, I turned the corner, laughing blissfully along with Ox and Frenchy, and ran into Grady. I instinctively took a step back as Grady locked eyes on me.

"Shit," I mumbled.

Ox and Frenchy looked at me but kept moving when Grady said, "Excuse me, boys, can I borrow this guy for a second?"

My heart stopped. I shook my head *no* ever so slightly in hopes the guys would refuse to let me leave their escort, but they moved on obediently, leaving me behind.

Grady walked me around the corner of the complex. "I wanted to talk to you about where you're going to be playing this year," he said.

"I figured," I said, dropping my head and bracing myself for bad news.

"We're going to put you on the Triple A roster. You've earned that. You had a tremendous year last year, and we're looking for you to repeat it."

My head shot up immediately, searching Grady's face for some hint of sarcasm, but there wasn't any.

"Now," Grady's rusty voice changed course, "that doesn't mean things can't change during the season."

"Of course." I nodded my head like a faithful player.

"I could see you picking up starts in Double A this year, if necessary. Or Triple A, perhaps. You'll be the long man, and you may move around a little bit, but Triple A is where you'll start."

"I'm not going to get a phone call tonight about how you've changed your mind, am I?" I asked.

"No," said Grady. "You can relax. For now."

I let out a sigh of relief. "That's awesome," I said. "Thank you for the opportunity."

"You earned it. Now keep earning it."

"I will," I said as the realization of what I'd done washed over me. I had made the Triple A roster. I was going to Portland. I was in line for a shot at the Show. I was going to get the extra pay I needed for a ring. Bonnie would get to see me sooner. Everything was lining up. This was fantastic!

"Try not to fuck it up," said Grady, "Now get out of here."

"Gladly," I said, and I went to pack my locker in preparation for the biggest season of my life.

Chapter Twenty-three

"I made the Portland squad!" I shouted into the phone.

"That's great, babe! That means"—Bonnie shuffled some papers in the background—"we can go by calendar A. I can see you in just over a month!"

"Calendar A?" I asked.

"I mapped out a couple of calendars around your possible team schedules."

"Wow," I said.

"So, are you going to be ring shopping now? Like, in the next thirty days?"

"Is that a heavy hint or what?"

"I'm excited, honey! You're going to Portland. I get to see you soon."

"Oh, is that it? For a second there it sounded like you were focused on a ring."

"I'm just saying, it would be nice." She dropped the charade. "Oh come on, I'm a girl, of course I'm excited about the ring!"

"Well, I will be ring shopping." Then, to throw her off the scent, "But it might be a few months till I have enough paychecks to get you the ring. We'll see. Speaking of a ring, you've been sending me pictures for ideas and they're all great, but I had some ideas of my own. First, is there a certain amount I have to spend?"

"Of course not. I want it to be nice, but you don't have to make it a pricey ring just for the sake of making it pricey."

"That's a relief. There is a guy on my team who bought three rings for three different girls during his career, and spent close to twenty grand on each of them."

"That's insane!"

"No, not really."

"Yes, really. Twenty grand for a circle on your finger? Ridiculous."

"Honey, put your baseball goggles back on. You're looking at a world where everyone is operating with unrealistic stereotypes and expectations. Why do you think the parking lot here is full of hundred-thousand-dollar cars when a well-appointed Accord would be plenty for anyone else? Guys make millions in this sport and still find a way to get into debt because it's all about image and excess. Wives aren't immune to it. They land an athlete and they get big expectations too."

"Not this wife."

"It's that very reason why I'd buy you whatever you want."

"I'd feel terrible lugging around a hunk of rock worth more than my car. However"—she paused for effect—"I would like it to be worth more than *your* car."

"My Corolla?" I objected. "Its beauty can't be quantified in dollars."

"It's a rusty pile of crap," said Bonnie.

"It got me to you all winter."

"That, or I want a diamond as big as an Escalade parked on my finger."

I bit my tongue. "Very well, my beloved, a ring worth more than fourteen hundred dollars. Next question: does it have to be a diamond?"

"What else would it be? Glass?"

"No, no, nothing like that. I was thinking, your favorite color is pink, so why not a pink sapphire?" I made a strong and robust case for the idea by expressing numerous facts about the hardness of the stone, its rarity, its beautiful range of hues, and the vast difference in price.

"I want a diamond."

"Come on, at least have an open mind about it. You said you wanted this wedding to be us, special, unique. I think it should be. How many people could say they have what you have? Also, you wouldn't have to worry about the whole blood diamond issue. Speaking of which, you should see that movie. It's got Leonardo DiCaprio in it. He dies in the end, just like *Titanic*—you'd love it."

"Alright. I'll think about it."

"Thank you, darling. Now, one last thing. Are you going to be okay coming to see me in an apartment that other players also live in?"

"I think so, why?"

"Let me rephrase that. Are you going to be okay with staying with me in an apartment that probably has only one bathroom and three men?"

"What kind of men are we talking about here? Boxed-set-porn men, or real men?"

"Portland is a pricey place to live, especially on a minor league paycheck, so I had to go in with some roommates. It was either that or putting off getting your ring until Lord knows when. I found two guys to room with, both really nice and married."

The two gentlemen in question were both position players. The first, Luke Carlin, was a catcher. We'd worked together in the past, a few days at almost every level in the system. When I first met him, he was a real tough nut. His parents were involved with the military, which I thought had to be the reason he had such a tactical feel to him. When he'd pay a mound visit, he'd march out like he was policing a firing range, explain to you that you needed to quit malfunctioning and execute, soldier. He looked remarkably like the liquid robot killing machine from *Terminator 2,* especially when he walked, as his head was always down and scowling like he'd locked on to John Connor. Over the years he'd mellowed substantially, which probably had something to do with getting married and having a daughter. Even the toughest soldiers tend to soften when they have a little lady in the house requesting their presence at an officers-only tea party.

Despite his military mannerisms, Luke had no ego, and never carried a grudge. He was always honest, especially about how much he hated Democrats, and he'd do his best to support you, even if his words of comfort were a tad blunt.

The other guy was named Chip. He was an outfielder who, in a former life, was a high-round pick on the fast track to big league glory. Things didn't go quite according to plan, however. He was definitely talented but, like many of the players who populate Triple A, he had a smattering of big league time but never seemed to stick there. Chip was also black, and although he was a really easygoing guy, I was nervous I would unknowingly say something racially insensitive and then wake up to a bat to the head. Aside from that, I didn't know too much about Chip because he was in big league camp and, while I had met some of the pitchers up there, I hardly met any of the position players. In the few conversations I had with Chip, he seemed funny and upbeat, and more worried about me being rowdy, since I was the one in the group who wasn't married.

In fact, the pair actually requested me to go in with them as a third. They knew I was a social dud, a trait they found appealing in a roommate. Back in the early years of pro ball when young studs were "living the dream" and looking to sow their wild oats with every baseball-crazy female who crossed their paths, a roommate like me was avoided like the use of a condom. Now, in the higher levels, where players have families and don't want all the drama of explaining why there are Bacardi bottles with thongs stuffed in them to their visiting wives, a guy like me is a hot commodity.

"Are these guys *married* married, or baseball player rules married?"

"They are good, trustworthy, faithful guys. And they both have kids, which means more alimony losses should they even think about crossing the line."

"That sounds okay, then."

"Yeah, but, depending on what kind of arrangements we land, we could all be there at the same time. Kids, wives, one big party—one little apartment."

"If there are more women there, I'd actually feel better about the whole thing."

"Okay, well, that's all I have. Everything else will take care of itself, though I really do hope you consider the pink sapphire. I think they look good, and if you agree the ring is a symbol of our love, I think that symbol should be distinct to us."

"I've already pulled up three sites online."

"Three? Obsess much?"

"It's my ring, I can obsess all I want."

"And?"

"It's unique . . . I like that."

"So, is it you? Is it *us*?"

"I think so," she said.

"Well then, maybe you'll see that ring when you visit after all."

Chapter Twenty-four

Holding on to the countertop for support, I stared at myself in the bathroom mirror at around four in the morning. My eyes were bloodshot and the skin of my face hung under the weight of its own fatigue. This was just the first of many rude awakenings ahead of me. In Portland, we would fly everywhere, and it would not be the friendly skies. Every away series Portland played would mean a seat on the cheapest red-eye flight available, headed to towns scattered all over the Pacific Coast League. I had traded marathon bus trips for sleepless nights and knuckleball flights aboard puddle jumpers and discount ferries. But it was an easy trade to make since, in a matter of hours, I'd be in Portland on the team built with the express purpose of reinforcing the big league squad. Even though I hadn't left the spring training hotel bathroom yet, I had never been closer to my goal.

The manager of the newly christened squad was Randy Ready, the same manager from last year's San Antonio team—he earned a promotion just like many of the players who served under him. His first edict as skipper was to mandate suit jackets and slacks for all team trips. He said that's what we'd wear in the big leagues, and, since Triple A was about getting guys ready for the Bigs, that's what we'd wear here. However, since I didn't have a suit, or even dress shoes, I had to borrow the necessary items from team members who'd been playing long enough to prepare for such dress codes.

Last year, when I broke camp with the High A team, I was the oldest guy on my new squad. This year, I was a young man once again. In fact, I could probably play for the next eight years and still not be the oldest player on my Triple A team. That's because of all the levels in minor league baseball, Triple A's player composition spans the widest range. On any given day, you can find rosters showcasing teenagers with phenom powers, as well as salty veterans who use their experience to make up for what their bodies can no longer do.

Equally diverse are the pay scales in Triple A, ranging anywhere from 16K for the first timers like me, to 120K for experienced players, to checks peaking in the millions for big league rehabbers. However, what makes Triple-A the most unique minor league level is not the variations in demographics or financials, but what lies above it.

As a Triple A player, there is no way to tune out the fact that the big leagues are just a phone call away, and with it all the powers, privileges, and money reserved for those lucky enough to receive it. This proximity to the Show influences everything—from kangaroo court rulings to dress code requirements. And living under its influence for a prolonged period of time can do one of two things to a player: make him very hungry, or make him very bitter.

Naturally, every player who enters pro ball wants to make it to the big leagues. Why, then, are some players bitter when they find themselves on the cusp of doing just that? That has everything to do with how they got there. For the hungry up-and-comer, the golden carrot they've chased for so long has never been closer. On the other hand, for the veteran who has tasted the fruits of the Bigs and now finds himself on the outside, Triple A is a poor substitute.

While it's certainly one of the most exciting leagues in the game, Triple A can also be one of the most bitter since it's crammed full of veterans who feel they should be in the Bigs, much the same way prisons are populated by criminals who swear they're innocent. The Brass factors this in when they assemble teams, especially ones with large amounts of rookie prospects. While most Triple A veterans are gracious about biding their time, helping their younger teammates until their own services are once again required by the big club, others turn venomous. And, since all power in baseball is reserved for those with seniority and service time, having a batch of bitter veterans on a team can be like living under a militant baseball dictatorship. That zest to achieve, which management hopes to nurture in its prospects, gets beaten out of them by a veteran with a chip on his shoulder. After all, it's not every profession that asks you to play nice with a guy who's making you obsolete.

I suspected this year's team would be more of a democracy, if only because there were so many young, approved Grady's boys on it. In fact, almost all of the players and staffing who made last year's San Antonio team so good were here, including Texas League Player of the Year, Chase Headley; Frenchy, the surgical lefty with a Bugs Bunny changeup; Matt Antonelli, or "Anto," who was making a run for future big league second baseman after hitting .500 for an entire month last year; Kip Freckles, last year's Texas League Pitcher of the Year; Caesar Ramos, the polished, left-handed first rounder from Long Beach; Nick Hundley, or "Hundo," an intense, power-hitting catcher with a watchdog arm; and Will Venable, consummate all-around athlete and son of the team's hitting coach, Max Venable.

With so many prospects being groomed for serious big league service, it was unlikely the management would weigh the squad down with toxic players. Indeed, those players returning for another year in Triple A were all upbeat, positive professionals, like Chip, Luke, and the organization's triple batting title holder, Brian Myrow.

Even the pitching staff, the group most notorious for being mad at the world for getting screwed—as well as the one I would be spending most of my time with—was a solid bunch of lively personalities. Abby, last year's San Antonio pitching coach, was back. His unassuming country-boy candor had a way of soothing even the most wild of pitchers' paranoia. Ox was with us again, in close proximity to his favorite Mexican Whoopee cushion, Manrique. There was the veteran lefty Hamp, who was often referred to as Quadruple A player since he'd been up and down so many times it was like he belonged in his own separate league. There was a mysterious and reclusive Latin pitcher who didn't speak any English named Zarate, whom we called "Z." There was Fish the tall, quiet, right handed split-finger specialist who was so long legged he practically strode to the plate while delivering. And finally, Chad Bentley, another Quadruple A player and our team pretty boy who possessed an uncanny knowledge of skin lotions, designer clothes, and luxury cars.

There was only one bad egg in the whole group: Dallas Preston. And when I boarded the shuttle bus to the airport, he was already talking the heads off of two rookie pitchers.

"The thing about this fucking league," said Dallas, "is the parks are fucking launching pads. If you get beat up, you can't feel bad because it's common to have a high four or a five ERA here. Like, last year, I had bad numbers, but it's because of the parks, mostly. I pitched good, I thought."

"I have heard this league is a hitters' league," said Frenchy.

"I heard that too," said Kip.

"Hell yeah, it is," affirmed Dallas. "Not like International League, where every park is a graveyard. I need to get my ass traded to the International League, snap!"

Kip and Frenchy exchanged concerned looks about their futures.

"You'll be fine," said Dallas. "Besides, I'll be here to help you, and the first thing you need to know is the chicks in this league are outstanding. Ain't they, Bentley? There are some sleeper towns in this league, huh?"

"I hardly think you need to be worrying about that, Dallas," said Bentley, who was reclined in a seat with a sleeping mask over his eyes.

"I ain't talking for me. I mean for these guys." Dallas turned back to a pair. "For my money, Salt Lake City has some of the finest girls on earth. Mormon chicks are hot, and they're wild. And then there's fucking Vegas."

"That's right, we go to Vegas in this league," said Frenchy.

"What's that like?" asked Kip.

"We play like shit, that's what it's like. Fucking, no one sleeps. Best home field advantage in baseball, snap!" Dallas noticed me sit down and immediately roped me into the conversation.

"Dirk, you drink now, right?"

"A little."

"You ever hit a bar called Dante's Inferno when you were in Portland?"

"I haven't."

"You gotta go, you'd like it."

"Why is that?" I asked, wondering what made him think I'd be interested in attending a place named after hell.

"There is just a lot of weird shit in there. You're into weird shit, ain't you? Like this one time"—he turned back to the pair of first-time pitchers—"this undead clown guy was hosting and he kept high-stepping around the place like a Nazi. Then there was this chick dressed up as a police officer and she was stripping. Her face was busted up but, damn, she had some nice titties." He reached across the aisle and grabbed hold of Z and shook him by the shoulder. "Some nice titties, Z, you like titties where you come from, don't you?" Z stared back at Dallas, mouth open, completely lost.

"Anyway, every day they have something crazy going on in there, people dressed up as spacemen and shit, stripping." He took a sip of his coffee, swallowed hard, then looked at me. "Come to think of it, you probably wouldn't like it at all. Hell, it's amazing what you think is interesting when you're drunk, ya know?"

"Uh, sure, happens to me all the time," I said flippantly.

"Oh, alright then," said Dallas, now locked on to me. "All these years and you're still a smart-ass, I see. Fucking Dick Gayhurst, everybody."

That comment woke me up in a hurry. How could he spend all that time dumping on me privately, and now that he had an audience, decide that he could insult me? I tried to think of something to say to all the faces waiting for me to retort to Dallas's jab, when Chip, my future roommate, broke into the scene.

"Watch out now!" shouted Chip. He was in the middle of the bus aisle moving to some music playing over the bus's radio. "This song right here, mmm, don't matter what time it is, you have to love it." The bus driver had tuned in a smooth jazz radio station—an odd choice for this early in the morning—featuring Al Green's "Let's Stay Together."

"I'll tell you what, mmm, I think I was made to this song." Chip continued to work it, acting like he was singing to us. We stopped what we were doing and accompanied Chip by snapping our fingers to the beat—all except Z, who just stared at Chip.

"Help me now, help me!" said Chip, calling out to all of us on the bus as the song built to its chorus. Then, if you were a bystander outside the bus doors, you would have heard a choir of Triple A baseball players singing, "Whether times are good or bad . . ." *Good or bad, indeed,* I thought, taking my seat as the bus pulled out for Portland.

Chapter Twenty-five

Our flight touched down around 9 A.M. A shuttle bus took us from the airport to the Doubletree Hotel next to the Lloyd Center Mall and Holladay Park. The hotel graciously put out fresh baked cookies for our arrival—we devoured them like a plague of locusts, then choked the front desk to a halt demanding our room keys. After which, chocolate chip stains around our mouths, we piled into the elevators until the weight alarms rang, thundered down hallways, slammed all of our doors, and cussed, loudly, when our roommates beat us to the toilet. That's right, Portland, your 2008 Beavers were in town; make way for your new role models.

Roughly half an hour later, or however long it took us to finish up in the potty, we headed out into the city. While it would stand to reason that most folks would sleep after getting off a red-eye, we knew that if we didn't get to the ballpark ASAP, we ran the risk of getting shafted with leftover uniform pieces. Also, the organization was only picking up three nights in the hotel, which meant the clock was ticking for us to find a new place to live.

Most of the team grabbed one of Portland's monorail MAX lines across town to PGE Park, home of the Portland Beavers, located on the edge of Portland's Pearl District, an upscale area with fine restaurants and high-end shopping. Players enter the park on the street level, through the main gate on the corner of Morrison and 20th. There is a secluded pull chain that allowed the gate to be opened; you can't see it unless you've been to the park before and knew where to look. This, ironically, was one of the reasons I was so shocked to find half the team already present and accounted for when I showed up.

"You're late," said Luke, sitting by his locker with all of his stuff unpacked and put away as if he was in mid-season.

"Late? How? We've been here for, like, ten minutes. What did you do, parachute off the plane when I wasn't looking?"

"I know the terrain. You'd better get your uniform picked out before you get stuck with leftovers." Luke gestured to the back of the clubhouse where the team clubby, Shane, kept all the uniforms.

For the 2008 season, the Portland uniforms were completely redesigned. That meant everyone would get new game pants sans sliding damage patchwork. However, because the pants were bought under the rule of Grady Fuson, they were custom-tailored to be painfully short, ensuring no one could test the "must show sock" rule that had become organizational policy.

You don't understand how unhappy a pair of pants can make you until you are forced to wear bad ones. At first, I thought, since each pair of pants was new, all of them would offer a perfect fit. I soon discovered that every pair of pants had one of two problems: either the pant legs were so short I looked like some baseball-playing hobo, or, the crotch was cut so low that when I lifted my legs up I was snared by my own pants leg.

I wasn't the only one to have pants issues, Frenchy marched around in his pants fuming, "They're pants!" He tugged at the mass of free fabric between his knees and his waist. "How long has humanity possessed the knowledge to make pants, and we still screw them up? Didn't anyone try these on before they ordered an entire team's worth?"

"You wouldn't be complaining if you had something to fill that space with," said Ox, gesturing to the same, decidedly occupied, area of pants on his person. "You can keep your plus changeup. I'll keep my huge cock."

"These are unacceptable," said Bentley. "I can't play in these, not after playing in real big league pants. And this show-sock rule, how juvenile. We're grown men, not infants. I'm going to order my own pants from Majestic. If anyone else needs the number, I have it. They know me there."

I picked out a pair that came as close to fitting as possible and stuffed it into my locker, along with the rest of my equipment. There was no practice scheduled for today, so this trip to the locker room was purely for the sake of getting familiarized with our new stadium, lockers, and uniform pieces. The rest of the day was ours to do what we pleased, though Luke had already decided how Chip and I would be spending it.

"Can we see it?" asked Chip, standing next to Luke at his locker.

"Yeah," said Luke, "the lady said we could come up anytime. There's nothing else to do here, so we might as well."

"See what?" I asked.

"Our boy Luke found us a place already," said Chip.

"What? How? When?" Since getting off the plane, I'd only had time to poop and come to the park. How was Luke already lining up apartment viewings?

"I put in a few calls before we left camp. Only one has gotten back to me so far. I think we should go check it out since it's hard to say when the others will let us get in. Besides, this one is in walking distance from the field, and they said they'd work with baseball players' leasing needs. It's about two clicks north of the stadium."

"Let's do it," said Chip.

"What the hell is a click?" I asked, but Luke and Chip were already moving.

We headed north, up West Burnside Street, to the place Luke had found. It felt like a long walk, but maybe that was because we were going uphill most of the way. As we walked, Luke pointed out relevant locations.

"If you need to get to the mall, you can take the MAX line to Pioneer Square. It's southeast of here. There is a Goodwill for travel clothes necessities, and a gas station, and a pizza joint. The trains go pretty much everywhere, and, as long as you're in the city, it's free," said Luke.

"I don't know about that train, man," said Chip. "I took that thing here this morning and there was a lady on board, head all buzzed, piercings all over, tattoos like crazy, holding on to a baby stroller with a plastic baby doll inside. She acted like the baby was real, bro. Like it was crying and she had to comfort it or something. I thought she was going to breast-feed it, just pull her boob out right there on the train in front all creation. She caught me staring at her and she looked back at me like I was nuts for looking at her."

Luke chuckled. "Yeah, you'll see some crazy stuff on that train. There's a saying around here that goes, 'Keep Portland weird.' Last time I was in Pioneer Square, there was a homeless dude holding a sign that read 'Need money for karate lessons—entire family killed by ninjas.' "

"Points for creativity," I said.

"Yeah, I gave him a buck for making me laugh." Luke slowed his stride. "This is the place here." He pointed at the towering apartment building in front of us.

The apartment manager took us up to the room we were inquiring about, which was located on the third floor. It was tiny and dated. The kitchen was galley-style with appliances that looked as if they hadn't been changed since the building was originally built. All the windows were single pane with rusted hinges and latches. The cabinets had been painted over multiple times, giving the wood a thick gooey coating, almost like a yogurt-coated peanut. There was only one bathroom and it had no counters of any kind unless you counted the tank of the toilet. There was also no air-conditioning. We were told that if we wanted to rent an air-conditioning unit to stick in the window, it was a hundred dollars extra a month.

"This is only two bedrooms," I said.

"I know," said Luke.

"This carpet looks like it's had it," said Chip.

"I know," said Luke.

"I don't know how we're going to put all our stuff in the bathroom," I said.

"Yeah," said Luke.

"It's gonna get hot in here come summer," said Chip.

"Yeah, you're right. But it's six hundred dollars cheaper than any other place in town, and that's with the short-term lease."

Chip and I stopped to consider the savings.

"And you don't have to ride the crazy train," said Luke.

"I kinda like the train," I said. "But I do need the money." I shrugged.

"You like crazy ladies breast-feeding plastic babies?" asked Chip.

"I don't know, it's like an adventure," I said.

"I'm good on adventure. I'll take the money. I'm in," said Chip.

"I suppose I can ride the train anytime. I need the money, too. I'm in," I said.

"Good, because I already told the lady we'd take it," said Luke.

After we did our paperwork and paid the deposit, we hashed out a rooming arrangement and a list of what we needed to turn our new apartment into a home away from home.

"Why do I have to sleep in the living room?" I protested.

"You're the youngest" was the mutual response.

"Fine, but I don't think I should pay as much as you guys do in the split since I'm not getting any privacy, and my room is also part of the kitchen."

"No, no. We've earned this. Someday you will too," said Chip.

"But you're both making more than me," I said.

"Yeah, well, I got two kids running through diapers like they going outta style. Come talk to me when you're in my shoes," said Chip.

"You should try potty-training them, Chip, we could get a bigger place," said Luke.

"Let me call my wife so you can tell her that."

"So I'm going to have to sleep in the living room, final answer?" I asked.

"We can rock, paper, scissors for it," suggested Luke. "That way it's fair."

"I'm cool with that. Just as long as if someone has family coming in, we can switch for a room so our queens can have their privacy," said Chip.

"Of course," Luke and I agreed.

Everyone put their hands in, and three fist pumps later I was still in the living room.

"Collusion!" I declared.

"It's meant to be," said Luke.

I paced around the living room. It was practically all windows, each providing a direct line of sight for other apartments around the building. "I guess sleeping in one corner is just as good as the other. I'll put my bed here, I think."

"You should probably put it over there so we can put a TV here," said Luke.

"Whoa, now you're telling me where to put my bed. I thought this was my room. What if I don't want a television in my room?"

"Yeah, but it's also the living room, so . . ."

"Shoulda went with rock, bro. You can always trust rock," said Chip.

"Well, we don't have a television, so, until we do, I guess I don't have to worry about it."

"What do y'all want to do about furniture?" asked Chip.

"I'll take care of that," said Luke. "I have some sources back at the field I can talk to. I should be able to get us everything we need."

Chapter Twenty-six

"Apparently, Luke's definition of 'everything we need' was a little less comprehensive than mine," I said, recounting the events to Bonnie via cell phone. Chip, Luke and I had moved out of the hotel and into the apartment, where I was presently wandering about with my laptop open, trying to find an unprotected Wi-Fi signal to pirate.

"Over the years," I said, "so many players have come and gone from this team that the clubhouse guy has collected a stockpile of furnishings at the field. Luke knew this, and 'commandeered' some stuff for us. He got us an ironing board, which we are now using as a kitchen table, a desk and, well, an ironing board. A collection of pots and pans that look like they've been dragged behind a car. Some plastic Tupperware that's been deformed from over-microwaving. A set of sleeping bags that I don't think have been washed since their first occupant who knows how long ago. Two lawn chairs, some clothes hangers, and a shower curtain—I feel like I'm living in MacGyver's apartment."

"So are you just sleeping on the floor in sleeping bags?"

"Since Luke has spent so much time here, he had his own stash at the field. He has an air mattress and a few items specific to him. I sent out a clubhouse guy to get me an air mattress as well, the exact make and model I have at Grandma's. I feel like I'm living at home, minus the crazy screaming gibberish. Chip is the only one who doesn't have a bed, and he said he didn't want one. He's sleeping on the floor in a sleeping bag with one pillow."

"Will you get more furniture? Can't you rent it?"

"We could, but what happens if one of us gets moved, who picks up the bills?"

This was one of the common issues with players renting or leasing anything. If one of the players in the lease gets moved, another player has to fill in before the payments get crazy for the remaining leasers. Everything that gets rented on top of that adds to the problem. When it comes to general issues, like a place to live or something to sleep on, it's not too complicated. But personal issues, like air-conditioning, furniture, Internet, and cable channels up the ante. If one of the guys in my apartment left, there was no guaranteeing that the player who replaced him would want to live in our apartment to begin with, let alone pay for extra utilities he had no part in selecting.

"Do you guys at least have food?" asked Bonnie.

"Oh yeah, we got, let's see here . . ." I opened the fridge. "A six-pack of Blue Moon, a jug of milk, some Coke Zero, and a couple boxes of instant mac and cheese."

"That's it?"

"I think there are some Doritos around here."

"Wow."

"It's not that bad, honey. We eat at the field a lot. Since we're paying the clubhouse guy twelve bucks a day, we eat all his stuff. At least guys in my earnings bracket do. The older guys who are making bigger money eat out a lot. It's actually understood that guys not making a lot are dependent on the clubhouse while the guys earning more eat out."

"Another of those baseball world rules?" asked Bonnie.

"You got it. Besides, even if we tip extra, it's still cheaper than buying all our meals. Also, they have free Internet at the field, which is really nice." I was holding my laptop above my head now, watching the wireless signal button flick on and off, practically toying with me.

"Are we going to get to video-chat?" asked Bonnie. "I want to see you."

"I want to see you too," I said. "I just don't want to pay for Internet."

"Today was a hard day," Bonnie said, rather deflated.

"I'm sorry." I stopped what I was doing to be more attentive to her voice.

"It's okay. I keep counting down the days until I'll be out to see you, but they don't go fast enough."

"Tell me about it." I sat down on my air mattress.

"I'm going to all these wedding venues and taking pictures for you, but you're not here . . . I knew it would be like this, but today I went to one of the venues I saw online and there was another couple there, and they were all lovey-dovey, talking about how their big day was going to go. Meanwhile, I'm trying to take pictures of the venue's angles so you can decide if you like it, and they won't stop making out long enough for me to get the shots I want."

"You should bring a squirt bottle and spritz them like bad dogs," I said.

"I should." She giggled, and some of the joy returned to her tone. "I love you," she said. "I know my mom doesn't like it when you make your little sarcastic jokes, but I love that about you."

"That's funny, when I talked to your mom and dad about officially having their blessing to marry you the other day, she seemed really supportive."

"You talked to them?" Bonnie shouted into the phone.

"Naturally, and even though your mom thinks my humor is inappropriate nearly all the time, she said she loves seeing how happy I make you and gave me her blessing. It was really painless."

"My mom?" asked Bonnie. "The same one who yelled at you for painting skulls and crossbones on Christmas cookies?"

"Christmas Pirates, they sail the Yule tide in search of Christmas booty—an often underrepresented part of the holiday season."

"That's great, honey. Wait, if you talked to them, that means you . . . Dirk Hayhurst, have you been ring shopping?"

"Maybe."

Not only had I been ring shopping, my first day out I found the perfect ring—a pink sapphire set in white gold, surrounded by little diamonds. I provided the down payment on the spot, my first real dollars-and-cents commitment to getting married. Everyone talks about the emotions involved in asking permission from the parents, walking down the aisle, and saying, "I do," but signing my name across the largest purchase receipt of my life was pretty damn emotional to me.

Actually, I didn't want to buy the ring when I did, especially since I didn't have enough money to pay it off. Chip, Luke, and I had to pay the first and last months' rent for the apartment up front, which emptied my bank account. I had to put the ring on my credit card, which made me very uncomfortable. I knew millions of Americans bought stuff they couldn't afford using plastic every day, but I'd never done it. I might have been poor, but I wasn't in debt—something I was very proud of. However, since Grady said I could get sent to Double A if the need arose, I felt it best to get the ring while things were stable. If I got off to a bad start, then ordered a ring, then got sent down, I could be on the other side of the country with a no address, no ring, and a looming credit payment, not to mention a very unhappy Bonnie.

"Have you or haven't you?" pushed Bonnie.

"I have. I found some nice rings, with beautiful pink sapphires. However"—this was kind of the truth—"with the up-front rent I had to pay, I can't afford one just yet. I know you're excited, but don't come out here expecting a ring. I don't want you to feel let down."

"I know. I know. I don't want to make you feel pressured, either. I'm sorry I keep asking. Really, honey, ring or no ring, I still love you, and I still can't wait to see you."

"And I can't wait to see you."

"Well, my plane tickets are bought, and I'm ready."

"I hope I'm still here when the time comes," I mumbled to my-self.

"When does the season start?"

"Tomorrow," I said.

"Are you ready?"

I looked around the apartment, at the air mattress, lawn chairs, and Dorito crumbs.

"As ready as it gets."

Chapter Twenty-seven

It was a terrible day for baseball. The temperature hit its lowest point since our arrival in Portland, which felt twice as cold considering we had just come from ninety-degree Arizona heat. Batting practice was canceled due to marble-size hail. Those courageous enough to venture onto the field for any kind of pregame activity were rewarded with soaked shoes, freezing fingers, and welts on their necks. We soon began to doubt the home opener would actually happen.

Self-amusement during weather delays is a fine art among baseball players, and while management debated over how much precipitation was too much, players broke out cards in the clubhouse. Many of the boys decided they would use the delay time wisely, sharpening their poker skills in preparation for the much-anticipated trip to Sin City. We weren't the first Portland team to think this way, which may have explained the clubhouse's rather robust collection of mismatched poker chips—leftovers passed down from generations of players hoping to beat the house. There was also a Connect Four game, Uno, a mangled Monopoly set, and some checkers that had poker chips being used as stand-ins to the normal chips.

Eating is another common use of player downtime. Those not

honing their gambling skills wandered in and out of the club-house's food pantry, where they grazed on sugar and fat like mindless cattle. Since players paid more in clubhouse dues in Portland, the snacking was better, offering a wider selection of ways to increase one's waistline: industrial-size tubs of cheese balls, Red Vine licorice, Oreos, Pop-Tarts, animal crackers, chips, chocolate, and a soft drink fountain featuring five flavors. If Stan were here, he would have had a heart attack.

In our boredom, we filled plastic party cups full of sodas and pantry snacks and parked ourselves either in the middle of the clubhouse at the casino, or in front of one of the clubhouse's two sets of televisions and couches located on either side of the room.

Presently, one television was showing a Cubs' game featuring Joe Morgan as the color man. The other showcased the latest VH1 reality show, *The Flavor of Love,* starring Flava Flav and his flock of debutantes.

"Where's the remote?" bellowed Myrow. "I can't take him any-more. We have to mute this idiot or change the channel."

"I hate it when people try to hold on to their fame in desperate ways. They should know their time has passed and move on. It's disgraceful to fight it," said Bentley.

"Never happen. This clown has too many fans," said Myrow.

"Only because they don't know any better," sighed Bentley. "They're disadvantaged, really. Your average viewer will believe whatever a celebrity figure tells them to believe. That's why they have so many guys like him doing this kind of thing nowadays."

"What y'all talking about?" asked Dallas, forcing his way into a seat between the pair.

"Joe Morgan," said Myrow. "He's terrible."

"And yet," added Bentley, "he's remarkably gifted at giving himself on-air blow jobs about how great he once was. If you drank a shot every time he started a sentence with 'I,' you'd die of alcohol poisoning before the fifth inning."

"Ain't fucking guys who are always talking 'bout themselves just the worst?" Dallas asked. "It just pisses me off when I hear a guy do that. Makes me want to smack 'em right in their fucking face."

Bentley lifted an eyebrow at Dallas. "Yes, well"—he rattled his plastic cup—"I think I'm going to refresh my cheese balls." He got up, leaving Myrow with Dallas.

"Listen to him!" Myrow pointed at the television. Morgan was saying something like, *I'm not going to lie to you, the only way to know if this kid has what it takes to be an everyday player is to see him play every day, someday.* "Gee, thanks for not lying to me about that, Joe." Myrow picked up the remote and aimed it at the television. "Why do people feel the need to ruin perfectly good baseball by letting Morgan commentate on it? Hayhurst," Myrow called to me, sitting on the clubhouse's sister couch with Ox, Frenchy, and Hamp. "What channel is Flava Flav on?"

"VH1, a few channels up," I called back.

Myrow changed the channel, crossed his legs, and smiled. "Now this is bold television. They should let this guy commentate for the Cubs, that would break that curse."

A few hours—and several cups of cheese balls—later, the weather gave up trying to defeat the ultra-weather-resistant turf field and allowed the home opener to proceed. To kick off of another year of Beavers baseball, several opening day festivities were held. The team was dragged up to the concourse to pass out swag to fans entering the gate. New graphics and player bios celebrating the team's new logo flashed across the video board in the outfield. First pitches were thrown by quasi-famous figures and, finally, our mascot, Lucky the Beaver, was presented in the grandest of ceremonies: a grounds crew member drove Lucky to home plate on a Gator brand ATV. The fans cheered moderately.

Kip Freckles got the start. He was absolutely paramount in our clinching of the Texas League last year, and this year, it was almost as if he picked up right where he left off, going a seven strong innings while allowing only one hit: a solo home run. This dominating start was great for Kip, but terrible for me and the rest of the bullpen crew who sat freezing our asses off in the pen. As night fell, so did the temperature. We heaped on all the spare clothes we had, anything to keep warm. We cut up socks to make headbands, used training towels as scarves and blankets, even huddled together to share body heat despite the fact that Ox nearly puked when he touched Bentley's ultra-soft skin. When the weather got ugly and spit out icy mist, we pulled up our hoods and took as much as we could before evacuating.

The Beavers' pen was situated down the left field line, completely exposed to the elements, which was a bad thing considering the weather. However, since there was a back door entrance to the clubhouse, this was easy to forgive. A back door entrance meant we could sneak into the comfort of our home locker room if the weather turned, or we needed a potty break, or we just got bored. We could gorge ourselves in the pantry, text-message our fiancées, or, like Dallas was fond of doing, fight with our baby-mommas via cell phone away from the prying eyes of the manager.

Equally nice was the amount of nooks, crannies, and cover the Portland pen provided us to screw around in. I'm not sure what it is about boys and forts, but I know that if given the choice, a reliever will always take the bullpen that feels like a fort over the one that doesn't. Luckily, behind the exposed portion of the pen was a towering wall of ivy behind which the grounds crew's equipment was stored. This was another fine development as relievers and power tools mix quite nicely, like last year in Tulsa, when the Double A relief crew made bets on what would explode when run over by a tractor. I love science.

Connected to the secluded ivy portion was a path tracing the hidden side of the outfield wall. Follow it and you could reach the hand-operated scoreboard in left field, or visit the opposing team's pen in right. Opposite the path was a staircase that rose to overlook the field. It was like a lookout tower, shielded from the elements, from where a player could watch the game and sip hot cocoa. Or, in the case of Dallas, an excellent vantage point from which to rate the quality of boobs in the beer garden, which, incidentally, also neighbored the pen.

"Why the fuck would you wear that out in this weather?" asked Dallas, staring down a young lady putting her own kegs on display in the beer garden. "That's what I hate about girls. They know what they're up to, they want you to look, but when you do, they get all pissed off at you for it."

"She can get pissed off at me all she wants," said Ox. "I might even let her smack me around a little."

"Oh, she's looking!" said Dallas. "Everybody wave." All of us waved hello to her. She did a double take. Ox even invited her over to the pen, waving his big mitts at her to join us. She smiled and refused, holding up her beer as an excuse.

"You can bring that," said Ox.

She shook her head no, then turned away. We kept staring at her, though, long enough that when she turned around to look at us again, she started to get uncomfortable. It was at this point a gentleman she was with moved seats to be next to her and block our vision. For his trouble, everyone in the pen booed him.

"Fucking douche bag." Dallas waved his hands at the noble gentleman blocking our eyes. "What the fuck's she doing with him? Look at him."

I looked over at the gentleman in question. He seemed like a decent guy, firm chin, dark hair, easygoing smile.

"Fucking rat-faced, white-trash pussy. You know she doesn't want to be with him. I mean, you can just fucking tell," said Dallas.

A couple of the guys laughed at Dallas's comment, at the unwarranted ferocious quality to his candor. It was like he took the whole thing personally.

"Jesus, man, you might want take off a few layers and cool down, Dallas," said Ox, slapping Dallas on the side.

"What?" Dallas looked at Ox. "It don't piss you off to see a hot chick with a fucking turd?"

"She looks happy to me," I said. The girl was laughing at something the gentleman said, though we were too far away to hear it.

"Then why's she down here in the fucking beer garden?"

"For the beer?" I answered.

"A chick with hammers like that can get beer in any bar in this town. She's down here 'cause she wants players to notice." He said it like a paranoid detective solving a crime that took place in his head.

"What if she's just here for baseball, and has nice hammers? No agenda?"

Dallas shook his head. "Girls always have an agenda. Even when you think they don't, they do. You can't trust women. This girl wants our attention. If I wasn't married I'd prove it to y'all right now. I could walk right over there and get that bitch's number like nothing." He snapped his fingers, still staring at the girl.

"While she's with another man?" I asked skeptically.

Dallas looked at me like I was incompetent. "Hell yeah. We're the ones in the uniform, man. We're the ones people pay to see." He leaned back and crossed his legs. "She might laugh or be embarrassed, but she'd give it to me. Besides, if she says no, there'll be another one tomorrow night, ya know?" He laughed after he said this, looking around to everyone else on the team as if to invite them to share in his mirth. I didn't think it was funny, though, and my lack of laughter did not sit well with him.

"Don't be so judgmental, Dirk. Fuck," said Dallas.

"What? I'm not," I said.

"I know what you're thinking," continued Dallas. He made a mocking face in imitation of my own, which, if Dallas's version was anything to go by, must have been one of smug contempt. "Like you never did anything bad in your life."

"I . . ." I threw my hands wide. "How did I get on trial here? I don't see things the way you do."

"You're judgmental, that's why."

"I don't think I'd make the same decisions as you, that's all."

"Better hope your girl sees things the same way you do while you're gone."

There was a collective tensing in the pen as everyone in earshot had just heard a statement that crossed the line. If I were Dallas and he me, fists would have been in the air by now and fellow relievers would have been fighting hard to pull us apart. Whether it was fear or prudence, I couldn't pull the trigger. I just sat there and took it.

"That's fucked up," said Ox, speaking for me.

"Yeah, Dallas, that's fucked up," repeated Hamp.

"I didn't mean nothing by it," he pleaded to his jury of peers. "I'm just saying the world ain't perfect. Shit happens." Dallas then smirked at me, begging me to counter.

The words were there, burning in me, but they caught in my throat as I knew what would happen if I said what I was thinking. Instead, I got up and left the pen.

Chapter Twenty-eight

We won the home opener game, soundly beating the Fresno Grizzlies 8–4, and Chip got his first homer.

"Nice poke, big man," I said to Chip as Luke, Chip, and I entered the apartment.

"Thanks, bro," said Chip. "Tried to get in on me, but he didn't get in there far enough." Chip took an imaginary swing and sent an imaginary ball over an imaginary left field wall.

"If you keep this pace, you'll hit 142 bombs by the end of the season. Think you can do it?"

"I'm gonna try," said Chip.

We spread out in the apartment's living room/bedroom. I sat on my bed, Chip fell into a lawn chair, and Luke, who didn't get to play tonight, took dry cuts with a bat he'd brought home with him.

Winding down after a game is different for each player. Some of the guys went out for drinks, others home to their families. Chip, Luke, and I sat in a living room on inner tubes and lawn chairs staring at each other.

We must have sat there for a good ten minutes in silent boredom when Luke, taking a final cut, announced, "This sucks."

"Yeah," I said, falling back on my bed.

"Oh," said Chip, moving as if he had the answer to our problem in the pack he carried with him to and from the field. He opened the sack and produced two cans of Gatorade protein shakes. "Breakfast," he said, and got up to deposit them in the fridge.

Luke's and my shoulders slumped: false alarm.

"You got a television in that bag?" I asked.

"Nah, bro."

"This sucks," Luke said again.

"Yes, I remember you saying that," I said to Luke.

Luke rested the bat over his shoulders and looked at me, "You know what we need?"

"Besides pretty much everything," I mumbled.

"We need some cards. You got any?" Luke looked at me.

"I'm sorry, I don't," I said.

"That sucks," said Luke.

"Maybe if we all take a piece of the locker room home with us, like Chip did, we could have all the best stuff from the locker room here by the end of the season. Chip, you think you can fit one of those barrels of cheese balls in your pack?"

"What are you going to do with a barrel of cheese balls, bro?"

"Smuggle one here and I'll show you. We could fill the bathtub—"

"Maybe the neighbors have cards?" asked Luke. He was scowling, indicating he was in deep, tactical thought about how best to secure cards.

"Oh, Lord. Look at the man's face." Chip pointed at Luke. "Luke's gonna go kill somebody for a pack of cards."

"Are you going to kill the neighbors, Luke? If you do, raid their fridge while you're at it."

"I wouldn't kill anyone for cards," said Chip. "Maybe for Monopoly. I'd dominate all of you at some Monopoly."

Luke did not respond to our helpful suggestions. He was too focused on the planning of Operation Card Game. Realizing Luke had checked out, Chip turned to me.

"I heard your boy Dallas was giving you some shit today."

"Where'd you hear that?" I asked.

"From him. His locker's next to mine. Dude doesn't shut up. It's gonna be a long year with him as a locker buddy."

"Tell me about it," I said, thinking of how not fun life in the bullpen would be this year with Dallas in it.

"If I was you, I'd tell him to worry about his own mess of problems and stop making up drama for you."

"You can't tell him anything, Chip. Me specifically. He hates me, always has. Always thinks I'm judging him. And, because of some violent history between us, he knows he can say what he wants because I'll take it. Because I won't fight him."

"Man, you don't gotta fight him. You just—"

"If I say anything he doesn't like, it will come to that. He's like my brother, you say something critical and his answer is to fight you. And I can't afford a fight with a prospect. If Dallas and I did get into it and the brass had to make an example of someone for fighting, it would be me. I need this opportunity, so I don't have a lot of choice but to take it."

"Okay, man, but shit . . ." Chip's facial expression tried to say what his voice couldn't. "Maybe we should have Luke here take him out for you." Chip looked back to Luke, who was still staring at the door. "You really gonna go ask the neighbors for a pack of cards?" asked Chip.

"Yeah, why not?" said Luke.

"Well, if you do, don't go ask these folks for any," said Chip, pointing at the far wall that served as the shared wall of Chip's room and the neighboring apartment. "Last night through the wall, I could hear them having sex."

"So?" said Luke and I.

"It's two dudes, bro."

"Oh." Luke and I cringed.

"They was going at it, screaming at each other." Chip raised his voice and put his hands up. "*You like that, baby, you like it when Daddy does that?*"

"Oh no!" Luke and I cringed harder.

"Yeah, they were getting after it. I just lie there like . . ." Chip made a face of stark, wide-eyed shock. "I almost came out here to sleep with you." Chip gestured to me. "You'd roll over and I'd be there, smiling at you."

Luke shook his head, returning to his thoughtful scowl. "I don't think that's a big deal, it's just cards."

"Alright." Chip kicked back in his seat. "Go ahead, then. Go on over there and tell them the three dudes living in a two-bedroom apartment right next door need cards at eleven p.m. 'cause we're bored. Next thing you know, they're gonna be knocking on our door every day, like"—Chip's voice and hands went back up— *"Hey, can we borrow a cup of sugar? Maybe a cup of penis?"*

"That's not going to happen," said Luke.

"Special delivery," continued Chip. *"We got something in this box, just for you!"* Chip pretended there was a box sitting on his crotch.

"What if they're black guys and they only like you?" asked Luke.

"Oh, no, no, they ain't black. I can tell you that."

"How do you know?"

"First, no black man, gay or otherwise, is going to squeal like them boys did." Luke and I laughed, but Chip pointed at me and said, "You laugh, but you remember what I said when your wedding night comes."

"Hey, my wife promised to be very gentle."

"Second," continued Chip, "I haven't seen any black people in this town since we've showed up. What are the chances of all of us living in the same place and two of us are gay?"

"He's right," said Luke. "Portland is a very white city. There probably are more gay guys than black guys here."

"Finally, y'all hear any bass? No. We been here three days now and I have yet to here any bass rumbling through the wall. They are definitely not black."

"Are you homophobic, Chip?" I asked.

"Pssh, no, I ain't homophobic. I'm hearing-dudes-have-butt-sex-through-wall-ophobic."

"So, you wanna switch rooms?" I asked, holding up my pair of earplugs.

"Uh-uh." He waved a tsking finger at my question. "I hit a home run tonight, I ain't changing a thing. I hope they have sex every night if it means I keep hittin' home runs. Hell, I might record it so I can listen to it on the road, if that's what it takes."

Chip hit a home run the following night. I didn't ask him if the noises on the other side of the wall had anything to do with it, since it was far more fun to assume that every time he had a good night with the bat, our neighbors did the same.

Chapter Twenty-nine

Shawn Estes, the veteran left-handed pitcher whose big league pedigree included the Giants, Mets, and Rockies, got the start the next day. He represented the most experienced player on our team and, in our opinion, was a big leaguer despite his current Triple A uniform. Competing more with his own age than superior talent above him, he missed the big league team's cut, losing out to a younger pitcher the Padres were hoping would blossom into a franchise player. Shawn consented to being a big league fallback plan since, in his years of experience, he knew it would take more than the twenty-five players who broke camp with a big club to make it through a season. Actually, that was something all of us were counting on.

Shawn's pitching performance was exemplary, though the weather was anything but. Fortunately, thanks to the backdoor pen entrance, the reliever crew spent most of the game hiding in the confines of the clubhouse and away from the nasty weather. If the team was younger, we would have set up a system of sneaking away from the pen when we thought no one would look down to check on us. We would move in shifts and make sure to exit during inning changes when player activity could mask our escape. However, since most of the relief crew was older guys who didn't care if anyone noticed if they were there or not, the bullpen sat completely unoccupied for innings at a time.

"I think I've put on ten pounds since I've been here," said Ox, casually flipping peanut M&M's into the bottomless pit that was his mouth. Many relievers did the same as we all reclined, watching television in the Beavers' training room, although Dallas, thankfully, chose to spend the free time arguing with his wife via text-message in the other room.

The training room was the closest part of the clubhouse to the bullpen's rear entrance, about forty feet closer in total, which, considering we were indoors and couldn't see anything happening on the field, didn't mean much. To keep us loosely up to speed on what was going on in the game, Fish pulled up the game's radio broadcast via Internet feed on the trainer's laptop. It was hard to say how much lag there was between what was happening live and the broadcast reaching our ears, but, when Estes himself came into the training room while the broadcaster was announcing the inning's second out, we realized the delay was substantial, a piece of news that stirred an immediate response from the relievers.

"Hey, Esty, could you wait on needing relief until this show is over? We're really into it," said Hamp.

"I don't know. Depends on what you guys are watching," Estes responded.

"Uh, we're watching . . . Shit, what are we watching?"

"A Japanese game show where people get the shit knocked out of them. It's fantastic," said Ox, who was completely enthralled with Japanese people getting flattened by giant boulders while people dressed like samurai clowns squirted them with fire hoses.

"Why can't we do shit like this in between innings? Instead, we have people spin around on a bat, or race the mascot."

"Hayhurst," Estes called at me, "grab a towel and wipe this off for me, would ya?" Estes turned and looked at me over his shoulder while gesturing to a huge smear of brown stretching across his ass crack.

"Did you shit yourself?" asked Ox.

"Slipped throwing over to first. Not my most graceful moment."

I hopped up and grabbed a training room towel, dampened the end of it, then started rubbing the spot on his ass.

"Get in there man, get after it," said Estes, staring up at me with his head between his legs.

"I have some neighbors you should meet," I said.

When it was clean, he checked himself and said, "You do good work." Then, instead of heading back out to the game, he plopped down on the floor, crossed his legs and looked up at the television.

"Get the Padres game on," said Estes. "I want to see how they're holding up."

The channel was changed at the senior's request. We sat with Estes and watched a few pitches in the Padres game. Estes seemed to see different things than us. He had almost ten years in the Bigs. He knew the umpires, the coaches, even the GMs sitting in their luxury boxes. When we asked him what he saw, he'd say things like "So-and-so is making more than so-and-so, but has worse numbers," or "This umpire loves showing guys up," or "I wonder how long they'll let him keep pitching like crap before they make a move." It made me feel like I knew what the big leagues were, but had no idea how they operated, even after spending nearly a lifetime in pursuit of them.

"Double play situation out there," said Fish, concerning the state of the minor league game going on outside.

"They might have already turned it," said Ox.

"Yeah, I suppose I'd better get back out there," said Estes.

"What's the rush?" asked Hamp. "We ordered a pizza."

"I should have been a reliever," said Estes.

"Still time," said Hamp.

"Not for me there isn't," said Estes, who jogged from the room.

"Go get 'em . . ." We lethargically cheered at Estes's departure, though it was hard with our mouths full of snacks.

"He sees the game pretty different than us, doesn't he?" I remarked at Estes's departure.

"Sure, he does," said Ox, "he's rich, he's got Show time and"—more M&M's went in—"he's left-handed."

"The Bigs are a different place, Ox. I believe that's what Hayhurst means," said Bentley.

"Yeah," I said. "It just seems like you guys who've been up there look at baseball differently than those of us who haven't."

"Of course, we've seen the other side of the curtain," said Bentley.

"What's it like?"

"It's"—Bentley paused—"different from what you'd expect."

"In what way?"

"It's everything you want, and yet, well, it's hard to say unless you've experienced it, which I have, of course, but that doesn't make it easy to explain to *you*."

"You sound like Joe Morgan, smart guy. Try again," said Ox.

We who had not yet ascended waited intently for Bentley to give us the tale of life in the Show. "Well, it's a lot more individualistic," Bentley began. "You know that going in, but it's strange how it shocks you regardless. There is, naturally, more money involved in everything. The lights are also brighter, the expectations higher.

"Stuff like this"—Bentley gestured to us strewn around the training room during a live game—"would never happen up there. Everyone is being measured by everyone else, constantly. Not everyone can make the adjustment to the expectations; that's why you always hear the saying, 'Getting there isn't the hard part, it's sticking there.' "

"Getting there seems pretty hard, if you ask me," I said.

"For some"—Bentley sighed—"but, compared to being here, it's like being alive for the first time. The money, the treatment—it's the way baseball should be played." Bentley stared off into a far-away land as he talked. "I should be there," he finished softly.

"Me too, asshole," said Ox.

"Oh, Ox, I hope you get there, but the Bigs can affect you in ways you didn't think possible. It's as much about survival as it is experiencing the dream. It can change you. Those lights can blind you."

"I'm perfectly fine with becoming a rich bastard, if that's what you mean," said Ox, turning his cup of munchies upside down and tapping all remaining food particles into his mouth. "I can't wait to be hated because I'm rich. I'm gonna be the next John Rocker."

"I don't mean the money, Ox, but I doubt it would be worth my time trying to explain to you the other parts of the big league experience."

"Probably." Ox burped. "How's the beef up there?" asked Ox, inquiring about the kind of women a baseball player had access to at the big league level.

Bentley smiled. "You can have any cut you want."

"That's enough motivation for me."

Chapter Thirty

Sunday: another terrible day for baseball. The sun poked out of the clouds long enough to tease the relievers into taking off their winter layers. Then, ten minutes later, the clouds came back and we had to suit up again. Rain delays had the groundskeepers rushing to get tarps on the dirt portions of the field, but once they were covered, the rain would stop. Then, once uncovered, it started raining again.

It was the kind of day when no one wanted to be out there, and it reflected in our play. Chip must not have had any homoerotic serenades during the night because he was a dud at the plate. We were all a mess defensively, and Caesar, the starting pitcher, struggled to find his rhythm, resulting in an early exit. Around the fifth, the game broke into a damage control situation, giving way to a merry-go-round of relievers wherein almost everyone in the bullpen got a turn, including me.

I came in around the sixth inning. Something about the first outing of the year always stands out. Maybe because stats are officially being recorded and evaluated. No, this wasn't the way I wanted my march to the Bigs to begin, but baseball doesn't wait to give you optimal circumstances. It gives you what it gives you, like frozen off-season workout facilities or sleeping bags on an unfurnished apartment floor. Then it tells you to make the most of it and be thankful for it. So sayeth Grady, this was my job. This was my first chance to impress, and, like most outings, just how thankful I'd end up being would hinge on how well it went.

I thought if I worked fast enough I would be able to get in and out before the weather, or my luck, went bad. I was wrong. I broke a bat but the ball found a hole. We missed a chance to convert a lifesaving double play. I went deep into counts only to give up hard hit balls, like a line shot that fell just feet in front of Chip in centerfield. Then, as if to prove that everything was against us, Chip made a beautiful throw that would surely have gunned down my first earned run of the year except that when the throw crossed into infield airspace, it bounced off the mushy, wet turf, just in front of the plate, where it ceased to be a threat to the scoring runner. I issued another walk, another hit, and soon, my turn on the merry-go-round was over. Not the start I was hoping for.

Post-game, the defeated Beavers sat around licking our wounds. Though there were nearly 140 games ahead of us, it's traditional for a team to sulk after a loss: the uglier the loss, the more vigorous the sulking. We know the key to being successful in baseball is moving forward and refocusing on the future, but we don't sulk because we're stuck in the past. We sulk out of respect for those who have reason to hang their heads.

Winning is great, but making it to the big leagues is the main focus of Triple A. Playing bad hurts because the proximity of the Show puts the price of failure in perspective. Because we can empathize with what it feels like to take a beating in pursuit of your dream, we pay reverence. How long that reverence lasts depends on the magnitude of the loss, the atmosphere of the clubhouse, and the expectations of the manager.

"Fuck, who died in here?" asked Ready, barely breaking stride en route to his office. "We won the series, didn't we? Someone turn the fucking music on."

And with those inspiring words, the first series of the season was concluded.

The boys pretending to be down got some life back in them. For those not quite ready to move on, things moved more slowly. Luke sat at his locker recording notes on some of the other team's hitters. Stansberry, who made a costly error, was still doing mental gymnastics about how his hands could betray him. Chip and Myrow, who had setbacks at the plate, sat on the couch next to me, all of us still in our wet uniforms, watching television.

Myrow glanced at Chip, then got up and checked to see if the coast was clear. He went over to his locker, opening his personal cubby. Inside was a bottle of vodka masked by a brown paper bag.

"Hey, Chip, you want some Kool-Aid?" asked Myrow.

"Yeah, I could go for some Kool-Aid today," said Chip.

"How 'bout you, Hayhurst?" asked Myrow.

"I don't know," I whimpered. "I've never tried vod—"

"Kool-Aid," Chip corrected me, looking around to make sure the wrong people didn't hear me.

"Uh, I never tried *Kool-Aid*," I rephrased.

Chip and Myrow exchanged skeptical smiles.

"Oh, don't worry," said Chip. "I'll fix you up right."

Chip went to the food pantry and got three red plastic party cups, put in some ice and Sprite, and came back. He then added generous servings of vodka to the cups for himself and Myrow, and about a third of that amount for me.

"Mmm." I took a sip. "That is some good Kool-Aid," I said to Chip.

"I told you, brother."

We all sat there sipping away, none of us talking. It was almost like the act of sharing Kool-Aid communicated the sentiment we were sharing telepathically. We all knew why we were drinking and not changing from our uniforms; no need to speak it.

After some time passed and the locker room cleared out, Myrow said, "I used to talk with my family back home after bad games, but they'd always try to coach me and it would just piss me off even worse. They always thought they knew what I was doing out here. They didn't, of course, but they always wanted to make it seem like nothing I did ever surprised them. They could never just tell me they were proud of me, they always had answers or coaching advice." He laughed to himself, then took a sip.

"I know what you mean," I said. I thought back to some of my earlier days in the game. "I'd call my dad from some town in the middle of nowhere and try and talk to him about bad outings. He'd start on about how he knew what I was doing since I did those same things all the way back in high school. I'd get mad and tell him I wasn't the same pitcher I was back then. He'd start screaming at me, or tell me he didn't care. All I wanted him to do was empathize with me but . . ." I took a sip and thought for a second about things back home. "Now I can't even talk to him."

Chip didn't say anything, he just nodded his head. Myrow talked about how you have to pick the right people to talk to about your career or you'll just end up frustrated. I agreed; it's a game you play in front of so many but share with so few.

"How about you, Chip? How does your family handle baseball?" asked Myrow.

"I love my family," said Chip. "I always play better when they're around. My kids were the best thing that ever happened to me. When I come home, even after a crap day, I'll see my little girl walking around and I can't help but snap out of my funk. She'll see me and I have to stop being bitter because she wants me to play and I can't spend the rest of the day being an asshole over something stupid like baseball when my kids need me to be Daddy."

Myrow nodded. "I hear you there. My girl looks at me so carefree and loving and I have to let it go."

I finished my Kool-Aid as they spoke. I didn't have kids, but I thought about Bonnie. I hoped that when I saw her beautiful face I always had what it took to let it go.

Chapter Thirty-one

Four days later, I awoke at 3 A.M. to Chip, smacking me on the top of the head. "Wake up, bro."

"Are the neighbor guys having sex again?" I asked, groggily.

"It's time to go," he said, standing over my bed.

Luke, Chip, and I had gone to bed only four hours earlier, after our last home night game. It was a travel day, and to get to our next destination, Salt Lake, we had to be up and back at our own stadium to rendezvous with the team bus by 4:30 A.M.

I sat up on the bed and stared bleary-eyed at Chip. He was already dressed with his bags by the door. I had packed most of my stuff last night but left my dress clothes hanging next to the bathroom so I could ready myself like a fast-moving assembly line.

I'd made a trip to Goodwill to get some travel duds of my own, and after suiting up and brushing my teeth, I came back to the living room with a terrible realization: I had no dress shoes. I hadn't taken the time to get them. I proceeded to have a minor freak-out, going so far as to wonder how I could disguise my feet by slipping dark socks over tennis shoes. I would never live this down, I thought. Ready would kill me and the guys on the team would have a field day.

"Shit," I said, pulling my just combed hair. "I got no shoes!"

"What size do you wear?" asked Chip.

"I don't know. Like, an eleven or something."

Chip went to his bedroom and brought back a pair of his shoes. "Here, try these," he said, handing me a pair of black leather shoes. They were really different from my style: polished, flashy, with no laces or buckles. I looked at them funny, wondering on what occasions Chip wore them. That's when I realized that Chip was wearing something that didn't look like a suit at all but like a really flashy bowling outfit, as there was no suit jacket, just matching shirt and pants with custom breast pockets and pleats.

"That's not a suit," I said, looking at him.

"It's dress clothes," said Chip. "For people with style."

"Oh," I said, taking in his style. He looked like he was going to lead a revival at a Southern fish fry. I turned my eyes to the shoes he gave me.

"What?" he asked, looking at me looking at his shoes.

"These are . . ."

"Careful, now." Chip eyed me.

"These are awesome," I finished.

"For sure they are. You gonna look like a pimp in those," he said, as if the shoes had made the outfit go from Cinderella's maid dress to the belle of the ball. I smiled at his enthusiasm, then looked to the shoes and wondered if he meant the usage of *pimp* in the literal or slang sense of the word.

"Thanks," I said. "They fit well, like they were made for me."

"Use 'em for however long you need."

Luke's door opened. He walked out in front of us with a pile of clothes in his hands and a scowl on his face, not bothering to say hello as he marched to the bathroom. I'm not exaggerating when I say that exactly one minute later the toilet flushed and the door swung open, revealing a perfectly dressed Luke, as if he were just taken out of his Republican action figure packaging.

"Damn." Chip looked at me, then back to Luke. "How'd you do that?"

"Do what?" asked Luke.

With no ride to the stadium, we pulled our rolling suitcases behind us all the way down Burnside Street, piercing the silent night with the sound of plastic wheels grinding over concrete and blacktop. As we got closer to the stadium, other street-walking players in their dress clothes joined us, heading the same way. Our ranks grew as we neared the park, a whole legion of curfew-violating, well-dressed, luggage-toting, twentysomethings staging a Jets versus Sharks–style choreographed dance fight in front of PGE Park. Shortly after, a bus arrived, collected us, and took us back to the Portland airport.

Flying was a real perk, or at least it seemed like one on paper. If you did the math, however, you'd realize you missed just as much sleep, if not more, doing the minor league airport shuffle. Players tend to compare travel times by how long they are in the actual vehicle. A three-hour plane ride is obviously shorter than a twelve-hour bus trip, but this says nothing of the layovers, security check-ins, baggage claims, and all the other bullshit that it takes to get a group of thirty men—some of whom don't speak English—trying to check bats and talking about "blowing up chicks," onto a plane in the post-9/11 era. By the time our plane skidded in to Salt Lake's airport, we felt like we'd been profiled as deviants, robbed by luggage fees, fed complimentary pretzels, and fired out of a cannon. Hurray for flying.

Standing at the luggage carousel, guys placed bets on whose bags would slide down the chute first. Our trainer acted like a bookie, holding the money until the luggage popped out. Hamp won. Instead of apologizing to everyone complaining about how he was a lucky bastard, he gloated, telling them they'd just funded his next trip to the strip club. Then, just to rub it in, he promised to waste the money on an ugly girl.

There was no bus to pick us up outside the Salt Lake City terminal. We were staying at the Sheraton City Centre, and it sent a shuttle to collect us. There weren't enough seats for everyone, so some had to stay behind. Who stayed was decided like all short supply items in baseball are decided, by who had the most service time, meaning I lost. It turned out that even if I would've made the first shuttle cut, I would have had to do some waiting because my room wasn't ready when I arrived. While everyone else was foraging for breakfast or catching a power nap before heading to the ballpark, I was stuck with my roommate, Matt Antonelli, in the lobby.

Players are given the option to select a road roomie at the beginning of the year, and I picked Anto because he was about as easygoing as they got. Usually pitchers room with pitchers since we operate on a similar wavelength, but after years of road roomies, I knew that Anto, a position player, had the makings of an all-star travel companion. Anto had the personality of a big, friendly dog. He liked being around people, but also liked lying on his bed. He loved to play a good game of ball, and then get fed. For Anto, life was very simple; as long as you didn't pull his ears, he'd be your best friend.

Anto had a few peculiarities. For one, healthy food was like poison to him. He couldn't consume plant life, or anything that consisted of less than 50 percent fat calories. In fact, the longer the nuclear half-life of his meals, the more he liked them. I've seen him turn his nose at seafood spreads furnished by big league rehabbers only to run to McDonalds for a Quarter Pounder. The man could eat Styrofoam as long as you covered it in hot sauce.

Anto was also a Bostonian, which made him partial to certain words, like *friggin'* and *retarded,* which he pronounced "retahhh-did." Used in a sentence it would sound like, "That's retahhhdid, it's friggin' one in the afternoon! Rooms should be ready by one in the afternoon."

"That's just the tiredness talking. This is a nice place, you'll like it."

"I'd like it more if they had cookies in the lobby. I'm stahhhv-ing."

"I'm sure the rooms will be ready soon. We gotta wait."

And so we did. Boredom made me run through the names on my cell phone. Anto texted his female counterpart on the other side of the country between pouts of friggin' disgust. Muzak played; I think it was supposed to be the Police, with Sting's vocals replaced by the splashy sounds of a tenor saxophone. Two hours from now the first shuttle would leave to take us to the field for batting practice.

"I hate this friggin' town," said Anto, clapping his cell phone shut. This was odd-hour anger speaking. A mixture of duress and fatigue compounded by the anticipation of expectation. He would have to start tonight, operating on hours of sleep you could count on one hand.

"It's not the town's fault."

Anto sighed again. He made for his travel bag housing his laptop. "Do they have free Internet, at least?"

"No, you have to pay for it. That's how you know it's a nice place: they make you pay for everything," I said cooly.

He dropped his bag back to the floor and slumped back in his seat. "This is friggin' retahhhdid! I'll bet the Red Roof doesn't charge us for Internet and we would have our rooms ready by now. I really hate this friggin' town."

"I can't begin to tell you how *tough* you sound when you use the word *friggin'* over and over like that. I'll bet if you drop a few of those angry *friggin'*s on the people at the front desk, they'll work faster."

He stared at me for a second and then said, "Shaddup."

I waved my hands dismissively and turned away. We continued our sit in, listening to the faux Police send their message in a bottle. My roomie mashed the buttons on his cell phone with fury, probably explaining his frustrations one text at a time. I got up and paced the lobby, amusing myself by trying to step on certain colored tiles but not others. I had picked my way across to the front door when a horde of large, beefy gentlemen came in. They filled the lobby, wide shoulders and boxy frames housing deep voices.

I recognized them to be a team, as they had all the characteristics of my traveling companions except they were much, much larger. Indeed, they were football players, the Chicago Rush arena team logo was marked on their luggage. *What are the odds a Triple A team and an arena football team would take in the same hotel?* I wondered. Salt Lake City was offering a lot of sports entertainment options this weekend.

The footballers joked about like my team did as they waited for their room keys to be distributed. Then they dispersed from the lobby en route to their rooms. My roommate and I remained, still no word as to how long it would be until our room was ready.

Shortly after the football team passed through, two more large men walked in; they looked very much like bodybuilders. At first, I thought they might be stragglers with the football team, but something was different about this pair: they were both wearing tiaras and holding hands. They strolled up to the counter and, in high, hair-stylist voices, inquired on their rooms. Theirs were ready. The deskman passed them their keys, they giggled, smooched, and headed toward the elevator.

I tried to act cosmopolitan. I didn't stare. Besides, they were bigger than me. My roommate did, though. He watched them sashay their way to the elevator doors and goose each other in. He watched them until the doors closed. The look on his face would make you think they just went through the doors of the *Twilight Zone*. He gawked back at me, across the lobby.

I smirked, and offered him a shrug. What else could I do? "That's something you don't see every day, huh?" I said to the deskman.

"Not every day. But you'll be seeing a lot of it this weekend," he said back, matter-of-factly.

"Why's that?" I inquired.

"There is a transvestite convention going on here these next few days."

The record skipped. "I'm sorry, what did you say?"

"There is a transvestite convention, going on here, until Monday. Sir."

"Oh."

On cue, a gentleman walked through the lobby doors wearing

super-tight jeans, a rhinestone V-neck, and a pair of heels. His toenails were done in a bright cherry red. He had large sunglasses on, and more than a touch of mascara. He had fake eyelashes and a mole and was carrying a mannequin head with a wig on it.

This time I stared. I mean, stuck to the ground like a lawn ornament stared. This new guy, or girl, or whatever, walked past me on the way to the desk but stopped to take note of my staring. He/she cocked his/her hip out to the side, adjusted his/her sunglasses down a tick, and peered over their rim. "See something you like, honey?"

"Um," I said, voice cracking like a schoolboy's, "no, ma'am."

"Well," he/she paused and looked me up and down, "I see something *I* like."

"Oh Jesus," I blurted.

I spun away like I had to answer my phone, or mother, or the voices in my head—anything to break eye contact. He/she didn't give chase, simply snorting at my cold shoulder like I was missing out on something fantastic. He/she then proceeded to the front desk, checked in, and went on his/her way, wig and all.

I glanced to Anto, who looked as if he'd lost his mind from the experience, mouthing the words, "I hate this town, I hate this friggin' town!"

I came back up to the front desk, looked the deskman in the eye, and in my toughest, tough-guy voice said, "You have got to get us our friggin' room ready now!"

"I'll tell you what. I'll just give you the keys and you can head up. I'm sure she'll finish with you in the room." He got the keys and slid them to us.

We made a beeline for the elevator. When the doors opened, Chip and Luke were standing there. We pushed past them, forcing our way into the elevator before they could exit.

"Hey man, what's the rush?" said Chip.

"Oh Chip," I said patting him on the shoulders, "are you ever going to hit well this series."

Chapter Thirty-two

Salt Lake City was Mormon country. Regardless of your views on the Mormon faith, there is one thing baseball players accept as fact: Mormon chicks are hot. I don't know what it is about them, but they are the closest thing to Scandinavian women that America has to offer. Blond, buxom, and, because their faith demands it, they are oh so sweet to gentlemen.

Because the bullpens in Salt Lake City are exposed down the foul lines, they provided open views of the field and its surroundings. This is a fantastic perk since Salt Lake's stadium is one of the most eye-pleasing places to watch a game in baseball. Your ticket buys you breathtaking views of the snowcapped mountains behind the stadium, as well as views of the blond-capped ones within it.

Thanks to the warmer weather, we weren't the only ones taking off our coats. Beautiful, and assumed Mormon, ladies flitted into the stands, sitting in giggly packs, waving at us when we looked their way. Naturally, Dallas was the first to notice the local demographic. He stared into the mass of blondes like a dog might watch his master eat at the dinner table. Lord knows what was running through his head, something starring Ron Jeremy as the leader of a polygamous compound, no doubt.

Two women came down and sat a few rows from where we

were. Dallas was glued to them. They wore skintight black shirts, pumps, bangles, and had their hair done up. The women were older, maybe scraping forty. They watched the boys on the field, yakking away, swinging their giant purses around like hammers. Then, suddenly, like spooked deer, they caught sight of us training our rifles on them.

"Why are they frowning?" asked Fish.

Before I could answer, Dallas was talking. "'Cause they think we're being rude. Fuck, this pair should be happy someone's looking at them."

Yet, instead of running, the girls' heads pulled back and shook as if they were talking about how inappropriate we were, and yet they stared right back at us.

"Mmm-hmm. That's just for show," said Bentley, sighing before looking someplace else in the stands. "Those girls are the worst variety of cleat chasers."

"There is a variety?" I asked.

"Of course, but you already know them," he said, dismissing my question. I continued staring at him to indicate I did not know.

"Hayhurst is a virgin," said Ox, like I had some condition explaining why I was so naïve.

"Oh. How quaint," said Bentley.

"Not for much longer, though," I said, proudly.

"Wonderful. At any rate"—Bentley cleared his throat, using his fingers to count—"you've got your whores, those are the ones who don't care if people know they want to land a player. They often look like prostitutes. You see them outside locker rooms mostly. They really like the Latin guys for some reason."

"The insiders," said Ox. "They work for a team. Tell you they love baseball and are in it for professional reasons, but they'll screw anyone on the team if the situation presents itself. Ha, I would know."

"The trophies," said Bentley. "You see more of these at the big league level. They go all-out to land a player. They're like big game hunters. They study you, what you like, and so forth. Then, once they end up with you, they let you foot the bill. They act stupid, but they're smart. And they'll trade you in for a better deal too."

"Horny host moms," said Ox. "I shouldn't have to explain that one."

"Princess Lay-mes."

"What?" I balked at that title.

"Princess *Lay-mes*," repeated Bentley. "They show up to the park, overdressed, but not slutty. They want attention, but act like they don't. They're a contradiction."

"Like these ladies here?" We looked back to the cougars a few rows in.

"Yes, except they're also cougars."

"So, Queen Lay-mes," I said, impressed at my wittiness.

"Very clever." Bentley nodded to me. "But it's all an act."

"You're sure?"

"Certainly. Look at them," said Bentley, and we all turned back to the women, who, again cocked their giant earring-wearing heads to the side as if to telegraph offense. "They go through this routine of being offended by obvious interest, so they can somehow preserve a shred of respectability, though they all want the same thing."

"What are you all staring at?" shouted the women, heads cocked skeptically.

"Observe," Bentley whispered to us. Then, to the ladies, "The girls behind you."

The cougars jerked 'round to inspect who Bentley referenced. Younger models sat there, completely oblivious to Bentley's call. When the cougars noticed they were once again competing with youth, they seemed more offended than anything our gawking could have incited.

"Could you get their attention for us?" added Bentley. "They're closer to our age and we're only in town for a little while."

"Hey now, we aren't as old as you think we are," said one of the women.

"See," said Bentley, folding his arms over his chest. "In Triple A, age isn't just a factor for the players."

"Yeah, and the best thing about cheating with an older chick is that your wife can't get jealous," said Dallas, trying to look cool like Bentley, folding his arms over his chest after he spoke.

Everyone's eyes left the girls and turned to Dallas.

"Jesus, Dallas, what the hell kind of comment is that?"

"What? Your wife can't get all hurt about it because an older woman is uglier and shit. You know, she can't feel bad about herself not being good enough, like she would with a younger girl. You know how girls can be."

"Do you even hear the things you say?" said Ox.

"Yeah, why?"

"How busted up a chick you bang when you're married isn't the point. You're married, you shouldn't be banging any other chicks, period."

Dallas looked at everyone in the group. An uneasy smile grew across his face. "Come on now, I'm just fucking with you guys. Jesus, every time I say something about girls, you guys freak out. It's like you all turn into Gayhurst here." He laughed to himself, despite the thick wall of *bullshit* looks surrounding him. "I think it's fucking hilarious. You guys are too easy." Dallas got up and walked over to the stands to start up a "harmless" conversation. We all watched him go, shaking our heads.

"So, Dirk, any of this made you consider a prenup?" asked Bentley.

I shook my head. "Nah."

"Are you sure? It's not as insulting as it—"

"I'm not getting divorced," I said, flatly.

"Of course, of course," said Bentley, appeasingly. "Though, if you do make it to the big leagues, remember, you're not the only person who makes it to the Show. Your wife can change too. It's funny how it works up there."

"What do you mean?

"I'd hate to see you in a situation like Dallas, that's all."

"Honestly Bent, I don't think *that* is ever going to happen."

Bentley dropped the subject,

"Nah," said Ox, throwing a paw on my shoulder. "Diggler here doesn't need a prenup. He didn't meet his girl in the baseball scene."

I never expected Ox to defend me on something like marriage. I gave him a thankful smile.

"And, since he's never used his penis for anything creative, he'll be afraid to cheat out of embarrassment."

"Thanks Ox, you're a real friend."

"Anytime, bud. Anytime."

Chapter Thirty-three

Later in the series, back at the hotel, the boys were starting to get paranoid about an entirely different category of cleat chaser. One of our infielders said he was cornered in the elevator by two transvestites who asked if he'd like to join them in the hot tub. Another player was catcalled by a guy who looked a lot like Bluto from the *Popeye* cartoons wearing a prom dress.

Anto, despite the hotel demographic, insisted I join him at the hotel bar for dinner. Anto couldn't eat the spread the team we were playing, the Bees, put out post-game. It was something covered in mushrooms, and a brown sauce he said would make him puke upon contact with his tongue. He said he needed a Philly cheesesteak and french fries or he would surely die of malnutrition, and then he said he needed me to protect him while he ate because if he got hit on by a dude his stomach would get queasy and he wouldn't be able to finish.

While Anto ate, a few male guests strolled in. Since not all of the transvestites in the hotel were wearing gowns, you had to look for signs. Anto stopped and watched them with suspicion.

"Give me a drink," said one of the new guests. "A stiff one, I mean *real* stiff. If I'm going to hit on one of the ladies out there, I'm going to need some serious 'help.' "

The joke made Anto's stomach settle, and he continued eating.

Meanwhile, the gentlemen passed the test and went about their business, talking about sports and cars and shooting horned animals, and all the other stuff men talk about at bars. However, as time passed, the bar slowly filled with odd-looking characters, but since none of them sat by us, Anto felt okay to stay.

"You guys want anything to drink with your meal?" the bartender inquired. I think I was making her mad as I was only drinking water and eating the free nuts while Anto stuffed himself with grease.

"We should probably order a drink," I said to Anto. We were eating at the bar, after all.

"You kiddin'? The prices on booze in this town are friggin' ridiculous."

"It's Salt Lake," said the bartender, acknowledging the exorbitant prices for liquor. "Not the best place to be a bartender." She said it sadly, like she never made any money doing her job because of the tyrannies of abolitionists. This, of course, motivated us to buy something out of sympathy.

"I'll have a Jack and Coke," said Anto.

"I'll have a . . . a Kool-Aid," I said.

"I don't know what that is," said the bartender.

"It's got vodka and Sprite," I said.

"And cranberry?" she asked.

"Sure, why not," I said.

"Oh, a blush," she said, and whirled away to mix it.

Soon the drinks were presented in front of us. Anto's brown drink and my own drink, as pink as the gem in Bonnie's engagement ring—with a little lime garnish.

"Oh, that's a nice touch," I said, taking the little lime out. "She even put a little sword in it for me." I swashbuckled Anto's arm.

The conversations across the bar stopped as the interest started focusing my way. I sipped my drink. Whispering broke out. I took another sip.

"Why are they all looking at me funny?" I said out of the corner of my mouth.

Anto, formerly oblivious to my drink in favor of his meal, gasped, "Dude, your drink. Stop drinking the drink."

"Are you kiddin'?" I said, imitating him. "The prices for booze in this town are friggin' ridiculous." I thought I was very funny.

"You're in a hotel full of gay guys and you're drinking a friggin' salmon-colored drink. And quit poking me with that friggin' sword." He smacked my hand away. "Either everyone thinks we're one of the queens out there, or they think you're going to bait the queens in here by drinking it!"

I looked around the bar. I had attracted a few disgusted looks, like that of the gentlemen who needed the "stiff" drinks, and a few stiff looks, like those from the gentlemen wearing makeup.

"So this is what it's like to be a girl who sits near the bullpen?" I muttered.

"Did you just say this is what it's like to be a girl?" asked Anto. "You're gonna find out pretty soon if you don't get rid of that drink."

"It cost seven dollars!" I said.

"Then hurry up and drink it."

"I can't drink it fast. I don't have good booze tolerance yet," I pleaded.

Anto shook his head and went back to eating, only at double the pace.

"Fine," I said. "Bartender, I can't drink this. Give me a beer."

"What kind of beer would you like?" asked the bartender.

"Oh, I dunno, give me something that tastes good."

"Oh my friggin' God. Who are you?" asked Anto.

"What? I just want to like what I drink, is that a crime?"

"Oh, come on now, guys, don't fight," said the new voice of a gentleman sitting down next to us.

Our new barmate was a taller fellow. He had a very, very close shave, nearly waxed. He had a little blush of his own, except his accentuated his cheekbones. His arms were shaved and adorned with bracelets. He wore a V-neck, which seemed to be the dress code around the hotel lately. He smiled at me very pleasantly. In the time it took me to acknowledge the man who sat down next to me, Anto started gagging, produced his wallet, put money on the table, and excused himself before he vomited, leaving me behind.

"Where is your friend off to?" asked the man.

"He's upset with me," I said, shifting awkwardly.

"Oh, that's a shame. But there's more fish in the sea. Some-times they just jump right in your boat, right?"

"I . . . Yeah." I finished my seven-dollar beacon of gayness in one solid gulp. Screw tolerances.

"What are you drinking?" my friend with fine cheekbones asked.

"I'm sorry. Really. I'm not interested. Excuse me." I slapped a ten on the bar and got up.

"You know," said my gentleman caller as I started away, "it's guys like you who are the worst. You pretend you're offended when it's obvious you're interested. Well, get over yourself. I'm not going to chase after you, princess."

Mouth open, I gaped back at him.

"Oh, too late now, honey. The bar's closed." He spun around on his stool.

Chapter Thirty-four

By the time I hit the mound in game three, it was already well out of control. Actually, that was probably why I was called in. Manrique self-destructed, walking six while allowing eight runs, all earned. It was one of those starts that's hard to watch, more an execution than outing. At least the pen knew to be ready early since it was only a matter of time before we took over. I knew I was going to be out there for a while, and this would afford me a real chance to shine. Unfortunately, shining is not what happened.

Whatever had attacked me back in Portland followed me here. I hit spots, but hitters put the bat on the ball anyway. Infield hits, broken bats, and then, when someone did get a solid piece of the ball—*boom*—ERA damage. I gave up five runs in three innings. I'd only made two outings as a Beaver and my ERA was already a 7. As the runs came in, I started to get increasingly angry on the mound and, when I was finally removed from the game, I voiced my frustration in a hurricane of glove-muffled swears.

On my way back to the locker room, I hung my head, wondering how long I would be in Triple A if I kept having outings like this. My confidence was starting to wane. Baseball wasn't the only thing riding on good outings. My mind shifted to Bonnie, the future, my parents, my grandmother—even the cocky face of that asshole Dallas.

"Hey, Hay, come here for a second, would ya?" Abby, the team's pitching coach, called me to his office for a private conference while the rest of the team stripped down post-game. "What did you throw to Sandoval?" Abby kept his own score sheet that had a column for recording which pitch was thrown to which batter. He kept his own records of every game, so he probably knew what I threw, though I answered him anyway.

"Curve," I said.

"Why?" Abby bluntly asked.

"Well"—I looked away, frustrated from reliving my costly mistakes—"because I trust it enough to throw it anytime I want." I thought this was a solid answer. Coaches always want to hear that you are confident in your stuff.

"That's just dumb," said Abby. "Weren't you reading his swings? He was behind on your fastball," he said as if everyone in the stadium knew this. "He pulled your change, but fouled the heater. You did him a favor, is what you did. Did him a favor with that curveball."

"Are you saying that wasn't a good pitch?"

"He hit it, didn't he? His bat told ya it wasn't a good pitch."

"Yeah, but hitters hit good pitches, that's what they get paid for, Abby."

"They get paid just as much to hit dumb pitches too, don't they?"

"Half those hits were luck! Infield cue shots, broken bat jams—"

"'Maz'n' how lucky them hitters is when you don't read their swings," said Abby.

"Fine, but I threw my best pitch in a count I was ahead in, and he hit it. I'd throw it again if I had to because I trust my stuff. Isn't that what pitching is about, trusting your stuff?"

"You can trust it all you want, but if it's the wrong pitch, you can trust it's gonna get hit."

I wanted to keep fighting Abby, not because I didn't believe what he was saying to me, but because I was angry about my outing and I didn't want to be shown the errors of my ways while I was fresh from making them. But Abby was right, and as easy as it would have been to say it was someone else's fault, that the other team was lucky, or that the Baseball Gods were against me, in the end, the blame was mine, and mine alone.

"Fuck"—my angry baseball player way of saying *you're right*— "I wasn't thinking about his swing, I was thinking about being nasty. I was thinking about strikeouts, I was thinking about try- ing to get to the big leagues . . ." I took a deep breath, then stood there in silence, bracing myself in the door of Abby's office.

Abby shifted back in his seat and looked into me.

I'd been coached by Abby for the last two and a half years, and I knew that nothing he told me was done so for vindictive reasons, even when my competitive frustration made me feel otherwise, even when I blew up on him. Abby wanted all of his pitchers to succeed, including me, a tall order considering no two pitchers are alike.

Some pitchers are hardheaded and need a firm ass-kicking to keep them on the right path. Some are doubtful and need a good coddling from their own minds to survive. However, no matter which part of the spectrum a pitcher spends most of his time in— belligerent or uncertain—at some point in his career, he'll experi- ence both extremes.

A good pitching coach knows this about his staff, usually from experience as a player himself. He knows that each of his pitchers requires a unique psychological prescription, and that the time and way the prescription is administered is just as important as the dos- age itself. Sometimes it has to come in the middle of a rough inning. Sometimes it has to come after the game is long over. And some- times, just like when a mother has to mix medicine with sugar to make it go down, it has to come in a way that's borderline manipu- lation, since there are pitchers paranoid enough to fry their brains trying to figure out why a coach is medicating them at all.

A quality pitching coach understands what kind of person his pitcher is, not just what kind of person he thinks his pitcher should be. He never lets his own fame get in the way, or cuts them out of a mold. It's a subtle art with relationships at its core, because if a pitching coach can't relate, he'll never get the dosages right, and the wrong medicine is worse than none at all.

"You're learnin', is all. You read them hitters next outing and you'll see a world a difference," said Abby. "But when you go out there, you can't think about nothing but what's in front a ya. The hitter tells you what you need to throw, and no one else."

"But," I said, "Grady likes it when I throw my changeup and hook."

"You ain't pitching to him, though, is ya? They like it better when you're a putting up zeros."

"Ya, I guess," I said.

"Ain't no guessing about it. You get outs pitching to that hitter, you'll always have a pitch they like to see."

I nodded my head at his simple logic.

"Can't lose your cool out there, though. That ain't you. When I seen you get mad out there, I says to myself, 'That ain't Hay. He don't do that.' Can't let things you got no control over get control over you."

"I just want to do good since the Bigs are so close."

"Shit, everyone wants to do good. Everyone wants to make it to them big leagues. You think pitching different's gonna get you there any faster?"

"No," I said.

"No," he concurred. "Alright. One inning, one hitter, one smart pitch at a time. Lot a season left—lot a season . . ." Abby's voice trailed off as he looked through his notes. "Get you some ice, Hay. You'll be back out there soon."

Abby dismissed me into the locker room, and even though I wasn't pleased with how things went on the field, I felt better about it thanks to our talk. Abby knew that I spent more time in the doubt-filled side of the pitcher psyche. To his credit, he never outright babied me, which would have been more insulting than anything, and he never browbeat me so bad I felt like pitching was pointless. What he did do was an excellent job of keeping me from going over to that dark side all pitchers feel the pull toward when they're close to something grand and feel like they're blowing it.

Chapter Thirty-five

On Monday, after losing a day game with the Bees, we packed up and hopped a flight to Colorado Springs, home of the Rockies' Triple A team, the Sky Sox. Sky Sox Stadium is the highest-altitude park in baseball, even higher than the infamous Mile High Stadium that houses its parent team, where ERAs commit suicide upon eye contact.

Like Salt Lake City, Colorado Springs offered gorgeous views of towering mountains. However, unlike Salt Lake, there were no pretty girls, or warm weather. We sat down the line on an unforgiving, bun-freezing aluminum bench. There were a couple of plastic lawn chairs, but only enough for the older guys who rested upon them like thrones.

The Sky Sox provided the pen with an oil-burning heater that looked like a miniature jet engine. It pumped out enough heat to melt our lawn chairs or set our uniforms on fire. Though its intensity was significant, its area of effect was limited, and we had to take turns standing in front of it to get warm, but not so close as to combust ourselves.

"Goddamn," said Ox. He was bending over, letting the heater warm his ass. "This feels tremendous. I might have to get one of these for the house."

"Careful, big man, or you'll melt a hole in your drawers."

"These fucking pants deserve to be melted. Besides, there's no one here to watch this game," Ox said, gesturing to the stands, which were virtually empty.

"Why people build stadiums in towns with weather like this, I'll never know," said Bentley.

"They say if you want to make a small fortune in minor league baseball, the best way to do it is to start with a large one," I said, standing up and taking a turn in front of the ass heater.

"Has anyone seen Zarate?" asked Hamp.

We all looked around. "No."

"Wasn't he just out here?"

"I don't know. I can't remember. He's like a ghost," said Fish.

"Did he get sent down?" I asked.

"No, he was definitely on the plane. I know because Reek has to help him out with all the English stuff."

"I don't think he speaks much English," I said.

"I don't think he speaks much Spanish," said Ox.

"I think he's part Aborigine," said Bentley.

"Maybe we should talk to him in clicks and pops?" offered Hamp.

"I never see him eat spread either. I don't know how he survives," said Bentley.

"He's probably out behind the stadium hunting feral cats with blow darts."

"Who gives a shit?" said Dallas. "He's a strange fucking bird. Yesterday, I saw him spray his armpits with fucking hair spray thinking it was deodorant."

"Yeah, but if the pen phone rings, he appears out of nowhere, like he was always there," said Fish.

"It's his witch doctor magic," I said.

"You think if we whistle for him, he'll show up?"

"He's not a dog."

"Just scream his name or something."

"Z!" screamed Fish. "Z!"

There was a rustling in the tree line just behind the bullpen fence. A dark navy jacket broke through and Z appeared, looking at us with wild eyes.

"Uh, Abby was looking for you."

"Ahbee?" said Z.

"Yeah, he wondered where you went," lied Fish.

"Ahh." Z nodded his head but there was no way of knowing what he had heard.

"What the fuck were you doing?" asked Dallas.

Z held up a couple of waterlogged baseballs he had found. Probably batting practice balls struck over the fence but never retrieved. He made his way to the pen with his new clutch, hopped the fence, and joined us again, showing us his collection.

"That's great, Z. You found some fucking baseballs. We got a whole bag of 'em right there," said Dallas.

Z nodded appreciatively at Dallas and sat down. We all sat down as well, exchanging *Twilight Zone* looks like we were sharing a roster with some alien. We half-expected Z to sit on the balls and try to hatch them when, instead, he picked up a long metal tarp spike, usually used for holding the bullpen tarp down during bad weather, and proceeded to bang the ball into the sharp end of it.

We all watched him as he worked the ball onto the spike, pounding it over and over again.

"Five bucks says he makes a shish kebab and roasts it on the heater."

"I may take you up on that bet," said Bentley, staring at Z.

"If something living comes out of that ball, I'm done. I quit," said Hamp.

We were all wrong. In the next strike on the ball, Z missed his mark and stabbed himself in the hand with the spike.

"*Ieeeee! Coño! Coño! Diablo! Mamma—heuvos!*" He grabbed his hand as blood gushed forth.

"Speaks Spanish about as good as any other Latin guy I know," said Ox.

"What a fucking dumb-ass," said Dallas.

"Z, go see the trainer. *Comprende?* Trainer?" said Fish.

"No, no," said Z. "Iz okay." He started wiping large splotches of blood on his pants legs, then sucking on the wound.

"Z, you need to see the trainer," persisted Fish.

Z got up, still sucking on the wound. He walked toward the heater, at which we all jerked back for fear he would stick his hand on the glowing red metal part and cauterize the wound. Z kept walking, though, hopping the fence and returning into the forest.

"What the hell?" We traded baffled expressions.

Minutes later, Z returned. He'd picked some vegetation from behind the fencing area and was chewing pieces of it in his mouth, and pressing it into his hand, which had stopped bleeding.

"Now I have seen it all," said Hamp.

"Where do they find these guys?" I asked.

"Iz fine," he said, smiling at us. "Iz okay. No trainer."

"I wanna know what he rubs on his arm after he pitches," said Ox.

After the game, we got our first paychecks of the season. They were sitting on our locker chairs waiting for us to discover them when we walked in from the field. It was a big moment for me since this year's paycheck would be the biggest paycheck of my player career—the first time I saw a comma in my earnings since receiving my signing bonus in 2003.

I carefully tore off my paycheck's perforated edging, opened it, and stared at the number. A nauseous surge of anxiety hit my stomach where glee should have been. I turned the paper over in my hands, then looked at it again. Then, in a cold sweat, I spoke aloud to the paper in my hands. "Is this right? This can't be right." I spun around to see the other players in the locker room. "Is this right?" I called to anyone who would answer.

Other players were looking upon their checks with wrinkled, angry faces. Heads twisted in confusion before going back to the checks for a second inspection. Fingers traced deduction lines, then silent counting indicative of mental math, then, like me, the desperate search around the room to see if someone was playing a bad joke.

"This can't be right," I said, answering my own question, then diving into my check again.

Chip spoke to me from a few lockers down. "Tax in Oregon is harsh, bro. And, don't forget, you're missing two days' worth of pay." He didn't seem upset about his pay, of course. His check was that of a free agent. A few hundred missing from a seventy-thousand-dollar-a-season salary is a lot different than a few hundred missing from a salary barely reaching fifteen thousand.

Chip was right about the two days missing, but, even after I factored those days in, my pay was still much smaller than I expected—almost three hundred dollars smaller. That was six hundred a month gone, over three thousand for the season! I sat down and gripped the check so tight I thought it might rip in two. In fact, if it weren't for my desperate need of the money, I would have ripped the check up in protest and fried it on the bullpen heater. But whom would I be protesting? My own stupidity for not considering the deductions for playing in a major city?

Guys around the room were having similar reactions, especially the first year Triple A players who seemed shell-shocked. Most of them had signed for large bonuses, one of the reasons they made it to Triple A so quickly, so I didn't feel too bad for them. In fact, I expected their checks to be less than mine, but when I asked them about what they made, it turned out to be more than me.

"How is that possible? How are you making more than me and I've been playing three years longer than you?" I asked Frenchy after consulting his numbers.

"I don't know, man. I don't know. Maybe there was a mistake?"

"There's no mistake," said Luke. "It has to do with the original contract you signed under, how it was negotiated, the way the pay level's scaled, and so on." He regurgitated this information in a sterile tone; then, looking at my devastated face, he offered a sympathetic frown and said, "Sucks. Sorry, dude."

My anger was building. It was my sixth year and this paycheck was less than what some of the third year players were making, and there was nothing I could do about it. What the hell was the point of all this time spent in the minors if you made less as you went up?

I felt like a fool. I didn't factor in the local taxes, the state taxes, and all the other deductions that get taken out of a paycheck when I blissfully planned out my future in Triple A. My outlook for the future crumbled, falling down on me. Reality set in. I had to pay off Bonnie's ring. I had to pay the rent. I had to save for a wedding, scratch up airfare, and provide for a wife I hadn't even proposed to yet. Where was this money going to come from? How did I not see this? I thought of my poor pitching numbers, my poor earnings, my poor living arrangements. Maybe my parents were right; maybe I had no idea what I was doing.

I meandered drunkenly back to my locker and sat down, collecting my head in one hand while squeezing my paycheck in the other. We were not playing at home and I was glad of it because, if we were, I would have needed some strong Kool-Aid to come to terms with what I was experiencing. When I finally had enough strength to lift my head again, I noticed my cell phone's notification light was blinking; I had a text-message from Bonnie. The message read, *"I found my dress!"*

My head fell again.

Chapter Thirty-six

An outdated team bus worked as a shuttle, taking us from the stadium back to the dilapidated La Quinta hotel the Sky Sox used as their hosting hotel. It was across town, a trek for the old bus as it groaned in protest on the mountainous grades. I sat in the back, as far from all the other occupants as I could, and dialed Bonnie. Her cheery voice came through the line, and I didn't dare start the conversation with my news and steal her wedding dress thunder.

"It's beautiful," she said. "I was debating on a few others, which were nice, but then this guy, who you'd swear just got back from that convention you told me about if it wasn't for the fact that his wife works there with him, told me to try some dress randomly."

"Uh-huh," I said, looking out the window. Snow was falling past the bus windows, and cars sloshed by on the slickened road. I sat low in my seat with my knees pressed up against the back of the seat in front of me.

"But"—she was getting excited now—"when I walked out of the dressing room, you just knew it was the one. Everyone stopped what they were doing and looked at me. The guy who suggested it said, 'Oh, girl, that's the one. You're a princess. A hot princess.' "

"Uh-huh," I said.

"I was worried it was a little too modern for my mom, but she really likes it."

"That's great," I said, rather disconnected.

Our conversation paused for a while. I wasn't faking my enthusiasm very well, and Bonnie was on to me. "What's the matter?"

"I got my first paycheck today."

"Oh? What are you going to buy with it? A ring, perhaps?"

"I don't know what I'm going to do," I said.

The starkness of my tone must have caught her off guard because her response was one of concern. "What do you mean?"

"The check is way short. When I calculated it for the season, it's thousands short. I didn't consider the taxes here. I just don't get it."

"Do you think they made a mistake?"

"No, I think I made a mistake."

"I don't understand. How could you make a mistake?"

I let my head hit the bus window. "I don't know, Bonnie, I saw the numbers before I signed this year. I knew what they were going to be, but this still seems wrong. Maybe I wanted to believe this year was going to be better than it really could be. Maybe I was being arrogant. Maybe I lied to myself. Maybe I knew this was going to be the situation and I just refused to accept it. I don't know."

"What are you saying to me?" The concern in Bonnie's voice shifted to fear.

"Maybe I bit off more than we can chew here. Maybe it was stupid for me to think we'd be able to do this."

"Babe, we've talked about this, you should pursue your dream."

"But I can't fund a life in the real world while getting paid peanuts in some dreamscape."

"Don't worry about the money," she said.

"I have to, Bonnie. Someone has to. We have rings to pay for, flights to book, hotel stays, and all the other stuff I haven't even thought of that I'm sure will pop up for the wedding."

"Don't worry about the wedding," said Bonnie. "I've got that covered."

"I'm not worried about the wedding. I could care less about the wedding. I'm worried about paying the bills!" My voice spiked over the rumble of the bus and traffic, pulling a look from a few other guys on the bus.

Bonnie didn't respond immediately, but when she did, "I'm sorry" was all she said.

"No, I'm sorry. I shouldn't have said that. I care about our wedding, honey. I'm just scared we're going to be in a bad situation financially trying to do this in the time frame we planned."

"Do you want to change the date?"

"No, I want to do this. I'm just afraid we're going to have regrets."

"I don't have any regrets," said Bonnie.

I sighed deeply, "I know you don't but . . ."

"But what? You do?"

"I just don't . . ."

"Don't what, honey? Tell me."

"I don't want to be my parents."

"Your parents have very different circumstances than we do. Your dad had an accident. Stuff like that changes a family."

"No, honey, you don't understand. The reason my dad got up on that roof in the first place was because of money. Before the accident, we still fought and that's what we fought about. We didn't have enough to pay someone else to roof the house, so my dad elected to do it himself. That's why he fell, that's why he's angry, that's why all the crap that has ever happened in my family has happened. Money. You can tell me it doesn't matter all you want because your family has always had it, but it always matters. I guess I just wanted to believe it didn't."

"What can I do to help?"

"Nothing, honey. Nothing."

Bonnie sat with me in silence for a bit. Then her positive tone came back. "Well, if we cut back on the ridiculous stuff we can save money all over the place. There are so many stupid, unnecessary expenses in weddings, I'm confident we can save whatever you don't make this year. We can make our own cake. We can make our own table decorations. There is a lot we can do. The more we save up front, the more my dad gives us as a gift, which will take the burden off you, right?"

"I can't do that to you. I can't rob you of your day because of my bad decision-making."

"It's our day."

"I'll feel terrible."

"Don't. Don't, it's one day. You need support and that's what I'm doing."

"Is there anything I can do to help?"

"Yes," she said sternly. "You can pitch great, honey. You can kick some ass for me."

Chapter Thirty-seven

Though Abby would have told me it was a mistake, I thought of Bonnie the next time I took the mound. I thought of what she asked me to do for her just before she offered to sacrifice her dreams so I could chase mine without distraction. I didn't visualize her face when I pitched, or hear her voice in my head, or some other Hollywood trick. I simply thought about not letting her down by doing what I had the power to do. I used it as motivation to focus on the present, the hitter, and my pitch selection. I wasn't just facing the hitter one smart pitch at a time, I was facing the rest of my life, one smart pitch at a time.

There are two parts to being a strikeout pitcher. First, you have to throw strikes. A lot of young pitchers seem to forget this part. They worry far too much about the batter hitting their throws before the count becomes a strikeout scenario. In short, they nibble, throwing as many balls as they do strikes. This means high pitch counts, early exits, and pressure situations wherein the pitcher must throw something in the hitting zone at the risk of walking the hitter if he doesn't. A strikeout is as much the first two pitches as it is the third and final pitch, even though it's the final pitch that gets the call.

The second thing a strikeout pitcher must do is know how to put a guy away. For some pitchers, this is done courtesy of their one nasty out pitch; the one they got drafted for; the one *Baseball America* raves about. For everyone else, getting punch-outs revolves around knowing what a hitter's weak point is, and setting them up to exploit it.

I had never been referred to as a strikeout pitcher. I always relied on forcing contact and letting my fielders do their job—this was the Grady Fuson way. However, if there was one thing that makes a pitcher stand out, it's Ks. I knew from experience I could throw enough strikes to get myself into strikeout situations; I just needed to convert them. Since I threw the standard four-pitch mix—fastball, curveball, slider, and change—I knew I had all the tools I needed to make those conversions happen if I read the hitter properly. The only thing I was missing was the conviction to rule information given to me from the hitter as more valuable than that given to me by the brass.

After I got home from our road trip, I went to work. I sped up on the mound, pitching with conviction. You could see it in my body language as I stalked around the mound. I borrowed Luke's scowl and Chip's swagger, and although the batter came to the plate with the weapon, I put him on the defensive. I attacked hitters, challenging them to fight me off or be retired.

There were times I lost the fight, but more often than not, I won. I threw up zeros and punched out hitters—more than I'd ever struck out any previous season. I never tried to do what I couldn't do. I just took what I had and attacked with it, processing what the hitter gave me and making adjustments as I went. Soon my strikeouts were twice that of my innings pitched, nearly five times my walks, and my ERA had shrunk to a 3. I was on fire.

Then, injuries started happening in the big leagues. Estes got a call to go up, just like we all suspected he would. Soon others headed north, fill-ins and backups mostly, but the Big Club was scuffling, losing twice as many games as they were winning.

The organization vigorously shuffled players, looking for people who could get the job done. New faces came into town, and the face of the Beavers started to mutate. Guys on the major league

DL came in to do rehab; guys from Double A came to fill in the upward domino effect; and guys from other teams got claimed off waivers. At one time, we had a bullpen with eleven pitchers on it, counting rehabbers. It was an exciting time to be a Triple A baseball player. There was lot of opportunity for guys doing well.

After a day game during a trip to Omaha, Luke got called in to the office and was told he was heading to the big leagues. After playing for nearly seven seasons, his time had finally come.

There was a line of players making their way up to Luke to congratulate him. Some talked at length with him, others simply wished him well and smacked him on the ass. I yelled at him and ran up to hug him like an excited mother. "Congratulations!"

"Thanks, man." Even his scowl couldn't hold up to my hug.

"This is great! I'm so happy for you!"

"Yeah, this is amazing. I can't believe it," said Luke.

"I can. You earned it."

"Thanks, bro."

"When do you leave?"

"I fly out tonight. Shane is going to come to the apartment and pack up my stuff and send it to San Diego to meet me."

"Wow, just like that," I said, marveling at it all.

"Yeah, this changes everything. I was really starting to wonder if I should keep going."

"Glad you did now, huh?"

"Affirmative."

"You know about the rule about picking up this month's rent since you're a big leaguer now, right?" I said, citing an obscure, but incredibly relevant to me and thus instantly remembered rule.

"There is no rule."

"Oh, I beg to differ. I heard if you get called up, you pick up the rent for the guys stuck behind since you'll make twice that your first night in the Show."

Luke's scowl came back.

"Come on, man, you're screwing Chip and me by leaving."

"Alright. I'll do it. If I'm up there for the rest of the month, I'll send you a check for the rent. It's on me."

"Awesome." I fist-pumped. "I knew living with you was a good choice. Does this also mean I get your room?"

"Oh, that's right"—Luke pointed his finger at me—"you got your girl coming into town in a few days, don't you? Talk about perfect timing. Are you going to propose while she's here?"

"Yeah, big visit coming up."

"How you going to do it?"

"I was thinking the Portland Rose Garden would be perfect. I walked up there once last year and it was beautiful. They have every variety of rose on earth there, and in the heart of it all is a spot called the Japanese Gardens. It's like another world there, with rock gardens and waterfalls. You can see the whole city from a lookout, and"—I started daydreaming about it all—"there is a little bridge that stretches over a koi pond, surrounded by Japanese maples in a kaleidoscope of colors. It's like something out of an ancient watercolor. I think I'm going to propose there. I'll hire one of the team's photographers to camp out at a certain time and photograph the whole thing without Bonnie knowing. The place is gorgeous and the pictures will really put it over the top. We'll immortalize it there, on top of the world and surrounded by flowers." I snapped out of the dream and looked back at Luke. "What do you think?"

"I think you should do it on a baseball field," said Luke.

"I think I'll stick with my plan, general. But I will enjoy the room while you're gone. You never know how valuable a door is until your girlfriend is coming to visit."

"Sure. But"—he raised an eyebrow—"I get it back if I come down."

"Deal. I hope you never come back."

Luke smiled. "Me too."

"Good luck," I said.

"You too. Don't screw up your proposal."

"I won't. Don't screw up your debut."

We clasped hands, bumped chests, smacked backs, and then we wished each other farewell. We both had big things ahead of us.

Chapter Thirty-eight

It had been nearly three months since Bonnie and I had last seen each other. We desperately needed this visit. Video-chats, cell phone calls, and texts were no substitute for physical contact.

Since players often go without seeing their wives for long stretches during the season, wife visits are often referred to as "conjugal visits." Yet, after these long-endured sexual frustrations are vigorously worked out, having a family in town can be a bit of a chore. The player is technically the host, though he usually doesn't have the means or the space to entertain. He's also working, so he has a routine in place and a job to focus on. The spartan accommodations he's adapted to can be an irritant to the guest, who is accustomed to one-thousand-thread-count sheets and down-stuffed pillows. Baseball is a grind, and visitors who haven't worked up the calluses necessary to endure it without complaints can make a player's life more distraction than satisfaction, not to mention sharing a bed after months of slumbering solo, can really screw up your sleeping.

I explained all this to Bonnie, how things would be a little rough around the edges, and she said that, after four years of traveling around in white passenger vans with no air-conditioning as part of Christian college ensemble groups, sleeping on the seats with moody girls whining about their periods, she could handle a few days in a crappy apartment.

But, she pointed out, she was sleeping with girls back then, not boys, a huge item of contention considering Bonnie's parents' views on anything remotely sexual before marriage. I tried all the classic arguments: that her folks didn't have to know about it; that we were going to be married soon anyway; and that we weren't going to be doing anything, but Bonnie still put up a fight. In the end, I won because we didn't have the money for a hotel, and as fate would have it, Chip's family was going to be in town the same time as Bonnie, thus stuffing the apartment with chaperones: Chip, his wife, and his two little girls.

With our temptation curbed, there was only one other issue: the players' wives. Just like coming on to a new team can present a period of adjustment to the rookie player, it can present adjustments to rookie wives and girlfriends. Being a player's wife is almost like being a player, and considering what I knew about being a player, I wasn't sure if I wanted my wife to be a part of that sorority. There are unwritten rules, seniority issues, periods in which rookies have to prove themselves. Of course, like all groups of women, players' wives can be warm, caring, and thoughtful in ways men will never know. But they can also be shallow, catty, and judgmental in ways men will never understand.

The day before Bonnie hit town, I brought this issue up to Chip, asking him if he thought it was worth connecting Bonnie with the other Beaver wives or not. For me, this wasn't an option since my teammates were my teammates, but for Bonnie, there was an association choice.

"I tell my wife to stay clear. There's more drama than there needs to be. You know how guys can be with rumors between teammates and who's getting called up and so on."

"Yeah," I said, thinking of the many times the pitchers have gotten together to figure out who deserved a call up when the opportunity presented itself. It was like attending a cult meeting when Estes got called up.

"Wives do that too, but way worse. When their husband doesn't get the call, they get mad at the wife of the player who did. They take it personally. That's what it all comes down to, really—they take a lot of stuff personally that isn't personal. They don't understand the game the way we do. Players come home and complain about their jobs, and all the wives know is what their husbands tell them, and then they think everyone is a back-stabbing, cheating, undeserving son of a bitch. I don't need my wife around that."

"That's a good point," I said.

"It's an elite club, bro. Being a player's wife makes you special. Just like the players think they're special. Wives get cocky too. Some of them even count service time, like they been there longer and they deserve better treatment because they're an older wife. It's crazy." Chip shook his head.

"Then"—he put his hands up as if he were telling someone to slow down—"they compete with each other. Buying stuff, dressing up, getting work done. I remember the first time my wife showed up to the wives' section and there were women dressed up like they were going to the club. My wife just got done changing my kids' diapers, and they all standing 'round like they on a runway. She came home and told me they was all outta they minds.

"Keeping up with the Joneses," mumbled Chip. "You know how you see players in the Bigs with their cars and clothes and stuff. Well, you don't really need all that. I mean, I like to look good, but I don't need to spend eighty thousand dollars on a car so my kids can grind Cheerios into the seats and spit up on the floor. They do it because the people around them do it. The game corrupts you. You don't need that."

"They aren't all like that, are they?"

"No, but just like it's hard to be your own person on this side of the game, it's hard to be your own person on that side. It's easy to follow everyone else. I like my wife just like she is."

"I like Bonnie how she is."

"There ya go."

"Do you think your wife would mind sitting with Bonnie, you know, showing her the ropes, like a veteran wife?"

"Your wife like kids?"

"Bonnie loves kids."

"Great, she can help my wife change their diapers."

Bonnie got in on May 27th, the first game of an eight-game home stand against the Sacramento River Cats and the Las Vegas 51s. We'd planned this out so she could have a good week with me before heading back home. I was planning to propose to her on Wednesday, the 29th, the second game of the stand, because that was the day the photographer was free and, according to the weather forecast, things looked promising for outdoor activity.

I met Bonnie at the airport with flowers. She met me with a hot yellow dress. Her aunt, who lived in the Portland area, drove me to pick Bonnie up and immediately regretted it as we started making out within seconds. We must have necked at least a hundred times before we finally made it to my room. It was pathetic, but it was absolutely what the doctor ordered, and we probably would have spent more time testing the waters of temptation if Chip's family wasn't at the apartment.

I waited until the last minute to leave Bonnie for the ballpark. After discussing where to pick up tickets from will call, where to sit in the wives section, and where to wait post-game, I decided she would be okay without me and gathered up my things for the park. Then, the instant the game was over, I rushed into the locker room in an effort to make a quick getaway and rejoin her. However, while I was stripping down, Abby pulled me aside.

"We're gonna start ya on this Wednesday. You okay with that?" he asked.

"Uh, yeah," I said robotically, thinking about the prospect of picking up a start on the same day I was planning to propose. "Of course I'm okay with that." Starting can be a real mind-bender if you're used to the pen, where life is lived on the spur of the moment. Starting gives you time to think about how things can go, all the what-ifs and happenings you can't control. I felt my mind sag under the weight of both a start and a proposal. I thought about telling Abby I might not be in the right frame of mind for a start, but I'd already given him all he wanted to hear, and then there was the golden rule of baseball reminding me to be thankful for the opportunity lest I never get one again.

When Bonnie and I made it back to my apartment, Chip and his wife were already in bed. Because the kids were sharing a room with them, they had to go to bed at the same time their kids did. Bonnie and I decided to retire as well so as not to disturb the scene.

Lying there on our squeaky mattress, in my air conditioner-less room, Bonnie told me she was sad I didn't pitch tonight.

"I'm sorry about that," I said, "but I have good news. I'm going to be starting on Wednesday."

"Awesome!"

"Yeah, you'll get to see me pitch, maybe more than you wanted."

"Is starting a good thing or a bad thing for you since you're a reliever?"

"It's good. It's priority innings. It means a lot to pick up a start."

"I hope you do good."

"Me too." I laughed nervously.

"I liked watching you in your little baseball pants," she said, changing subjects while walking her fingers across my chest. Soon she was kissing me on the side of the cheek. "I wish I could see you in them now."

"Oh, maybe I should bring a pair home with me?"

"Then I could take them off of you."

"Someone's a little frisky."

"Well yeah, we've only been apart for nearly three months."

"I know, frisk away, baby," I said, rolling to meet her affection with some of my own.

"Don't you ever get tired of waiting to, you know, have sex?" she asked.

"You have no idea," I said.

"What if we just said to hell with it and had sex right now?"

I pulled back and looked at Bonnie. "Are you sure you're feeling alright?"

"It's those pants, I'm telling you. You turn me on as is, but after watching you in those pants, grrr, my little baseball player." She started rubbing my chest. Then, she smiled at me and said, "We could totally do it. No one would ever know."

"I'm pretty sure the family of four one bedroom over would hear us. I've been told it's remarkably easy to hear sexual activity in this building."

"I could be really quiet."

"Bonnie, we're not going to have sex."

"Are you scared?"

"No, I'm not scared! Why does everyone keep asking me if there is something wrong with my desire to have sex with a woman—including the woman I intend to have sex with?" I sat up on the mattress. "We have waited this long to get it on, we can wait a few more months to do it right. I can even bring the pants home with me. Besides, I pictured my first time being someplace a little more romantic than on an air mattress in an efficiency apartment with no AC." I lay back down. "Every time this thing squeaks I feel like my grandma is going to burst through the door and scream at us."

"You're right. I'm sorry."

"Oh no, don't be sorry. I like it when you're frisky." I kissed her. "I'm just asking you to bottle it for me until we're ready to pop the cork in grand fashion." I started rubbing her slumped shoulders. "I promise it will be worth it," I said. "Not a day goes by around here that someone doesn't try to give me tips."

Chapter Thirty-nine

On the day I got engaged, I ate blueberry pancakes. I remember it because it was one of the few times I had breakfast that wasn't hijacked from the field. While treating Bonnie to whatever she wanted, I decided to spoil myself a little too. Then, as we let our food settle, we talked about how wonderful it would be if I kept pitching well and made it to the big leagues. How, if I made it up for a long enough chunk of time, we could go house shopping. The talk of a house gave way to furniture, then dogs, then kids, and then guessing all the superpowers our kids would have. Finally, after checking the time, I curtailed the conversation and suggested we head up to Washington Park and visit a special place I'd discovered.

Hand-in-hand, we walked up the hill to the International Rose Test Garden, where we strolled around, reading placards and taking frivolous pictures. I played as casual as I could, hiding all my glances to my cell phone clock. At roughly 11:30, I "casually" led us into the Japanese Gardens. Little did Bonnie know, I had already paid one of the Beavers' personal photographers to pose as a tourist reading a pamphlet on the south end of the koi pond with the bridge on it. In fact, Bonnie was so taken by the sights of the garden, she didn't notice me nod at the photographer as we walked by, en route to our mark.

"It's a beautiful place, isn't it?" I said, squeezing Bonnie's hand as we walked toward the bridge.

"It's great. I think we should have one of these at our house. A little one, with a little pond full of fishes."

"Right," I said. "To go along with our expertly trained dog, our modernly appointed house, and our MENSA-candidate child who will be both an All-Star athlete and a concert grand pianist. Is there anything else you want while you're at it?" I stopped in the middle of the bridge and looked across the pond at the photographer, who put down her pamphlet and picked up her camera, and began adjusting the lens.

"No, I'm a simple woman, with simple needs."

I chuckled and put one hand in my pocket, tracing the edges of her ring with my finger.

Bonnie looked around on the bridge a little, taking in the views, and then she slid in next to me, leaning on the railing.

"Bonnie, I love you," I began.

"I love you too, sweetheart."

"I can't wait to spend the rest of my life with you."

"Mmm . . ." She snaked her arm around mine and rested her head on my shoulder. "It's going to be great."

"It is. But I think it's time we made it more official." I uncoiled her from around me, stepped back, and took a knee. My pose widened her eyes as what was happening set in on her.

"Bonnie, I've never been as happy or as confident in my life as I have been in the few months that we've known each other. There is no doubt in my mind that you're the woman God made me for. I love you, and with this ring I promise you that I always will. So, even though I've already asked you this question before, for the sake of our dog, house, and koi pond, will you marry me?"

Bonnie was tearing up, but she was smiling and giggling. She reached out her ring finger and said, "Yes." I slid the ring onto her finger, and then, in one smooth motion, stood from my knee, wrapped my arms around her waist, and picked her off the ground, spinning her around on the bridge. I set her down and we kissed on the bridge to the sound of a few onlookers in the park clapping.

"It's beautiful," said Bonnie, admiring her new ring.

"I'm glad you like it. I was a little worried."

"I love it, it's perfect. You did good, honey."

"Oh yeah, and there is someone I'd like you to meet."

I waved to my photographer to come around and join us. I explained how I'd arranged to get the whole thing on film, which made Bonnie happier than the proposal itself.

"I may not understand just how significant the wedding experience is to a woman, but I do know that capturing once-in-a-lifetime moments are a big deal. Now your family can see, and we'll have these pictures for generations."

"Yeah, that's great," said Bonnie. "But more importantly, I can put these on Facebook and brag to all my girlfriends. This is awesome!"

"Well"—I ran my hand through my hair—"that's what marriages are all about, bragging on Facebook."

Chip and his wife clapped for us when we got back to the apartment. Bonnie showcased her ring. Then she started calling her family and announcing the big news.

"Congrats, bro," said Chip, as we stood next to each other listening to Bonnie relate the story in four-part harmony to her parents.

"Thanks," I said.

"You gonna remember it the rest of your life."

"I hope so. I don't ever want to forget these days."

"You won't. Neither will she. That's why it's so important to do it right. Days like this will keep you both sane during a long season."

"I think I did good."

"You did great, bro. You can tell by the way your girl acts. She's one happy princess right now. She's gonna be calling all her friends until you pitch tonight. Heck, she's probably gonna be calling while you pitch. You gonna look up in the stands after you get an out and she's gonna be yakking away with no clue what's going on. It's like she just got called up to the big leagues."

"That's probably a good thing. If I know she's not concentrating on me, I'll probably pitch better. I can't stand pitching when I know my family is there because I can almost feel them looking at me. I know what they're thinking. I can't seem to focus on the game because I'm always aware of them. Do you know what I mean?"

"Not really. I always play better when my family is around."

"That's right. You said that. Well, not me. I play terrible. I almost always pitch bad when my folks show up. The last time my parents were at a game, I took a line drive in the crotch. The last time my extended relatives showed up, I gave up seven runs in a third of an inning. It's uncanny, man. Anytime I know people are watching with big expectations, it's like I'm cursed. Thank goodness they only see me pitch once every three years or so. I hope I don't do the same while Bonnie is here."

"It's probably not them, it sounds like it's you."

"Probably, but I don't know what to do about it."

"Be confident, that's what. Don't worry 'bout all those other eyes. You got your queen in the stands tonight, she loves you no matter what. She don't want you worrying about her while you're pitching. You just keep doing what you doing."

"I'll try."

"Probably not a good time to tell you that this is a TV game, huh?"

"What?"

"Yeah, you gonna be on television tonight, baby."

"That's just great."

Chapter Forty

After spending the last few years running out of the pen when my number was called, it felt weird to lead the team onto the field from the dugout. It just wasn't natural. However, once I got on the mound and started warming up, things felt right. I was able to find my minor league rhythm, that familiar dance of winding and delivering.

I knew Bonnie was in the stands. In fact, she was almost right behind home plate. In PGE Park, there are boxes behind home plate, and one of them is always reserved for players' families. Bonnie could see me from it, and I her, but she did not wave or call to me as I prepared for the game. Now that I was on the mound, she stayed in the shadows, watching from a distance so that I wouldn't read panic on her face should I get into trouble. She was a performer herself and understood just how nerve-racking it can be to have people in attendance who know you.

There were also some radar guns in the stands. They belonged to scouts. For whom, I didn't know. It was getting close to the All-Star break and soon after that would be the trade deadline. Scouts were out hunting down marketable talent anywhere they could find it. It reminded me that my own team wasn't the only route to the big leagues. If I pitched well today, I might have a shot with someone else.

The stage was set, and when the umpire said, "Play ball," I punched my time card and went to work, pumping the zone full of strikes. I pitched like a reliever, moving fast on the mound, trying to keep the pace uncomfortable for the batter. Most starters move slower since they know they'll be out there for a while, but I reset as soon as I got the ball, shook, wound, and fired again.

I struck out the side in the first inning. I did it again in the third. By the time I came out of the game in the fifth, I'd punched out nine hitters and allowed only one run. It was a stellar performance, one that ended only because I'd hit my pitch count and had to come out. Abby told me he'd love to send me out for another inning, but then he'd lose his job if I got hurt. Safety first, he said. "You want that arm to last the whole season, don't ya?" Then he slapped me on the butt and picked up the phone to call in the cavalry.

When I made it back to the locker room, I went to my own phone. Bonnie had texted me several times, like an emotional game log of what I was doing and how she was reacting to it. Each message was full of congratulatory sentiments followed by lines of exclamation marks. After I read through all fourteen of her messages, I started to realize how big this day was for her as well. Not just because of the engagement, but because she was going to be my wife, and as such, she'd be tied to my highs and lows on the field for as long as I chose to play this game.

After putting my arm in ice, I went into the underground tunnel outside the lockers and called Bonnie.

"Honey!" she screamed. "You did awesome!"

"Thanks, honey. Where are you?"

"I'm above the dugout."

"You're not in the wives' box?"

"No. Oh my God, you were right. They're ridiculous. One of them accidently spilled wine on one of the other players' wives, I don't know who, she had fake boobs though, had to have, they defied gravity. Anyway, the one who got wine on her had a fit. She screamed about the cost of the shirt and how so-and-so was going to buy her a new one. Ugh. I am so glad Chip's wife was there. She showed me how to get out, subtly."

"Do you know how to get back into the service tunnel?" I asked.

"Yeah, why?"

"Look down the left field line." I had walked down to the pen's rear entrance and was peeking out with my phone against my head, waving.

"I see you! Hi!" She waved back.

"You wanna come down here and make out with me, during a game?"

"I'm on my way," she replied instantly.

"I'll meet you at the security—" The line went dead and when I looked back toward the roof of the dugout, she was gone.

"She's such a wholesome girl," I said to myself.

I met Bonnie near the security checkpoint and snuck her down the tunnel and out toward the bullpen, tiptoeing behind the relievers in the pen. We ducked behind the outfield fence line between the giant ivy-covered stone wall and the outfield fencing. We passed the scoreboard and the batter's eye, and went all the way to where the centerfield cameras were set up. From there we watched the game for a bit, me in my uniform pants with my shirt damp from ice and sweat, she in jeans and a hoodie.

"Was it fun? Watching me pitch?"

"It was great. At first I was so nervous, but then, when you started kicking butt, I was like, *Oh yeah, that's my future husband!*"

"I'm glad. I can't believe I pitched that well. Nothing satisfies quite like a stellar outing. I think that's why guys hold on in this game so long—it's such a good feeling."

"Well, you pitched awesome." She put her head on my shoulder. "I hope you get the win."

Some of my fellow relievers were in the game, and things were starting to unravel. The River Cats were making a comeback, slowly but surely.

"That doesn't matter to me. I'm just glad I pitched good," I said. "I'll go back in the pen after this outing, and wins don't matter for relievers, just quality appearances."

"I still hope you get it. You earned it."

I didn't debate her on that. Instead, I asked, "Did you make any friends?"

"I don't know," said Bonnie. "I don't know what having those girls as friends means. I got along with some of them. Some were nice, but some were just putting on a show. It's like there were ways you're supposed to behave but no one tells you what they are. I mean, the whole concept of meeting a group of random women wherein a veteran wife has to show you how to act even though you supposedly can act however you want? Isn't that weird?"

"You have no idea," I said, musing to myself over my years of experience with the same matter, only with a different gender.

"Some of the girls were snobby, others were nice. Like, I showed my ring to some and they were happy for me, and congratulated me. Others were like, *Oh my God, it's pink. Did you tell him to get you that or did he mess it up?*"

"Wow, they said that?" I asked.

"Yeah. One of them said they wouldn't even think about saying yes unless there were at least two karats on her finger."

"I'm not surprised. It's like that on the team too. We sit in the bullpen and talk about how important cars and shoes are. Stuff that has no bearing on our life at all but is suddenly very important because we're all stuck with each other and comparing."

"Well, I don't care what anyone else says. I love my ring. I think it's great. I like that it's different, it's ours. And I love you because you're different, and you're mine."

"I love you too," I said, putting a soggy arm around her.

"And I like that you are still wearing those pants."

"Yeah," I said, putting my nose on her head.

"Yeah," she said.

"Why don't you come back here and help me make the most of them?" I tugged Bonnie back behind the outfield fence and out of sight.

Chapter Forty-one

"I fucking hate my wife," roared Dallas, like he was smacking her as he said it.

The team was in Fresno now, and it was only a few days from the break. I had put Bonnie on a jet some weeks ago after our exquisite visit. We made the most of our time together, enjoying the many fine virtues of Portland while mapping out post-wedding ideas. We even went to an Ikea furniture store together, where I counted walking through the place as post-start conditioning.

But, as it always seemed to do, our time together came to an end all too quickly. I kissed her good-bye and watched her board a plane back home while I hopped a flight to another minor league town, Fresno, California, home of the Grizzlies. We'd see each other again soon, however, as I'd bought a ticket to head home and help finalize some of the wedding details over All-Star break. In the meantime, it was back to life as usual in the Portland Beavers pen, where, presently, I was trying to survive another emotional tirade brought on by Dallas's married life.

Dallas had just come from the lockers where he was texting his wife. The conversation must have gone badly, though no one asked Dallas to elaborate since, by this point in the season, we'd all learned not to get him started. Unfortunately, we'd also learned that what we wanted rarely had an impact on what Dallas did.

"She never fucking lets me do anything," he kept going. It was like listening to a child complain about how his mommy won't let him go hang out with his friends.

"What do you want to do?" asked Bentley.

"I just want to go out with the boys after a game. You know, just go to a bar like I did in the old days and shit. But she fucking gets all pissed off about it, like she doesn't trust me."

"You did get another girl knocked up in your first year of marriage," said Bentley.

"That was over a year ago," pleaded Dallas.

"One year isn't that long a time for something that big."

"It ain't just that, man. She fucking nags me all the time. She's never nice, like she's so fucking smart and I'm so fucking dumb. And she ain't got no friends."

"Try killing her with kindness, bro," offered Bentley.

"I'd just like to kill her," said Dallas.

"A lot of times girls pick up on your lack of affection. I'll bet if you went out of your way to make her feel like you loved her, she'd change her ways."

"I'd like to get out of the city and then send her the divorce papers and say, 'Yeah, it's like that, who's hot shit now?' That'd wipe that look off her fucking face."

Bentley sighed, and uncrossed his legs. "I don't know what to tell you, Dallas. I think you two should see a counselor."

"I tell her that all the time, I tell her she needs to see one." Dallas spoke rapidly, pleased to find himself in agreement with Bentley for the first time in their conversation.

"No, the both of you," corrected Bentley.

"Why? What the fuck did I do that I need to see some shrink?"

There was a collective groan by the guys in the pen. I stood up and went to the watercooler as I couldn't take it anymore. Dallas had always been promoted by this time in the season, or, conversely, I had been demoted. Not since our first year had Dallas and I been on the same team this long. I always wanted to keep up with him, but now I realized that being separated from him was actually the better scenario.

Our communication had become increasingly strained of late. I was like his alter ego, actually. The more he talked about living it up in the moment, the more I hunkered down on the value of responsible, big-picture decision-making. While he complained about his married life, I talked fondly of high hopes for mine. But maybe the biggest factor was that I was pitching better than him. Dallas always had the money, the girls, and the numbers; now it seemed the tables had turned, and he did not like it.

It's common for players to hope other players, even teammates, fail. This is because we know there are only so many spots available at the top and, even though we like our teammates, we want that spot for ourselves. On the days I had to back up during big league camp, I wanted other players to fail because it meant I'd get some playing time. During the season, I hoped to outpitch my teammates so that I could get the call. With Dallas, however, I was hoping he would outright blow it so his career would end. The way he spoke without thinking, his absence of filtering, his complete lack of self-awareness—it was almost as if Dallas didn't want anyone to respect him. I know I didn't. At best, I could only nod and agree, and that was only to keep him from getting pissed at me.

While I was standing at the water cooler, mulling over how much I wanted Dallas's arm to explode and force him to disappear from the game, Abby popped out of the dugout and looked down to the pen. He gestured to his open mouth with his left hand, folding one finger like a hook had caught him and was tugging him from the water—it was Fish's warm-up signal.

Immediately, Fish jumped up and started preparing for action. Though Fresno's bullpen is far down the line, it's exposed to the field. The pitcher and the catcher are both open targets for balls struck foul while they work. To protect them, other occupants of the pen stand off the side of the pitcher and catcher, gloves on, ready to take a bullet for their buddies. Though only two bullpen dwellers needed to get up, the entire bench cleared, taking the opportunity as a way to escape from Dallas's impromptu therapy session. I stood by Fish, while a few other guys went down to protect the catcher's back. Some even ran down to use the dugout bathroom.

Dallas was the last to get up, but when he did, he came over and stood next to me. I focused on the field to make it seem like I was locked on to the game, oblivious to Dallas. But it didn't matter what I did with my body language, or what our previous history was. If he wanted to talk, I was going to have to listen.

"Women just don't understand how hard this lifestyle is," he started. "It's like having another family full of brothers and shit, and we do more than just hang out on the field. I mean, going to a bar and blowing off steam together is part of our fucking, you know, our fucking . . ." He labored for the word, which is how he sucked me in.

"Culture?" I finished for him.

"Exactly. It's our culture. It's what we fucking do. It don't mean nothing."

"I guess it means something to your wife."

"Yeah, but it don't mean the right thing," said Dallas.

"What is the right thing? The thing we players share, or the thing you and your wife share?"

"What we share," said Dallas, gesturing to the immediate surroundings. "That's what I try to explain to her, but she don't understand baseball players."

"But you're married to her, shouldn't her definition matter more?"

"You're starting to sound like her," said Dallas.

"I just mean that the biggest part of your life shouldn't be controlled by one of the smaller parts. Baseball's definition shouldn't control your marriage, right?"

"That's easy for you to say, you're pitching good right now."

"What?" I turned to regard him for the first time in our chat.

"I'll bet if you were pitching like shit, you wouldn't be so quick to say things like baseball ain't a big thing."

"I didn't mean it wasn't a big thing, I meant it wasn't the biggest thing."

"Then why the fuck are you playing it?"

I was starting to get angry. "How did this become about me? I play because it's a once-in-a-lifetime job with a major payout if I succeed. It doesn't control me."

"Bullshit. I remember what you were like back when you were in A ball. I remember how busted up you used to get about it being hard for you 'cause of the atmosphere. You can't fucking pull the high-and-mighty shit on me now, like you're above baseball and shit."

"That was six years ago," I said.

"Now you got it all figured out?"

"If you don't like what I have to say, don't talk to me."

"Sounds like you think you got it all fucking figured out and think you can tell me what I should do."

"You're unbelievable. It's always about you, isn't it?"

"I didn't ask you to judge me."

"I'm not. I just disagree—no, no, that's it." I'd had enough and I waved my hands as if to say the act was over. "I *am* judging you and you're fucking guilty. You read into everything more deeply than you need to because you know you fucked up your life and now you want everyone to feel as shitty as you do. Well, guess what, you fucked up and I don't feel a damn bit sorry for you."

"Baseball changes you. You think it doesn't, but it does."

"Baseball changed you," I said.

"You're still a judgmental asshole, that ain't changed."

"And you're a martyr no one feels sorry for."

"Start getting money and attention and see if it don't make you do crazy shit. You've never been in my shoes. Hell"—he started laughing to himself—"it don't matter, you never will be, you aren't going to make it anyway."

"Fuck you," I said, squaring up with him.

"Oh, you wanna fight, motherfucker? I'll beat your ass like I did back in A ball." We were locked eye-to-eye, fists clenched, ready to throw down on the edge of the left field foul line.

I took a step back, not sure I had what it took to finish what I was starting. "I don't want to fight you. I got nothing to prove to you," I said, shaking my head and backing away.

"You're a pussy, that's what you proved. You're a fucking pussy, you've always been a fucking pussy."

I wasn't much of a fighter, but even if I was, the fact that we were on the field, in uniform, in the middle of a game did not escape me. No matter how good a reason I had, breaking a teammate's nose in broad view of fans would severely damage what I'd been putting together this season.

"You're lucky we're playing right now or I'd straight whoop your ass," taunted Dallas.

"No, *you're* lucky we're playing a game right now," I said.

"Oh really"—Dallas laughed—"you think you can take me, huh? All right, we can do this in the locker rooms right now. We can do this in the hotel, bitch. We can do it anywhere, anytime, fucking pussy."

The other guys in the pen had turned to inquire why Dallas was screaming at me in the outfield. They saw me standing there, frozen and unable to call Dallas on his bet to fight. They say the bigger man walks away, but I knew from years of experience on a team that you can feel pretty small when the occasion you didn't stick up for yourself is shared by a team of onlookers. But I didn't want to fight, at least not as bad as Dallas. I just wanted to see him get what he deserved. I wanted him to see himself for what he was.

"Fucking pussy," he said again when I failed to move.

"I feel sorry for you, Dallas."

"Why's that, pussy?"

"Because you need this game. You need it to save you. If you didn't have baseball, you'd just have your fucked-up life off the field with no way out. If you wanna fight later on, that's fine, but no matter what you do or say to me, it's never going to be as bad as what you've done to yourself. You might kick my ass, but it will never hurt me as bad as it must hurt to wake up to the life you live every day."

Fish had to stop warming and pull back a rabid Dallas. That's when I walked away, to the safety of the dugout, with Dallas shouting slurs and challenges at me from behind. I acted like I didn't feel his words hit me, not from the outside at least. I felt them inside, where they practically begged me to turn around and spear him and beat on him until we were separated by teammates with both our faces bloody from trading blows. I felt them all the way into the dugout, where I sat down, calm and controlled like I'd just been pulled from a bad outing. I felt them after the game had finished, after I talked to Bonnie, and every time Dallas and I passed each other in silence the next day. However, I did take some small satisfaction in knowing that as frustrated as his words made me, it wasn't half as bad as what my words had done to him.

Chapter Forty-two

Abby held the door open for me as I walked into Ready's office in the Fresno visitors' locker room. The whole of the visitors' locker room was a small space, including the offices, but Ready's office was large enough to sit the three of us for our private, closed-door meeting.

It was at least an hour before stretch, and there was no rhyme or reason for this meeting that I could think of beyond the possibility I was getting sent down or, dare I say it, I was getting called up. The thought of the latter had me on the edge of my seat.

"We've already sent up Myrow, Luke, and Estes, and we're real happy about that," said Abby.

"Me too," I said, anxious to hear if I was going to be joining them.

"The problem is, they were our selections fer the All-Star game. Now we have to find someone to replace 'em with." Abby's smile widened as he nodded to me. Mine shrank as I sat back in my seat, knowing full well what was coming next.

"We get to choose who the substitutes are and we both were a think'n you'd make a fine replacement. You've pitched real good all year, that's what I said to Ready, didn't I?" Abby turned to Ready. "Didn't I say he pitched real good for us?"

Ready raised an eyebrow. "Yep, that's what you said, Abby."

"We'd like you to go on account of you earning it, but it's up to you if you wanna do it. I don't see why you wouldn't, though."

Making an All-Star team is great news, except when you've bought plane tickets to head home over the break. Like many of the other boys on the squad, I was planning to skip town and get away from the baseball scene for a couple of well-earned days off. Besides, Bonnie had lined up visits to the wedding and rehearsal party venues, and tours of potential apartment complexes where we might make our home. After all she'd done solo, I couldn't leave her hanging now.

On the other hand, this was the Triple A All-Star game, not some A ball hoopla for youngsters with several seasons ahead of them and the big league roster. This was the best players in Triple A, a roster representing players who could help a big league club right now—maybe I'd be helping Bonnie more by going to the All-Star game than going home.

"How big for me is this, really?" I asked.

"It would be a real feather in your cap," said Abby.

"Would it help me make the big club?"

"It wouldn't hurt."

I gritted my teeth. Abby had been so supportive of me all year; I felt guilty for not taking his offer as soon as he gave it. I was hoping he'd tell me the All-Star team wouldn't make a damn bit of difference. It was just a show team, after all; everyone would only pitch one inning and it didn't matter who won the game. Hell, I wasn't even the first choice! I searched the room for an answer other than the one on Abby's face.

"But I made this promise to my fiancée months ago, and we already bought the tickets. They're nonrefundable."

"Have her change 'em and come see you. I'm sure she'll be proud."

"She's got work, and, well, we were going to look at wedding decorations together."

Abby looked at Ready with a baffled face, as if asking him if he really heard me say I was giving up an All-Star game bid for a chance to look at wedding décor.

"Maybe if this wasn't last minute, I could have planned for it better," I said, trying to recover.

"This only happens so many times," said Abby. "When other teams come looking at ya, they'll always see this. It means more than ya think."

I dropped my head. "I understand."

"So you accept?"

"No. I can't."

Abby and Ready exchanged looks of astonishment.

"Yer sure?" asked Abby.

"No. But this is what I'm going to do," I said.

After a long stretch of silence and a resigned sigh, "Alright then," said Abby, his demeanor suggesting I just did something really, really stupid. "Well." He picked up a stack of papers and shuffled through them. "Send Dallas in here, would ya please?"

I swallowed hard and bitter at his words. "Sure," I said.

I left the office, found Dallas, and told him that Abby wanted to see him. Then, faintly, I added, "Congratulations."

"You should have gone!" said Bonnie, driving us from the airport to her parents' house on the east side of Cleveland. I was going to stay there, in their guest room under their watchful eye for the break. Bonnie picked me up early the morning of the fourteenth as I'd flown through the night, leaving as soon as our final first half game against Tucson ended.

"Oh, don't say that now. I already feel terrible."

Bonnie shook her head. "I feel like I did this to you. It's my fault."

"You didn't do it, honey. It just happened at a complex time, that's all."

"I would have understood if you had gone. Next time, you should go."

"There might not be a next time." I thought about the finality of my own statement, then, as if to combat it in my own mind, "I wanted to set the precedent that baseball doesn't get between us. It was a hard decision, but we made plans, and I don't want to break our plans for baseball if I can avoid it. Besides, the title of All-Star next to your name is nice but it doesn't really mean anything."

"Are you sure?"

"Sure I'm sure." I wasn't. "How many people do you know who don't have to pay taxes because they made a minor league All-Star team?"

"None."

"Exactly."

"But if you could have gone, if we didn't plan this visit, would you have? Would you talk about it like it was a great accomplishment that was going to really help your career?"

"Absolutely."

"Now I feel bad again," said Bonnie.

"Honey, one of the best skills a baseball player has is his ability to rationalize things in his favor so he can always be on the winning end. For example: Missing the All-Star game was a key maneuver in my ascension to the Bigs. It's a chance for me to recharge and come into the second half fresh."

"Do that again. Rationalize something else," said Bonnie.

"Okay. Here is a classic one: Pitching badly today will help me in the long run as it exposes the things I need to work on to make me better. I'm actually glad I failed because now I can improve. Winning just covers up opportunities for improvement."

"But what if you don't improve?"

"Then you're just lying to yourself. That's the key to rationalizing, you have to follow through."

"Okay then, we need to make the most of the experience while you're here."

"Agreed. So, let's relax, see the venues, and find a great place to live."

"I think you should talk to your parents," said Bonnie.

"Excuse me?" I rolled my eyes over to her.

"I talked to your mom about the guest list a week ago as she was upset."

"With what?" I barked, my tone one of irritation.

"I know you don't like to deal with them, and I didn't want to bother you with this while you were playing, but she's mad you didn't call her to tell her this. She feels like you don't want them to be a part of the wedding." Bonnie cringed at how I might respond to the news.

I slapped a hand over my face. Oh, the irony, I thought, first Mom doesn't think it's going to happen at all, now she's upset because I'm not making her a bigger part of it.

"I'll never understand her. It's like whatever she says to me, I should assume the opposite."

"I think she's just upset you haven't called to check in on your dad. She dropped a lot of heavy hints about it."

"She's not very subtle," I said and stopped there, choosing to sit in silence for a while instead of talking about what I might do concerning my parents.

"Families are a big part of the wedding process, babe. I know people say you aren't marrying the family, but you kinda are. I think you should at least try and make peace with them before-hand, just so they can all enjoy it. It's important they feel like they're a part of it. You *do* want them to be a part of it, right?" She let the question float for a second before tacking it down with, "You don't want to look back and have any regrets."

There was that word again: funny how it seemed to be showing up so much lately. "Would you regret it if my grandmother wasn't there? Do I have to go make peace with her too?"

"I sent your grandmother an invitation to my bridal shower, then she called my mom and told her she was pissed we even considered her. We can leave her out of this process. But I think you should go see your dad."

"I came here to see you, honey, not to go fight with my parents."

"You're not going to fight with them."

"You don't know that."

"You're right, I don't, but if you go when your mom is out of the house, you and your dad can talk without interruption."

"Can't I just call them?"

"If they find out you came home and didn't visit, your mom will be twice as pissed, and since I'm the one who has to run all the wedding details past her and listen to her complain, I want you to do this for me." She reached one hand across the car and took hold of mine. "Do it for us."

"Fine," I said. "But this is not going to help me with the restful, recharging part of my rationalization."

"I know, but it will help me with my *I made you come home for reasons bigger than an All-Star game* rationalization."

I gripped her hand. "Well played, Mrs. Hayhurst, well played."

Chapter Forty-three

I pulled into my parents' driveway in Bonnie's borrowed car. My Corolla was parked under the tree next to the house, covered in buds and twigs from the onset of spring. I'd asked my parents to watch after it since I was afraid of my grandmother sabotaging it like she did my last one. I'd also asked my parents to drive it every week or so, but it looked like that direction had been forgotten, or at least I suspected it was until I peeked in the window and saw empty fast-food wrappers scattered around the backseat.

Neither my brother's car nor my mother's was in the drive. They were both at work, allowing my dad and me to be alone without any interruption. When I came through the front door, I could hear music playing from the stereo in the living room. It was a Bob Dylan album, my dad's patron saint.

He was surprised when he saw me, but before he could talk I explained that it was the All-Star break, and that I'd come home to help Bonnie with the wedding arrangements.

"Your mom never told me anything about you coming home," said Dad, surprisingly conversational but still sitting in his customary chair at the kitchen table, complete with a cigarette in his hand. He didn't get up to turn the music off.

"That was by design," I said.

"Ah," he said.

"How are you feeling?" I asked.

"Better than I was," he said, taking a pull and puffing it out.

"What's that mean?"

"I don't know. I didn't feel like me much before." He took another pull of his cigarette. "You ever feel angry 'cause you're hungry? You know why you're angry, because you haven't eaten, but you can't stop feeling mad even when you tell yourself not to be. Well, I felt like that a lot, but there was nothing I could eat that would make it feel better. Nothing I could buy, or say, or do. I felt angry, irritated at everything, and knew I had no reason to be. Just real mad at everything. And then, when I'd blow up and get it all out, I'd feel so terrible about what I'd done I couldn't stand myself. I'd see my life and how I had no control and I'd wanna be dead, 'cept I was too scared of it to do it."

"You don't feel that way anymore, right?"

"I don't feel such highs and lows, but I still feel the pull of it. Your brother still does stupid shit. The dog still won't shut up. Your mom still nags me. Your grandma still gets on my nerves. It ain't like your mother and I are smoking dope by the fish tanks again, if that's what you're asking."

"Maybe you should try that."

"Yeah." My dad laughed. "Maybe I should." He took a final pull from his legal cigarette and mashed it into the ashtray in front of him. "I gotta stop smoking these anyway."

"Your mom told me, after the last time she talked to you, she expected you to get married and never come home."

"That was my plan."

"Why the hell are you here, then?"

"Bonnie," I said. "She talked me into it."

"She did, huh?"

"I didn't want to come back. I had it all justified in my mind. I still do, honestly. I'm tired of this place."

"Can't say I blame you," he said. "Most days none of us want to be here."

"Then why are you? Why don't you guys just move, turn over a new leaf?"

"Where else would we be, Dirk? We had some bad luck, and now we're working it out. That's how life is." My dad's hair was brushed and flipped up on the side like he'd combed it with a balloon. He passed one of his crumpled hands over it like a paw, trying to smash it down, but it wouldn't be beaten. "There are some things we could have done differently, I suppose."

"You mean, like when you got up on the roof?"

"No, not that. That was an accident. Wish it had never happened, but it did. I couldn't control it."

"Then what?"

"The stuff after. Stuff I said. To your mom, to your brother . . . to you."

I looked down at the floor. "It's all right."

"It's been so long since I've felt normal, or close to normal, Dirk. I don't much know who I used to be. The music helps, though." We sat there for a while, listening to Dylan saw away on his harmonica. Then my dad said, "I knew you'd come back, though."

"Why do you say that?"

"Your car."

"I got keys of my own, I could get that anytime," I bluffed.

"I got all your crap in the basement," countered my dad. "All them childhood toys and stuff you couldn't live without."

I smiled. "Yeah, I'd miss my old toys, I guess."

"You wouldn't miss any of us, but you'd miss them toys," said Dad. "And you'd miss this place. You don't realize how much things mean to you when you're young, but when you get older, it's funny what sticks and what don't."

I didn't say anything. Instead, as if testing his words, I got up and strolled around the house, absorbing it in a way I hadn't been able to do for a long time. We didn't have central air-conditioning in the house, just windows that were open now to let spring air in. I walked to each of them and gazed through them, like I was looking back in time. This was the first time I'd seen my home in the summertime in seven years. I forgot about what the lilac bush looked like covered in blooms, what the broken concrete driveway looked like with grass shooting through the cracks. Then, there was the old mound in the backyard, covered in grass instead of snow. Not since I threw off it in 2003, before I finalized my contract and left to play, had I seen it in such a state.

"You remember the last time I saw you pitch?" I asked Dad, looking through the window.

"What's that then?" asked my dad. "Back in slow pitch softball?"

"No, that day in the backyard. After that start I had in high school?"

"Oh yeah. That day you thought you were gonna knock that wall down on account of Central beat'n you up?"

"Yeah."

"I remember."

"I shouldn't have stopped you from throwing."

"Ah, that don't mean nothing," said my dad.

"It meant something to me. You just said it's funny what sticks with you and what doesn't, and that moment has stuck with me for years now. I think of it more than you know."

"Why?"

"Because I felt like I took something from you."

"What?"

"I don't know. Something. Like I robbed you of a chance to be you again."

"You didn't take nothing from me," he said, shaking his head.

"I never saw you pitch after that."

"Yeah, but that wasn't on account of you. I could have went down there and pitched anytime I wanted to."

"Why didn't you?"

"Ah . . . I just didn't. Don't worry about why, it wasn't your fault," he said. "Ain't nothing you did to me, and you don't need to keep thinking about it."

Though I wanted to know his reasons, I decided it best not to push it, not now with other, more pressing things. I sat back down at the table, reached across and took the stereo remote, and turned off the music.

"Are you okay with me marrying Bonnie?" I asked.

"What does my opinion have to do with it?"

"Yes or no?"

"Yeah, she's nice," he said, looking at me like I was crazy.

"Anyone can say that."

"She's good for you, and we like her. I got no problems, Dirk. But I ain't marrying her."

"What does that mean, Dad?"

"It means you don't need me to tell you what's good for you. I was wrong to tell you otherwise. You're your own man now, Dirk. You're going to work out your own decisions. Parents have trouble with that, your mom especially, but that's how moms are. You can make your own choices. I think you made a good one." He pulled out another cigarette and lit it despite saying he wanted to quit. He took a fresh puff, and blew the smoke from his nose. Then he smiled and said, "Besides, Bonnie's got good taste in music."

Chapter Forty-four

When I got back to Portland, I was about as happy as I could be. The place Bonnie picked out for our wedding was a beautiful outdoor space that would be absolutely dazzling when the colors of the fall came. We found a small but affordable apartment not too far from her work, and a gym where I could train. My family, though things would never be perfect, had finally stabilized, and my dad and I had made peace. Finances were still tight, but Bonnie and I were enjoying the discovery of how creative we were in putting together a wedding on a shoestring budget. Though the experience was only four days in total, peace of mind was worth missing the All-Star game for, and, just like I rationalized, I was returning to a successful pitching campaign fully charged.

In fact, my first week back I pitched so well, Luke called and left me a voice message explaining how, after every game up in the Show, a packet of game notes showing minor league stats gets passed around. He said people up there knew who I was, and that I should keep doing what I was doing because *they* noticed. He said they were looking for a reliever and I could very well be their guy. His voice mail pumped me up so much I was convinced it was only a matter of time before Luke's prophecy came true and I got the call.

Then, one evening while I was lying on my perfectly adequate air mattress, in my perfectly adequate apartment, enjoying the prospects of my perfectly adequate life, Chip knocked on my door.

"Yeah, buddy, come on in," I said.

"Did you hear the news?"

"What news?"

"Your boy Dallas got called up."

Suddenly, I wasn't happy anymore.

I called Adam as soon as Chip convinced me the news wasn't a really cruel joke. It took Adam a few moments to recover from my ambush of fresh, hot outrage when he answered the phone, but soon he had me calmed to the point he could understand what I was angry about.

"How does that happen, Adam? I've been the hottest reliever on this team for a month and a half now."

"I know it, they know it. It doesn't make sense," Adam soothed.

"I know this game isn't fair, but, well, that's not fucking fair!" I whined.

"No it isn't, Shizzle."

"I want you to explain how I can outpitch Dallas and still not get the call."

"He's on the forty-man roster and you're not."

"Screw the forty-man!"

"You'll like it when you're there. I get this call at least ten times a year, Shizzle. Guys just like you, pissed for the exact same reasons. But when it comes down to a choice between two dirtbags and one is on the forty-man, even though he has terrible numbers, he wins. That way the big club doesn't have to shuffle the guys currently on the forty-man roster and risk losing a guy they like by running them through waivers. They take a guy off to put you on, they could lose him."

"I wish they'd lose Dallas," I grumbled.

"Don't worry, in September, if you're still pitching like this and he's still pitching like crap, they'll get rid of him and call you up."

"September is almost three months away! What are the chances I'm still this hot then?"

"You're a machine. You'll be fine."

"Machine, my ass. I don't want to have to be perfect for three months when I've earned the opportunity now."

"Oh, I know, you're the best, baby. You're the man. You'd be a terror up there. But the game isn't fair, no matter what league they play it in."

"Will you quit saying that?"

"As soon as it becomes fair, I'll call you, I promise."

I slouched into the wall and tried to calm my breathing. Chip peeked in the doorway and indicated he was going to the ballpark, and I waved him off to go without me.

"What do I do now?" I asked Adam.

"Keep doing what you've been doing."

"And if I don't? If I never do this good again?"

"Don't think like that. You've made your mark in this league. You're an all-star here."

"Don't say that word. That could be the reason I wasn't called up and Dallas was."

"Why do you say that?" asked Adam.

I hadn't told him I turned down the All-Star game to go home to be with Bonnie. Admitting it to him made my stomach turn. Instead of the whole truth, I said, "Dallas made the All-Star team and I didn't, that bastard."

"Yeah, it makes him look better," said Adam. "Makes him look more valuable for a trade."

I slapped a hand to my head. *I knew it!*

"But don't worry. Teams know who you are, Shizzle. If you don't make it this year, what you've done will put you at the front of the line next year. You just get your mind back into kill mode and this won't even be a blip on the radar."

"You sure about that?"

"Of course I'm sure. I'm your agent, would I lie to you?"

* * *

Weeks passed. Angry, bitter weeks in which I spent a lot of time pissed at baseball, cursing it and Dallas, and the brass, and the whole goddamn industry. Ironically, I pitched better than I ever had before. I struck hitters out in bunches and threw harder too. It was like every time I took the mound I did so with the intent of striking out Triple A altogether. I wanted to show anyone up there watching that they made a mistake, that I was the right guy and they should have picked me. But it was pointless. I wasn't going anywhere, and the harder I tried the more frustrated I got.

Then, after the anger ran its course, I began to feel sorry for myself. That's when I let my guard down. In Vegas I took a beating so bad it ruined my entire first half of work. I gave up seven runs in a third of an inning; another pitcher and I combined for nearly thirteen runs in the same inning, all earned—a league record. My ERA, which was holding steady in the 3s, shot up to a high 5. It would take me a couple months of uninterrupted success to get it back down to something respectable. Now it was no longer a question of whether I could be perfect for the rest of the year, but a requirement for me to be perfect if I was going to convert this season of success into the fulfillment of a big league dream.

The pendulum of my life in ball was on the downswing again, and the regret everyone warned me about started to take over. I feared that refusing my bid to the All-Star game was another mistake, just like not going to Winter Ball, or attempting marriage and baseball at the same time. I could feel my window of opportunity slipping shut, and it felt like a lie—a big, fat, heavy lie about how the best player always gets promoted. It tormented me with its injustice, and nothing Bonnie or Adam or even Abby said to me made it any better.

Weeks turned into months, and soon the end of the season was in sight. Making it to the Bigs, however, was just as far out of view for me as ever. Chip got called up, then sent back down. Hamp went up, then Bentley. Hundo went up, Headley too, and several others came and went. I, *naturally*, remained behind. I told everyone who got their wish granted I was excited for them, but I was seething with jealousy. As happy as I was about being a player in Triple A at the beginning of the season, I was now equally bitter for the same reason. The only occurrence that brought me any marginal satisfaction was that Dallas, as predicted by Adam, pitched poorly, got traded, and then, got sent down again. He was out of the system and I'd never have to deal with him again. Still, he'd made it, after all the shit he pulled, the son of a bitch made it—something I now feared I'd never be able to say.

Chapter Forty-five

With about two weeks left in the season, I marched into the clubhouse's weight room after I was pulled from another bad outing. When I arrived, I was already working out the numbers of my failure in my head, calculating my new ERA, totaling up fresh hit to strikeout ratios. I had worked my statistics back into something respectable after the Vegas blowup, not what I had before the All-Star break, but maybe good enough for a September call up, I hoped.

I started running on the treadmill, shooting for a mile, or whatever distance it took to catch up with peace of mind. Numbers and possibilities chased after me as I ran. I kept thinking about how many days there were left in the season, and if this outing would be the one that knocked me out of the running, or would it be the next one?

I hit a mile without remembering how I got there, then stopped the machine and let the slowing treads eject me from the back of the mill. Wiping sweat from my brow, I looked at my reflection in the mirrored walls of the weight room. In my heart I knew numbers weren't the issue. I needed more than that. I needed someone to say I was the right guy, someone to say I was worthy, someone to say yes. I needed someone to look at me and say yes, goddammit, yes, this guy is worth the call up, this was the guy worth rearranging a roster for.

The game ended. I sat at my locker as the other players filed in, throwing down their equipment and peeling off their sweaty clothes. Runoff from the ice my arm was wrapped in dripped down from my elbow and formed a wet spot on the floor next to my own dirty cleats and damp hat. My God, I thought, I was so close—did they see how close I was? Did they understand how much this season meant to me, that if I didn't make it after all I'd accomplished this year, it would be like lifting an impossible weight to convince myself I could do it next year when the strike-outs might not come and bats might not break?

"Dirk." Abby came behind me and laid a hand on my shoulder.

"What's up, Abby?" I asked, returning from the abyss.

"Oh, Ready wants to talk with you about that play."

The pitches, hits, and results rolled through my mind. "Which play?" I asked.

"He'll tell ya. He just wants to make sure your head's in the right place."

My head is where I need it to be, I thought as I went grudgingly into Ready's office. I was focused on my job, so focused I was practically strangling it.

When I crossed the threshold of Ready's office, Abby shut the door behind me, effectively saying this was going to be a bad meeting. I did my best not to show my anger with the timing of a private chew out by the manager, even though we were out of the hunt for the Triple A playoffs by a dozen games. Ready was not a manager to be trifled with. If he sensed I was bitter at him, he'd step on my neck for the rest of the year and not let up.

I sat in front of Ready's desk. He looked at me with tired, annoyed eyes, as if this meeting was a waste of his time, one he wouldn't have to hold if I hadn't gotten sloppy.

"I know it's late in the season, but you give up a knock, you got to back up the bag," said Ready.

For Christ's sake! I screamed inwardly, *I was in the vicinity. Who cares if I didn't form a perfect eclipse with the outfielder's throw? Come on, Ready, is this necessary?*

"I know," I said. "I'm sorry."

"You're better than that. I shouldn't be having this meeting with you."

"I know," I said, and dropped my head.

He sighed through his nose, then leaned back, crossing his hands behind his head. Abby didn't say anything, just sat there, quiet, looking at the floor.

"Okay," said Ready. Then, just as tired and annoyed, "This Saturday you're heading to San Francisco to pick up Maddux's start in the Padres' rotation."

My head snapped up and my focus narrowed in on him. His face was so placid, I thought I had imagined the words. I looked to Abby, who simply looked back at me with the same casual look.

"What?" I asked, tentatively.

"You're flying out Friday to join the big league team in San Fran," repeated Ready.

"I'm going to the big leagues?" I asked.

"Yes," said Ready.

"Yep," said Abby, and he patted a hand on my shoulder.

"Congratulations," said both of them.

The walls started to bend and ripple as reality and fantasy collided in real time. Something like vertigo hit me, though I was still sitting in Ready's office chair.

"I'm going to the big leagues," I repeated to myself, saying it out loud as if checking it to be real. Ready and Abby stood up. I shook their hands, thanked them for the opportunity, guidance, support. Then I hugged Abby, and thanked him for putting up with me.

"I told ya things would even out," he said. "Now go up there and keep doing what you been doing."

"I'll . . . I'll . . . I'll do my best."

"I know you will," said Abby.

I stood there for a second, taking it in. I had no idea what to do next. I had spent all my life waiting for this conversation to happen, but now that it had, I had no clue how to act.

"What the hell are you still in here for?" asked Ready, finally smiling at me. "You got a lot of people to call."

Chapter Forty-six

It was nearly 11 P.M. by the time I made it out of the spontaneous locker room party held in my honor. Everyone wanted a turn at whacking me on the back and telling me they had a feeling I was going to get the call. Ox told me he was proud of me and that I'd better go shove it up someone's ass in the Show to make them sorry for waiting so damn long to call on me. Other guys said good luck, offered their best, and gave me unsolicited advice. It wasn't until one of the older journeymen players told me my news was just as much my family's as it was my own that I had the wherewithal to break out of the festivities and make some long distance calls.

I pushed open the dugout doors and made my way out onto the field's turf. The sound of blowers herding stadium trash into piles on the stairs echoed through the place. The light arrays that illuminated the field were cut down to only a handful of lightbulbs, under the glow of which the grounds crew raked and pounded dirt. To avoid the noise, I walked down to the home bullpen, to my favorite spot next to the ivy. There, I pulled my cell phone from my uniform pants rear pocket and dialed Bonnie.

"Hello?" came the groggy voice of my fiancée. It was 2 A.M. her time.

"Hey, honey, were you sleeping?"

"Yeah . . ." she mumbled. There was the sound of ruffling blankets followed by the distinct din of head plopping onto pillow. "It's okay, I was dreaming of you." Her breathing hissed through the receiver indicating she'd probably laid the phone on the pillow next to her head.

"Well, sorry to wake you but I've got some—"

"We're getting married," she continued mumbling. When she's not really awake, her voice has a drunken fairy quality to it, sweet yet incoherent like she was high and about to pass out.

"Yes, yes, we are, but—"

"I wish you were here," she said, chuckling to herself before adding as naughtily as she could muster in her state, "in my bed. I was having a sexy dream about you."

"I wish I was there too, but—"

"Less than fifty days," she said. "Then we can have sex."

"Uh, yes. Yes, we sure can."

"We're going to have lots of it."

I looked around the stadium, paranoid that someone else could hear where this conversation was going. "Of course."

"I'm excited," she said, though the words came out like someone mumbling in their sleep.

"Me too, but—"

"What are you wearing?"

"Bonnie, I've got some *big* news."

"That's great. Are you wearing those baseball pants? I like those."

"Bonnie, I need you to wake up and think about why I would call you this late at night to tell you I have big news."

After a moment or two, her pillow breathing stopped cold. Then, all manner of fabric noise from her overstuffed, princess-quality comforters reverberated through the phone. The creaking of the bed told me she was sitting up. Finally, the loud voice of a fully awake and head-against-phone Bonnie surged through the line. "You're going to the big leagues! Oh my God, you're going to the big leagues!"

"You know, I've only been waiting my entire life to say this to someone and you just go and steal my thunder."

"You are!" She got hold of herself. "I'm sorry, you're right. You say it. Let me hear you say it."

"Bonnie, I'm going to be a big leaguer. I got the call."

Screaming caused me to take the phone away from my head. There was the sound of jumping and ecstatic laughing. Then, when she calmed down, she brought the phone back to her head. "I have to tell my parents. I have to wake them up!"

Bonnie ran down the hallway and blasted through her parents' bedroom door. I was standing in the middle of left field now; I'd wandered there during Bonnie's attempt to turn the call into an X-rated chat line. Though I was very much in the Portland outfield, I was also very much in Bonnie's parents' bedroom. From my dual location, I could hear stadium trash collecting commingled with the sound of Bonnie's mother freaking out that someone had broken into the house. Bonnie rehashed the news, and though I didn't catch much, I did hear Bonnie's mother say, "Praise the Lord," followed by Bonnie's father saying, "Amen. Now go back to bed 'cause some of us have real jobs."

Bonnie exited as instructed before telling me, "They both said congratulations."

"Did you tell them you were excited to have lots of sex with me?"

"I would never say that to them. My mom's head would explode."

"I think you should have led with that, kicked the bedroom door open and screamed it at them. That would have gotten their attention. It got mine."

"This got their attention just fine." She shut her door. "Oh my God, and now you're a big leaguer! I'm so proud of you! This is so awesome."

"Yeah, it's so surreal. And they say the pants up there are ultra-sexy too."

"Who else have you told?"

"No one. You're the first person I called."

"You didn't call your parents? Honey, you have to call them. You can call me back. I won't be going to bed now!"

As instructed, I got off the phone and dialed my parents. The phone rang and rang and finally, just when I thought I was going to get kicked to the answering machine, my mom picked up.

"What's up?" she said, tailoring her greeting to the caller ID.

I tried to play it cool. "Took you long enough."

"I was watching the SciFi Channel and I couldn't get up from the recliner. Whaddya want?"

"Is Dad up?"

"No, why?" A munching noise came through the phone indicating she was eating.

"What are you eating?"

"Just the popcorn stuck to my shirt. What do you want or did you just call to ask what I was eating?"

"Go wake Dad up."

She scoffed, "What? Why? Your dad's in bed."

"Well then, get his ass out of bed. I want to talk to him now!" I demanded outrageously.

"Jesus, Mary, and Joseph, alright, hold on." Mom marched upstairs and woke Dad.

"What?" he asked, his voice surprisingly awake, probably from being trained to wake on command from the days my brother stumbled in drunk.

"Put me on speakerphone."

"Alright." He took the phone from his head. "Christ, I can't find the button. Pat, what button is it? Don't know why they have to make 'em so damn small." After much laboring, the phone clicked over to speaker. "Alright, go ahead."

"Mom, Dad," I announced majestically, "your son is going to be a big leaguer."

"What?" Mom stammered, though she'd heard me fine.

"I got the call. I'm going to the Show to replace Maddux in the rotation on Saturday."

"What?" This time Mom screamed it.

"I said I'm going to the big leagues!"

My mom started wailing like a hysterical idiot. "Oh my God, Dirk. Oh my God, Sam! Sam! Sam!" Her voice was deafening over the speakerphone.

"What, what, what? For fuck sakes, woman, I'm right here. I heard him."

Mom got real close to the phone so it sounded like she was shouting at me. I had to tell her to talk at a tolerable volume on multiple occasions as she mined every single detail of the event and what it meant for the future of the free world. As I recounted the whole thing to the pair of them, some of the guys walked out of the dugout entrance heading to their cars and shouted at me, in emotional, schoolgirl voices, *"Oh Mommy, Daddy, I'm going to be a big leaguer!"* Then they made kissing noises. I gave them the finger.

"Maddux, huh?" said my dad. "Well, that's good." He cleared his throat. "That's real good. You earned it, kid . . . Replacing Maddux." He was happy, I could tell by his voice, which seemed genuinely touched to the point of breaking into emotion. I could just see him nodding his head and smiling like he did when the good music played, repeating to himself the verse about me taking Maddux's spot in the rotation.

"This came at a great time. What a great wedding present," said Mom.

"I know, right?"

"We're going to have to get the MLB package now so we can watch you," said my mom. Then, as she realized what it meant. "Oh my God, Dirk. You're going to pitch on television—in front of millions of people. Millions of people! Oh my God, *oh my God!* I'm going to have a heart attack watching you pitch. Jesus Christ almighty, this is going to kill me."

Chapter Forty-seven

It was pathetic how little I had to pack. I could fit my entire wardrobe in my suitcase, which, though new at the beginning of the season, was now beat to hell from a full year of red-eye flights and playing demolition derby with twenty-four other minor leaguer suitcases.

The only outfit I didn't stuff into my battle-damaged bag was the suit I'd cobbled together from pickups at the Goodwill and Chip's donated shoes. That's what I was traveling in. I'd spent the whole season wearing it with no concern about what anyone might think of me, but that changed today. I was on my way to a world of luxury automobiles and custom apparel; I would be like a peasant boy standing before the royal court.

I was supposed to fly out on Friday and meet the team in San Francisco. Though I was arriving well before the Friday night game started, I was told explicitly not to show up at the park before the day of my start. I wasn't sure why this was such a big deal. In fact, I thought it would be a good idea for me to get there the night before and get my feet wet. I didn't dare question it, though, lest I sounded ungrateful and undeserving.

Because my flight was on Friday but I got my news on Tuesday night, my last few nights in Portland were like being stuck in limbo. Though I was both a big leaguer and a minor leaguer, I wasn't allowed to play with either team. Every time I goofed around like normal, practicing new pitches or conditioning by throwing the Aerobie with the boys, I got yelled at by players who thought I was crazy for risking my dream job. "What if you hurt yourself?" they'd ask. I'd tell them it was no different from any other day I'd have fun at the park, that this was all just part of my routine and it was important to treat life as normal, but they insisted it wasn't normal. They insisted I was a big leaguer now and I was just tempting fate to screw everything up. They told me war stories of guys who cut themselves on beer cans the night before their plane flights, guys who twisted ankles or pulled obliques, guys who tore their labrums playing catch. I believed them, of course, why wouldn't I? I had everything to lose at this point, and soon I started treating myself as if I was made of porcelain.

It was great to know I was going to the big leagues, but finding out three days ahead of time turned out to be a bad decision. With nothing to distract me from the impending climax of my crucible of a baseball career, I started to get nervous. I started asking other players with big league experience for comfort. Instead, I got admonitions grounded in hearsay and wives' tales about what I should do up there under penalty of rookie death, as well as things I should never do under penalty of rookie death. Often these tales contradicted each other, but the one thing I took away from them was that, if I could be sure of nothing else, I could at least be sure the experience was probably going to kill me.

When Friday morning came, the Beavers' clubhouse crew came and gathered up all the apartment furnishings. There was the possibility I'd go up to make the start and then get sent right back to Triple A after the game, but since the apartment lease was up at the end of the month, I'd have to move out, regardless. In fact, Chip, via the aid of his short-lived big-league paycheck, had already moved into a hotel a few days before. I watched the furniture loads leave the building, one after another, the disassembling of my last moments as a career minor leaguer. My air mattress, Memory Foam, and linens were all donated to the Triple A stockpile of home furnishings. Our pot, pan, and the ironing board on which we shared so many meals. Our television that distracted Luke and Chip's kids. The lawn chair I got drunk off Kool-Aid in while watching *Harry Potter*. Even the extra paper towels we used as bath towels because we forgot to buy actual bath towels. Seeing it empty made the place feel barren. Not because of a lack of furniture, but because of a lack of memories. Or, maybe it felt that way because when my air mattress left, it revealed how clean the carpet was before we moved in since we'd failed to vacuum during the season.

When it was time to leave, I put on my suit, hefted my bags, and took a cab to PDX. As we rolled along, I watch Portland pass from the back of a cab. The nervousness subsided for a moment and I slipped away. It was not the trees or the buildings I beheld; rather I saw my life projected on Portland's landscape like it was some giant screen showing my history as the feature presentation.

I could see myself playing T-ball, running the bases in the wrong direction. I could see my Little League teams eating ice cream, even after we lost. I could see summer leagues where my parents fought favoritism to get me playing time, the awkwardness of high school, the donning of a letterman's jacket, a scholarship to college.

Then, the memory of my initiation into professional baseball. I was drafted in the eighth round. The contract came overnight in the mail. I signed with shaking hands and went out to celebrate with my family at a cheap Chinese restaurant. It was the last time I could remember everyone in my house being excited enough about my baseball career to put aside the drama. I had made it into the elite. I was going to get paid to play baseball, and though I didn't know how little I'd make at the time, I didn't care. I would have walked through fire for the chance to play and, indeed, I did.

I paid the cabby robotically and checked in at the airport in a fog. On an escalator inside the airport, people buzzed by like worker bees. Did they know what I had just become? Did it matter to them that I had been made sports royalty? A treadmill spit me out in front of my gate, and as I stood there in front of it, in front of my future, I couldn't help but think of the years of my career spent spinning my wheels to get here. I remembered the demotion I took to spend my fourth year in A ball. That feeling of helplessness, and how all the hope I had to keep fighting slipped away. I remembered the anger and outrage, doubt and pain. I remembered the consuming jealousy as those around me moved forward while I was left behind, written off as a washout, told I was a bust. I remembered what it was like to resent baseball, to hate it.

How many times had I gone through airports like this? Traveling away from home and loved ones to try my hand at being a better string of numbers than the next guy? How many times had I sat in the back of cabs, navigating unfamiliar streets for a chance at a chance? How many bus trips to nowhere towns for nobody teams? I'd seen six years of my life pass by staring out windows, looking into an uncertain future with nothing to hold on to except the old cliché, "As long as you have a jersey on your back, you have a chance." I was a long shot, a non-prospect, and if the things websites wrote about me were true, I wouldn't be standing here. I had turned my career around and put myself back on the map. I had beaten the odds and refused to be written off. I had learned. I had grown. My dues were paid in full, and it was time for me to take hold of my purchase. The culmination and inspiration for every dream, doubt, and drop of sweat was waiting for me at my destination, and I was flying to meet it first class.

Chapter Forty-eight

Compared to the bargain bin motels that touted Frosted Flakes in turnstile dispensers, the big league hotel in San Francisco was a palace. Granite countertops and cherry desks with ornate lamps and bonsai trees; chandeliers of gold and crystal; life-size murals, mood lighting, and Muzak that didn't make you want to rip your ears off. The plane had crashed, I was convinced of it. The plane had crashed and I was dead, and at any moment, angels were going to throw me out of the place.

There was a store in the lobby where you could buy a suit or an expensive watch, and a restaurant that promised excellent steak if you had an excellent bank account. Marble beneath my feet, crystal above my head, surrounded by smiling, well-groomed people who stood ready to assist me. I wanted to fall to my knees to kiss the floor of this temple. In fact, there was a strong feeling that at any moment the whole scene could break into spontaneously choreographed dancing with me twirling around the place singing my joy as bellhops pushed high-note-hitting waitresses around on luggage carts.

The lady behind the check-in desk greeted me with, "How may I help you, sir?"

I stared at her in wonder, and then I got to say words that made me feel like I was declaring, "Let there be light," and actually had all the power to back it up. "Yes," I began with a smooth, deep voice, "my name is Dirk Hayhurst, and I'm a player on the San Diego Padres. I believe you have a room for me?" Boom, that just happened.

I expected the words to knock the woman behind the desk over with their sheer awesomeness, but she stood firm and replied, "Oh, wonderful," before punching away at the keyboard.

"Looks like I do have a room for you, Mr. Hayhurst." She handed me my key and gave me directions to the door it would unlock. "Would you like someone to take up your bags?"

My bags were parked beside me with the one marked with the giant Padres logo sitting prominently on top. I made sure all the tags and labels faced out as visibly as possible. If bystanders didn't recognize me, at least they would recognize the logo, and maybe do the math that I was a player, and then whisper about me in that way I'd always dreamed about, ever since the concept of celebrity through sport had first entered my brain. If I would have had a big league ID card, I would have dropped it in the middle of the crowded halls announcing, "Silly me, always dropping *my big league ID. Us big leaguers* can be so clumsy sometimes." I wanted to be noticed. I wanted to shout and tell the whole world that yes, Dirk Hayhurst was a big leaguer, the approachable, praisable kind who carried his own luggage!

"No thanks, I can handle it." I left the front desk and paraded my way to the elevators. I kept note of every stray look that lingered on me or my luggage and even of some that didn't. Then, while strutting down the hallway, I ran into Luke.

"Hey!" we shouted at the same time.

"Congratulations!" Luke followed up. We traded a man-hug. I knew he was here, of course, and had we not run into each other in the lobby, I'd have searched him out immediately.

"Thanks, man, wow, I can't believe this is for real." I grabbed his shoulders with both hands and squeezed them in my excitement.

"It sure is, man, you earned it. When I heard you were coming up, I was so happy for you—told you to keep your head up, didn't I?" He whacked me in the side in that atta-boy way.

"I know you did, thanks. What a great time for this to happen, huh?"

"Is there such a thing as a bad time to get a call up?"

"You know what I mean."

"Sure. How's Bonnie taking it?"

"She's ecstatic."

"That's great. That's just great." Luke's words meant a lot, but his face said the most important stuff. The knowing way he smiled while looking off to some familiar memory told me he was recalling the moment he was in my place. Every player who has been through the experience knows just how wondrous it is. It can't be summed up in one moment but through a series of them chained together as we players enter our new life as a big leaguer in its full spectrum. The first-class flight, the big league hotel, trying to get people to notice your team bag: they were but the tip of the iceberg. Luke recalled these moments when he saw the elation on my face; those, and many more I had yet to know.

"You're starting tomorrow, right?" Luke looked back at me. His face changed, indicating he knew something I didn't.

"Yes."

"Nervous?"

"Oh my God, am I ever." In fact, every time I thought about it I got shaky.

"I got something that can help you with that. Come with me."

We got into an elevator with glass panels exposing views out over the city and its historic buildings, bridges, and bay. It all seemed too surreal. I'd been to San Francisco once before, but not like this. I was a tourist then. I thought buying crap in Chinatown was the coolest thing ever. Now I was a reason people toured.

Luke watched me as I took it all in. He chuckled to himself.

"You going to be my catcher tomorrow?" I asked.

"Nope. I'm not even going to be here tomorrow."

"What! Why?"

"Got sent down. They told me last night. I leave for the airport in about thirty minutes."

"Was it to make room for me?" I felt terrible. I knew who came up and went down was out of our control, we were just pawns. Still, Luke was a friend, and it was hard to know if I was mixed up in his descent.

"Not your fault. Tactical decision by the brass. Bard's coming off the DL. Don't worry, I'll probably be back in a couple of days when they expand the roster for September."

"And you are cool with this?"

He shrugged. "I made it, I caught Maddux's 350th win, and I'll probably get to come back in September. I can hang out in Portland for a few days. At least this way I'll get to play every day again."

I had forgotten that Luke's main role in the Bigs this year was to sit on the bench. He seemed excited to play again, even if it was in Triple A, which I'll admit baffled me because we'd always joke about how we'd happily collect splinters in our ass as long as we were collecting the Big League minimum. I didn't articulate those thoughts, since now didn't seem like the right time for such talk.

The doors opened on Luke's floor. We exited the elevator and made our way to Luke's room. He opened the door to a stunningly appointed suite: a king-size bed with heaps of throw pillows, a desk with a glass tabletop, panoramic views of the city, a Jacuzzi tub in a bathroom with marble floors, and a forty-two-inch flat screen television—a good one I couldn't afford even with my store discount at Circuit City.

"How on earth did you manage a room to yourself?"

"What do you mean? We all have our own rooms here."

"Are you serious?" Like I said, all the good stuff about being in the Bigs doesn't hit you at one time. "This just keeps getting better!"

"Yeah man, it's great." There was a certain bittersweet candor to Luke's tone, seeing that his bags were packed next to his bed. While I wandered around the room inspecting the place, he opened one of his suitcases and fished out a pill bottle. He shook out two blue pills and handed them to me. They looked like little blue diamonds, which made me think they were Viagra. I wasn't sure what he was insinuating. I'd heard the big leagues change people, but how Luke could go from a devoted family man to a dude popping Viagra to do Lord knows what so fast was beyond me.

"I don't think I need any Viagra, Luke. I know it worked for Palmero, but, uh."

"They aren't Viagra. They're sleeping pills. Blue Bombers, we call 'em. We can get them up here because the doctors come right into the clubhouse and write you a prescription, if you need them. It helps us regulate our sleeping when we do the harder traveling. Or"—he raised his eyebrows—"when we're nervous as hell."

I rolled the pills in my hand. I knew some guys who took them in the minors and they would talk about how magical they were. I was always jealous of them because while I'd sit crunched on the rumbling buses unable to sleep, they'd pop one of these and knock themselves out. We'd cover their sleeping bodies in discarded garbage wrappers as a punishment for slumbering while the rest of us suffered.

"Awesome! How do I take 'em?"

"Stick 'em in your mouth and swallow."

"I know, but when?"

"Before you want to go to bed. They'll help you sleep through the night. Trust me, tonight might be the hardest night you've ever had in baseball."

"Thanks, dude."

"Sure. And good luck tomorrow, I have to get going now. I don't want to miss my flight."

"No other sage advice for me?" I asked. I was a little sarcastic when I asked this, but that was just to hide the real, nearly tangible anxiety that had been building in me since I got the news. Once Luke left, I'd be alone in this hotel with nothing but the do-or-die tales of life in the Bigs as recounted by the guys back in Portland to keep me paranoid and terrified. I was nearly as afraid of violating the unwritten codes as I was of taking on the Giants in front of a national audience tomorrow.

"Keep the ball down, pitch like you have been, you'll be fine."

"I'm not talking about that. I'm talking about not screwing up big league etiquette and getting crucified. I've heard"—I swallowed—"stories."

"The only thing I can tell you for sure is, don't take the team bus anywhere."

"Why not? It says I'm supposed to." I took out my travel itinerary and tapped my finger on the sheet.

Luke shook his head. "I know what it says, but don't take the bus, trust me. Unless you got like ten years in the Show, take a cab."

"Why have a team bus if you can't take it?"

"I have no idea. Just make sure you're not on it."

"I don't understand why they wouldn't just say that on the itinerary if—"

"Welcome to the big leagues." Luke smiled. "Oh, and get used to hearing that every time you don't understand something but you still have to do it: 'Welcome to the big leagues.'"

"Wonderful, what other traps await me up here?"

"Just do what all the other young guys do. They'll show you. Keep your mouth shut, keep your head down, do your job, don't piss anybody off, don't get on the team bus, don't forget to . . . Oh, you'll figure it out. Just worry about tomorrow."

"I've got worrying more than covered, thanks."

"You're gonna be fine. Relax."

That seemed impossible now that I knew there were punishments and thrashings mismarked on the itinerary. I kept asking Luke to explain, but he had no concrete answers for me. He kept saying I'd just have to feel it out.

"Alright. I gotta go. Do great, I'll be following." He gave me another man-hug, wished me luck, then made his way to the door. Before it shut, he caught it, looked back in, and said, "Oh yeah, one more thing: if Jilly tries to hug you in the shower, just let him do it. Seriously, it will be better for you in the long run if you do."

"What the hell?"

"Welcome to the big leagues." The door shut, and Luke was gone.

Chapter Forty-nine

My room was actually better than Luke's. It was the same room, but it was clean and pressed with everything in perfect order, and it was mine. The bathroom with all the little soaps and oils and towels folded into the shape of swans was mine. The bed with forty-seven throw pillows and 300-thread-count sheets was mine. Even the private view overlooking downtown San Francisco and the Bay that made it famous—mine. The bill for it all, however, was the Padres', and on that thought, I dropped my bags, kicked off my shoes, and leapt onto the bed like a stage diver. The pillows and comforter swallowed me up, and I lay there sinking blissfully into Egyptian cotton heaven.

Breathing facedown in the luxurious fabric, I started laughing to myself. A player sleeps in a lot of places during his baseball evolution. I'd slept with other teammates on road trips in high school, four of us in one room, two of us per bed. Of course, this would happen around the same age when most teenage boys have a strong paranoia of what homosexuality entailed; thus, those nights were hardly comfortable, with who got beds decided on everything from card games to gladiator fights in the parking lot. Then, college days landed me in dorm bunks, budget hotels, and leftover host family mattresses. In the minors I laid my head on everything from bus floors to backwater budget bungalows. And there was Grandma's house, where praying to the squirrel gods was a must if you didn't want to be up at 6 A.M. This king-size slice of nirvana made me as giddy as a schoolgirl. I rolled over on the bed and did a snow angel in the fabric, spraying pillows and laminated information cards all over the floor.

I spent about an hour milling about the room, counting all the goodies in the well-stocked minibar, looking at prices on the room service list, flexing in the mirrors with my shirt off to see if being in the Bigs actually did make me look sexier. I had a lot of time on my hands, and I didn't want to leave the hotel room because I was afraid I'd break some rule I was not aware of, at least not while anyone else on the team might be in the building.

When I was sure everyone affiliated with the club was at the ballpark, I left the hotel and wandered the streets of the city looking at sites and foraging for food. I called friends and family, and we freaked out about how I was really in the promised land. I called Bonnie and freaked out about how awesome the hotel was. She told me her family freaked out about how she was going to be married to a big leaguer. And we both freaked out about how close we were to saying "I do." There was a lot of freaking out going on.

After food and phone calls, I was back in the hotel room, where I started to feel the tick of the clock. I could only eat so much, or wander so far, or freak out to so many people. My debut was coming, and as bad as I wanted it to come, I was terrified of its arrival. The future was large and looming, and I was running out of distractions. In a matter of hours, I would be in front of the biggest crowd I'd ever known with friends and family all over the world watching.

Anxiety started to take over, and soon I was pacing, hyperanalyzing, looking for omens, searching for signs. What if I was a huge, embarrassing failure tomorrow? *No, no, don't think that way, you're gonna be fine.* Then I made a deal with God that if a certain number of pigeons flew by the window, I'd pitch great. When that didn't happen, I changed the deal to no pigeons, then to clouds in the shape of pigeons, then to just clouds.

That was when I realized that I'd not played catch today. In fact, I'd done nothing baseball oriented at all. As a creature of habit, this did not sit well with me. Under normal circumstances I might have relaxed on this issue; I mean, I have spent entire off days in front of pizza boxes and video games without worry of what my lack of physical activity would mean come the next game day. But this was no ordinary off day. If I wanted to feel like vintage Dirk for tomorrow's game, the game of all games, I needed to throw. I didn't have a lot of options, and I wasn't about to call down to the front desk to ask if there was some nice young man on staff who wanted to come up to my room and play ball, not with a pocket full of blue diamond-shaped pills.

In my equipment bag were my glove and a ball. I pulled both of them out. Next I took all the pillows and sheets off the mattress and flipped it up against the wall. I stripped down to my underwear so as not to stink up my dress clothes since I didn't know when I'd be able to wash them. Then I ran in place, did some jumping jacks and a few light stretches. Glove on, ball in hand, I came set about eight feet away from the upturned king-size mattress. I took my sign and tossed a ball at near point-blank range. It collided with a soft thud, then fell to the floor. If it were a lesser mattress with lesser memory foam, I'm sure the ball would have ricocheted into a lamp or window, but once again, life in the big leagues was better, even when it came to something as mundane as playing catch with a mattress in a luxury hotel in your underwear.

I turned the television to the Padres/Giants game. Cha Sueng Baek was pitching for the Pads. When he came set, I came set. I dug into the pile of the hotel carpet with my toes, watched Baek throw a fastball down and away, then wound up and pretended to do it myself. There was just the center of the mattress for me, but my arm wouldn't know the difference. As far as my arm was concerned, I had a perfect game going through two innings. Then Baek threw an absolutely filthy slider that painted the outside of the strike zone, and the hitter took it off the wall. I stopped and stared at the replay. A bastard pitch peppered off the wall with the flick of the wrist. That just wasn't fair. I looked at the ball in my hand, then to the mattress—I was doomed. I turned the game off.

I was starting to panic. Six years in the minors and I still wasn't ready for this moment. I had to relax. I called Bonnie and told her I was having trouble keeping it together, and she told me I needed to take a bubble bath and listen to music because that always helped her relax. I told her I couldn't take a bubble bath the night before a big league debut start, and she said, "Aren't you the one who says that in this sport it doesn't matter how you get it done as long as you get it done?"

"Fine. You win. But do I have to use bubbles?"

"Yes, they're part of the magic."

I followed her advice and ran a bath, but added so much complimentary bubble formula that by the time I had two inches of water in the tub, bubbles were spilling over the rim and onto the floor. I had to stop and wait for some of the bubbles to melt before I could soak, which took agonizingly long. In the meantime, I went to plan B: the minibar.

Alcohol makes me sleepy, which is why I poured two mini bottles of vodka and a can of Sprite together and slammed it. I'm not sure how much was there, at least enough to make it seem like there was no Sprite in the mixture, but it didn't matter. I had no tolerance for alcohol, and no idea how to make mixed drinks. Chip and Luke always did it for me back at the apartment. A lot or a little, I would feel it, but I decided to err on the safe side by consuming way more than usual. I thought for sure it would put me under, but hard liquor swilled quickly doesn't have the same effect as when it's sipped in a calm, unforeboding, the-rest-of-your-life-doesn't-hinge-on-this type of environment. About fifteen minutes after consumption, I was irritable, confused, and lashing bubbles off the tub with a towel spun into a whip. I still wasn't tired, which led me to believe I didn't have enough. I went back, grabbed another bottle, and bombs away. Shortly afterward, I was floating in some dreamlike state while water and bubbles gushed over me and onto the bathroom floor. I knew what was going on, but I didn't know exactly why, nor did I really care. I was warm, wet, and things were great. I was gonna be a big leaguer tomorrow. "Hell yeah! I'm gonna be a fucking big leaguer!" I yelled in the bathroom as I pressed the warm, foamy bubbles into my face in an attempt to cover my head like a sheep.

About this time the phone in the bathroom rang. I don't remember picking it up, but sure enough, I was talking and the water had stopped running. The organization's pitching coordinator's raspy voice grated through the receiver. I was shocked to hear him and tried to calm the wavy ocean of alcohol my brain was adrift on long enough to sound coherent.

We hadn't talked in a long time, but he was calling to wish me luck, the most awkward luck I've ever been wished. It's strange getting a call from an old coach out of nowhere, but even more so while you're in a bubble bath, wasted, and obliviously taking a piss while it happens. I had enough sense not to say much, but I can't be sure if I really did keep my mouth shut or just can't remember what I said. I think we had a good conversation, actually. From what I recall, he kept repeating a lot of baseball clichés like, "It's the same game, pitch like you are capable," and "Do what you did to get yourself there." He also kept telling me he was proud of me, how he really wanted me to make it after all I'd been through— how I had a good head on my shoulders. He just kept saying the same stuff over and over again, which led me to believe he'd been drinking. That pissed me off. I mean, what kind of boss calls you up buzzed to tell you how proud he is of you while you're drunk in a bathtub? Have some self-respect, for God's sake. Then I dropped the receiver in the water.

By the time we finished our conversation, the tub water had gotten cool and I was aware enough to know I needed to sop up what spilled on the floor. I threw some towels down, dried myself, then slid into bed. I was sleepy, but just in case the alcohol wore

off before I went under, I had the pièce de résistance: Luke's sleeping pills. I popped one and minutes later my head hit the pillow
like a sledgehammer.

I heard it chirping at me from far away, like some annoying
bird that needed to be shot. I was warm and safe and cozy in a
black abyss of pills and alcohol, floating beyond the bounds of
space and time. All was good in the universe except for that goddamn bird that would not shut up. It persisted, growing louder
until it didn't sound like a bird anymore. It sounded like a phone.

I woke up to the phone ringing beside my head. It was about
12:30 A.M. I had only been in bed for an hour, if that. Who the hell
was calling me? I didn't give a shit how happy my pitching coordinator was for me, so help me God, if he was on the line I was
going to tell him to shove his advice straight up his ass. It probably
wasn't him; it probably was some jackass fan who asked the hotel
for my room so he could call and harass me about how bad I was
gonna get my tail kicked tomorrow. It was my stupid fault, I
should've seen that one coming, should've changed my name at
the front desk to Harry Rosinbag or something.

I picked up the receiver with an intense fury but what came out
was a groggy, illegally medicated, "Hellope."

"Dirk, this is Darren Balsley." The big league pitching coach.

"Oh, hey," I rubbed my face, perking up instantly, "how are
you?" I pulled myself from my cocoon of blankets and sat upright.

"I'm fine. Did you see the game tonight?"

"Yes," I responded immediately. "Yes, I did." An interesting
first question; it made me seriously wonder if there was going to
be a quiz about the game. Was he going to ask me about what
pitches were thrown to whom or if I memorized the hitters'
stances and scouted them for weaknesses? I couldn't remember
my last name at this point. Is that what they do the night before—
have phone conferences about hitters? Why didn't Luke tell me
that?

"What are you up to right now?"

Oh Jesus, they do. Was he on his way up to my room now? "I'm in bed, actually. I went to bed early because I knew I'd have trouble sleeping tonight. This is one of the most nerve-racking nights of my life. Tomorrow is kind of a big deal for me." I offered a nervous chuckle at the end. I thought it sounded very committed on my part, like I took the job super-serious to get to bed early, but his tone was vacant.

"Yeah, right. About tomorrow, try and get to the park at a decent time. You only get to experience this day once, so try to slow down and really take it for all that it's worth." It's hard to explain, but the way he said it made it feel like he didn't really care much if I took it all in or not, as if he was just saying it like a legal disclaimer.

"Right, absolutely. Once-in-a-lifetime thing, gotta enjoy it. I want to be ready for this." More nervous laughter.

There was a strained pause in the conversation, then, "See you at the park tomorrow."

"Okay, see you there."

"Good night."

I lay down again and stared into the dark of the room. I could feel the pull of all the depressants in my system, but I could not fall asleep. I wanted to so badly, but I couldn't. The more I thought about sleep, the more I couldn't do it. I kept checking to see if I was falling asleep, which made me wake up. Then my mind began to break free of the downers, and I began surging with paranoia again, thinking about the start, the brief phone call, and how it didn't feel right. I lay there for hours, tossing and turning, uncomfortable in the most comfortable bed I'd ever been in.

Chapter Fifty

I took a cab to the park as not directed by my itinerary. Upon my request, it drove me to the players' entrance of Giants' stadium. It was a small, unassuming gate. Even so, there were fans staking it out in anticipation of players' arrivals. Some of them even knew who I was when I got there, shouting my name and holding up my minor league card among other items they wanted signed. I wondered how they knew who I was, not to mention how they knew I'd be there when I myself didn't understand why I wasn't allowed to be there until this very moment.

A security guard asked me for my ID, even though there were people calling for me by name. He took my driver's license and searched his sign-in roster. As his finger slid up and down the list, I worried I wouldn't be on it yet and not allowed in. He found me, though, and directed me inside. I awkwardly gestured to the mysterious people calling for me, explaining I was sorry I had to go pitch and stuff, and couldn't come sign for them just yet.

Like Portland's stadium, the Giants' ballpark had a large service tunnel winding through its underbelly. Supply carts carrying buns and cups and kegs of man-soda zipped around me. I walked along, weaving and dodging until I arrived at a sign that said VISITORS' CLUBHOUSE. I stood there for a second and caught my breath. This was it, I thought, it was time to go to work.

In all honesty, I don't remember the order in which things happened next. It came at me like sensory overload, like I was a dog with a million new things to sniff. I pressed through the locker doors and found myself surrounded by new faces, not all of them players. There was a legion of trainers, clubhouse attendants, and non-player personnel. Someone, not a player, came to me, welcomed me, and took my Padres bag, and then disappeared with it. A few players I didn't know said welcome, while a few players I did know did not. There was some type of computer system that housed several terminals where players sat and looked at videotape. Guys in their underwear milled around with plates of food. A gentleman asked me if I wanted something to eat. Someone asked me if I needed a jacket for the game. Then the food question again. What size pants did I wear? A hat was handed to me. Someone talking in Japanese. Loud laughter. The cafeteria coolers housed beer, and lots of it. A variety of pants options were handed to me. A towel was thrown into a bin just over my head. Cussing at a SportsCenter report: "Can you believe they gave that fucking guy eight million?" More Japanese. Guys on cell phones at their lockers arguing with wives. Trevor Hoffman, standing in front of me, shaking my hand with his huge paws, saying welcome, congrats, good luck, and have fun while I gagged trying to articulate words to him. A trainer told me if I needed anything before the start to come see him. A huge guy with a shaved head poured powder from a canister into a mixer bottle and drank it. A former minor league coach was congratulating me. My stuff was unpacked and organized in my locker. My locker. My name. "Holy shit, that is my jersey! My big league jersey!" Several snaps with my cell phone camera, and then, like someone took their hand off the fast-forward button, a player was standing in front me saying, "Have you talked to Bud Black yet?"

"Oh crap. No, I haven't." A cardinal sin I was warned about making. The first thing you always do upon a promotion is talk to the manager.

"You should probably go and check in."

"Right, of course, where is his office?"

I was pointed in the direction of my new skipper. I took off the new Padres hat I'd put on sometime during the preceding events and went straight to the manager's office. It felt like I had been in the place for an hour, but when I checked the clock I'd only been there about fifteen minutes.

Bud Black was sitting in his office at his desk when I arrived, knocking at his open door. He looked up to me, realizing instantly who I was, and invited me in.

"Dirk Hayhurst," he said in a heralding way, as if he'd heard a lot about me. He shook my hand then sat down, inviting me to do the same before shuffling a stack of stat-riddled papers on his desk. Then, sitting back quite relaxed like we were going to have a chat about muscle cars over a can of beer, he said, "Congratulations. Welcome to the club, we're excited to have you."

I didn't really believe he was excited to have me. I don't know why I didn't, maybe it was because I was nervous as hell or that I hadn't done anything to help the club yet. Maybe it was because stuff like, "We're excited to have you" is traditionally part of the introductory ceremony. Even so, Bud's face was so intensely affirmative I was starting to believe he meant it. In fact, his ease and interest in me made me relax for the first time in several hours. It also made me realize I was just staring at him, mentally debating his words instead of talking.

"You're a Golden Flash, eh?" continued Bud. "From Kent State?"

"Yes, sir," I said.

"The Golden Flashes," he repeated. "And you're a writer?"

"That's correct."

"I've read some of your stuff."

This could go badly. "Oh?"

Bud smiled. "It's good."

I sighed in relief. "You've really done your homework on me, haven't you?"

I wrote a column for *Baseball America,* one of the country's premier baseball publications, called "The Non-Prospect Diaries." I picked the title because I felt it captured the essence of my baseball career. I didn't want baseball players reading it to think I took myself too seriously, since I was a real nobody when I'd started writing a year ago. Now, however, as the skipper of a big league team who would no doubt be sifting every ounce of my competitive character stared me down at the edge of my debut, it mattered big-time.

"Of course," said Bud, "I like to know about my guys."

"I . . . Uh . . . Well, that's great."

He continued smiling at me in that disarming way. "How's Randy doing?"

"Good. He sends his best."

"Good," remarked Bud. "So, you ready for today?"

I didn't know how to respond to that. How can anyone be really ready for a day like this? I knew what the smart, patriotic lie answer was, but I also knew what the real, jumbled, emotionally-out-of-control answer was. Thankfully, Kevin Towers, the team's general manager, knocked on the open door before I had to give either.

As with Bud, I had never met Kevin before and the experience was uncanny. In effect, Kevin had been my boss for years, though we'd never actually communicated before this day. Bud and Kevin were just people, like me, and I knew that. But they were also elite people in my baseball world, people at the top of my profession. I had to earn access to them, and now that I had, I didn't know how to communicate with them in a way that didn't let my whirling emotions come gushing out like a crazy person.

"This is"—I collected myself—"this is amazing. I can't believe I'm really here."

"Well, I need to get your signature on a couple of things before it's official," said Towers. He produced my major league contract and put it in front of me. "This contract will look a little different from your last one," he said with a wry chuckle.

I started reading the contract, looking for what was so funny. When I found it my heart stopped. I hate math, but on that day I fell madly in love with it. Next to the place my name went was a number so large it meant the end of air mattresses, rusted cars, and red-eye flights. The end of value meals, winter retail jobs, and Goodwill suits. It meant life, flexibility, and freedom. They say you can't put a number on happiness, but this one made me feel pretty damn happy. I was to be paid $400,000 to play baseball. Divide that over a full season and that meant I made about $1,800 a night—more than I made in a month in Triple A! It was one of the most beautiful things I'd ever seen in my life. All I had to do was remember how to breathe long enough to sign the contract.

Balsley found me shortly after I inked my name to the end of poverty. Our conversation was brief, sterile, and mostly about hitters. He gave me a quick rundown of the Giants' lineup, who I was going to face and how I should pitch to them. He handed me a sheet that had hitters' hot and cold zones and tendencies to steal. Then, after he briefed me, he said I would be throwing to Bard and I was basically to follow Bard's lead. That was the best part of the meeting, actually, as I wasn't sure what kind of mental state I would be in once I was out there on the hill, but I was pretty certain that calculating swing path data would be the last thing on my mind.

At the end of our conversation, Balsley told me my main priority now was to do whatever I needed to do to get ready, and when I was, we'd head out to get loose. I didn't tell him I didn't know what I needed to do to get ready since I wasn't really a starter. This was only my third start of the year, for a total of five in the last two years. During the other starts I just wandered out to the mound and started throwing to a catcher as if it were mid-game and I got the get-up call to get hot in the pen. That was a routine I knew; however, I didn't think it would go over very well at the big league level, so I formulated a more starter-centric program on the fly. I got a back rub in the training room, drank a protein shake, walked around looking moody like other starters I knew. I looked over the opposing hitters' hot sheet, trying to retain any details I could considering my overstimulated brain. In the end, it was all for nothing as all I could really focus on was the clock, and the fact that in a matter of minutes I would be out in front of the biggest crowd of my life for the most important pitching experience of my existence.

Deadtime is the enemy in moments like this. I wanted to be distracted but, when you're a starter, other players are trained to stay away from you so you can find your "zone." Some starters can't stand being interrupted when they are getting their mind right before a game. Me, on the other hand, if I'm left alone with my mind, it will devour me whole. I suppose I could have talked to someone, but how exactly would that conversation have gone down? "Hey, Hoffman, I'm scared shitless right now, would you mind holding my hand and helping me do some Lamaze?"

When the time finally came for me to head out to the field and warm up, I was thrilled. Pitching is about the moment, and it can create a mental shield made from competitive will focused on the task at hand. But when I walked onto the Giants' field, my defenses were instantly breached.

The stadium was just so big. In fact, the scale of everything was massive. The JumboTron was the size of a house. Seats went on in endless rows. The crowd wasn't even close to capacity, and yet there were more people in attendance here than any of the minor league games I'd ever played in. Walls stretched up to touch light poles, which reached out to tickle the chins of skyscrapers peeking into the park to inspect the new guy. The sound system was louder, the light boards were brighter, abundant concessions, legions of workers, and dozens of cameras. All of it here just for today, an idle Saturday between two basement clubs. It was all disposable, all routine, all absolutely terrifying.

Nothing felt familiar: the ball, my glove, the earth itself. Everything was new, like I'd never seen or touched it before. But it didn't matter. I was to pitch today. I would take that San Francisco mound as a pitcher or a sacrifice to this beast in motion all around me, but I would take it nonetheless.

Bard and I started to play catch in right field, which quickly degenerated into a game of trying to get the ball to Bard. All my life I'd been trained to hit my catch partner in the chest and, for the life of me, today I could not square Bard up. I skunked the ball into the grass in front of Bard. I threw it over his head into the stands. Balsley, standing by with his poker face, replaced the ball as needed, but it wasn't the ball. It was me, and it was labor to even do the simplest of throwing tasks.

When we were finished playing warm-up catch in right field, we went to the mound. Before I threw my first warm-up pitch, I tried very hard to break my funk. I dug out a hole for my feet. Took a deep breath. I marked a place for my landing foot to hit. Took another big breath. I licked the rosin, tried to clear my mind, and focused on my breathing. Coming set as calmly as I could, I gestured for Bard to get down, wound up, and promptly stood Bard up again with a ball over his head.

Usually the visiting starter paces the home team's starter, but Barry Zito had a very different program from me, which is to say, he had a program—I was just trying to learn how to pitch again.

After about twenty errant throws, I started to get some semblance of myself. I even produced a few good pitches, including a changeup that made Balsley say, "I didn't realize your changeup was that good." Understandable, as it's hard to realize someone has good stuff when 90 percent of their throws are in the dirt or the stands.

Balsley's words did make me feel a little better, like, if nothing else, I could throw all changeups today. Trouble was, it took me thirty tosses in the pen to find a good one, a ratio that would have me out of the game before the first inning. I worked as hard as I could to replicate my good fortune, but I was running out of time. Indeed, time was up. Zito was done warming and the Giants were about to take the field.

I got the ball back from Bard, flipped it to Balsley. He handed me a towel, and a bottle of water. We walked into the dugout together and took our seats. The next time I would exit that dugout, I would be a big leaguer, for better or worse.

Chapter Fifty-one

I was naked and scared, stranded atop that patch of red dirt like an orphaned child. A crowd of loaded expectations surrounded me, eyes trained on my every movement. Twisted, scrutinizing faces pressing down, squeezing my breath into short, labored gasps. Cameras zoomed in past the cold sweat on my brow, past the darting eyes under the bill of my hat, and right into my soul. My teammates, whom I'd known for all of the last four hours, stood impassively at their posts waiting to see if I'd survive, or self-destruct in a flourish of pants-wetting and vomit. I was now a cog in the machine of big league baseball, simultaneously the greatest and the least in an industry that devours its weak. The more I tried to look confident, the more I was reminded I wasn't. It was pointless to pretend this was the same game I'd played for the last twenty years of my life. It was not. It was the only game in the only league that would ever truly matter, and I was tied to the hood of it as we barreled recklessly into my destiny.

At this point I think it was safe to say I'd lost my mind. Not in the sense I was insane, although it very well could be construed that way as my thoughts were no longer mine to control. Up they wandered into the press box: to the strokes of the pens recording my "mound presence"; to the minds of my pitching coach and the general manager; to the lips of fans belching, "Who the hell is this guy?"; to the clicks of the cameras and even to tomorrow's headlines—all of this struggle would be summed up in a paragraph pronouncing me a success or a failure.

I wanted it all to stop, but since I knew it wouldn't, I wanted the first hitter to get into the box so I could put my body on autopilot and forget about the world around me. If I could just close the hatches and dive under the chaos of the big league experience, I could disappear into the current of pitching. The rhythmic action of winding and releasing, of focusing on the moment, that routine would become my savior. But the extreme speed at which I was moving blew the hatches wide. I couldn't get a grip on them, or myself. There was no shutting it out, no taking control, just the umpire saying, "Batter up!"

Four seasons ago, in 2005, when I was in class High-A in Lake Elsinore, California, Dave Roberts joined the team on rehab assignment. He'd just been traded to the Padres from the Red Sox where, so the legend goes, he stole the most important base in the history of playoff baseball. The Red Sox were facing certain death at the hands of the Yankees in the 2004 playoffs. Roberts, a short, quick guy, was brought in to pinch run for Kevin Millar, a round, slow guy. In the bottom of the ninth, Roberts took second with two outs at the risk of ending the season for the Sox. He put himself in scoring position and was later driven in to tie a game the Sox would go on to win. This event is believed to be the spark that lit a history-changing fire. Not only did the Sox come back from a three game deficit and win the next four, which had never been done in the playoffs till then, they also went on to win their first World Series title since 1918 via a four-game sweep. Dave's stolen base was considered the "Steal of the Century" and helped break the infamous "Curse of the Bambino." The dude was a Red Sox legend—hell, he was a baseball legend—and there he was sitting in his underwear eating a PB&J in my minor league clubhouse.

The 2005 season was a terrible one for me. It crushed my confidence and left me wondering if I was truly meant to play baseball. Naturally, I took Dave's arrival to be a sign from the heavens. I *had* to speak to him, he was a world champion, after all. Surely his words would be prophetic, and, if not, at least I could get a ball signed.

If he were a pitcher, we might have shared some type of transcending bond, but he was a position player, a fast, muscular, position player—we had nothing in common. I was too afraid to approach him in the wild, so, from a safe distance, head bowed in reverence, I asked if he would tell me even a whisper of what it was like to play in the big leagues. With class and clarity, he set down his sandwich and spoke to me of the marbled halls of the Bigs, where the chosen sat on golden thrones around shrine-like lockers. Where fortunes were won and lost in seconds and inches. Where the masses cheered their champions to victory, and spent ludicrous amounts of money on domestic booze.

When he finished, with starry eyes I asked if he thought poor, pathetic me could ever be one of those great men someday. This was what he said: "Don't let anyone sell you short, you can make it to the Show. But when you get there, no matter what the reason is, remember you've earned the right. You're a big leaguer and you belong. It's a state of mind." I thanked him, tucked his deep and powerful words away, and then ran to a computer to see the worth of his autograph on eBay.

Ironically, Dave Roberts was not only the first active big leaguer to tell me of life in the Bigs, but also the first batter I would face there. As he strode into the box, I thought of our special conversation. Was he thinking of it right now too? I wanted to call time and remind him of the moment we shared: me, young and naïve; him in his underwear with peanut butter. I wanted to tell him that even though I could have gotten about fifty bucks for that ball he signed for me, I didn't sell it. Maybe he'd be moved by my sentiment, and since he'd already made a boatload of cash in his career and would retire a legend, would he be a real chum and strike out? I had to put those thoughts out of my head, however, because Bard was throwing down fingers and it was my cue for my first big league fastball.

Considering how sloppy I was in the pen, how much I'd dwelled on what could go wrong, and how Dave Roberts was baseball royalty, it should come as no surprise that the thought chugging through my head as I wound for my first pitch was, *Don't hit him, don't hit him, don't hit him.* Dave seemed to take on the characteristics of a bulls-eye as I kicked and uncoiled on the mound. Out flew the most distracted, anxious, and uncommitted pitch of my career. The pitch that would punctuate the sentence after my name in the annals of baseball record books was in the air, and a split second later it was caught—ball one, not even close.

Roberts squatted, spun his bat around showing bunt, and might have if it wasn't such an obvious miss. Bard flicked the baseball back to me and I reset. Even while I was getting the sign for the second pitch, I kept thinking about the first one. My brain tried to make sense of it all while my body kept going forward, propelled by adrenaline like some amped-up pitching zombie. Before I knew it, the second pitch was out of my hand and the count was two balls and no strikes.

My second pitch was a bigger miss than my first. The ramifications of walking the first batter of my big league career on four pitches danced in my head like demons around a funeral pyre. I stepped off the back of the mound and went to get a lick of rosin. I tried to calm down, but even as I licked the rosin, I felt the umpire watching my rosin-licking technique. I became acutely aware of every nervous twitch or touch, and even though I vigorously licked my fingers, my tongue was too dry to assist me. Soon I was winding again and ball three was out of my dry, rosin-less hand and into the stretching glove of Bard. Three balls, no strikes.

Time was called. *Oh, for Christ's sake, three pitches in and I'm already getting a mound visit?* Bard jogged out to me, packed the ball into my mitt, and told me to work down in the zone. An explosion of thoughts went off in my swirling head. Guilt for disappointing him; anger for him telling me to work down in the zone because where the fuck else did he think I was trying to work, the backstop? Fear: I wanted him to tell me it was going to be alright, that I was going to survive this, maybe hold me for a few seconds before he left; betrayal because Dave Roberts didn't seem like he knew me, after all we'd been through, that bastard!

"I gotcha, bro, I'll get it down, no problem."

The next pitch was a strike but a merciful one, more gift from the umpire than rediscovery of my ability. In response to this, Dave stepped out of the box and took a breather. *What the hell do you need a breather for, Roberts? I haven't thrown a pitch below the belt yet! Get back in the box you . . . you . . . you false friend!* Dave leisurely dug back in and I took the next sign, wound, and promptly missed for ball four.

Dave scurried off to first base, where he was an even bigger threat than at the dish. Every chastisement I'd ever received from coaches about how lead-off walks score rained down on my confidence like a shower of clubs. I took a deep breath, thought of some advice Hoffman once gave me concerning pulling bad thoughts from my head and throwing them away when pitching in a rough situation, then dismissed it. I wasn't about to lay hands on the snarling swear words snapping in the kennel of my brain.

Ivan Ochoa dug in at the plate while Roberts led off first. I was told before the game, should this situation happen, to expect bunt, but also to expect steal, to pitch fast but remain under control, to be careful but aggressive, to defend but attack—complicated even if I wasn't drunk on a cocktail of hyperexposure. Soon it was two balls, no strikes again.

What the hell is wrong with me? This is just ridiculous, I thought. *My first start in Triple A I punched out the side, now I can't even throw strikes!* I got the ball back and stared down at it in my glove, screaming at it telepathically, demanding that it obey.

Ochoa dug in. Roberts led off. I watched Roberts, Ochoa watched me, Bard watched Roberts, Balsley watched me. Somewhere my mom lit up her third menthol. Roberts inched off the bag. I thought about doing the "slide step" to home, but scratched the idea because I wasn't throwing strikes, and when you aren't throwing strikes, it's not time to be Mr. Fancy Pants with your motion. When I made my pitch, Roberts broke for second. I ducked Bard's tardy throw and Roberts slid in safe. *Dammit!*

After his theft, Roberts called for time as he'd gotten some dirt in his eye from sliding. I wanted to run over and tackle him and put my fist in his eye. *Wouldn't that be something,* I thought. *My first big league game and I go nuts beating on Dave Roberts?*

Dave was just doing his job. He was a good guy. Expecting him to remember an inconsequential little leaguer like me was ridiculous. I had to let it go, it wasn't personal. I had a job to do. If Dave was on my team, I'd be proud of him—I'd hock his signature on eBay all the time, but I'd be proud of him. However, when he took third on a bunt single the very next pitch, I wished to God I'd tackled that false-friending son of a bitch at second!

Chapter Fifty-two

With a man on first and third and no outs, and only one strike thrown, for the first time all day a singular concept took over my mind: making it out alive. Some refer to this moment of a pitcher's clarity of purpose as "locking in," although this is usually accompanied by a pitcher doing something authoritative, like punching out the side. Me, I fell behind on Randy Winn before trading a groundout with the scoring of Dave Roberts—the first out of my career, a force at second. I gave up a double to Aaron Rowan right after that, which scored Winn. Next came a long fly out by Pablo Sandoval, a dude everyone called Kung Fu Panda. With two outs and a man in scoring position and Bud Black standing next to the bullpen phone, I finally ran into the first batter I knew from the minor leagues, Travis Ishikawa.

I liked Travis, especially right now. As strange as it sounds, he was the closest thing to a friend I had at the moment. I didn't know him, never talked to him once in my life, but I liked him because I knew I could get him out. I'd done it before in the minors. The rest of these guys were immortals as far as I could tell, but Travis was a guy trying to get a foothold in the Show, just like me. I found my confidence against him, as well as my breaking ball, and got him to dribble a grounder to second for the third out.

Music played to mark the end of the inning. The fans cheered the Giants' good fortune. I walked off the field trying to look strong and impassive, but I was a wreck. I took my sweaty glove off and sat on the bench. A trainer handed me a cup of water and a dry towel, which I used to swab my head down with. That was the longest inning of my life. It felt like I'd played nine full with how emotionally exhausted I was. I sipped the water and looked out onto the field, watching my guys fight their guys, knowing I was supposed to be leading and not panting to keep up. Zito was making it look easy, throwing strikes, probably using his well publicized yoga training to keep his mind from self-destructing. He had two outs by the time I finished drinking one cup of water.

I crinkled my empty cup and tossed it to the floor. Chase Headley, aka Chase the Magnificent, was up to bat. Chase's arrival in the big leagues was foretold by prospect magazines and media guides for the last few years now, and he'd never failed to deliver. He was an organizational building block, and he had the luxury of knowing it all season long. I, on the other hand, was not. My time here was as much an audition as it was anything else. Yet, we were both here. No one could ever take today away from me. I would always be a member of the elite fraternity of big leaguers, prospect or otherwise. I could always say I got to wear the uni-form, and bore my grandkids with repeated tales of how it was the scariest, longest, most mind-blowing day of my life.

But the goal now was no longer to make it to the big leagues. Now the goal was to stay there. The hype on who would make it to the Show might not matter anymore, but I realized as Chase stood arguing a called strike three to end the inning that the hype on who would stay could matter a great deal. The way I got here meant I wouldn't have the luxury of second chances if I didn't pull myself together. As Chase slammed his bat into the rack, I put my hat back on and ran back onto the field. I had seven warm-up pitches to figure out what the hell I was doing.

It took me half an hour to get through my first half inning. It took Zito less than ten minutes to manage his second. Thankfully, my second went much smoother. Fellow Kent State standout Emmanuel Burriss flicked a single up the middle, then stole second base, but relief came in the form of the pitcher.

I could say that I struck out Zito to end the inning, but no one says that. Zito's the pitcher, and anytime a pitcher comes to the plate, they are generally acknowledged as an automatic out. There are a few athletes out of the bunch who can hit and pitch, but they're a dying breed. Now we are trained strictly to bunt so as not to be completely useless, but to sacrifice bunt only since we are a bigger liability on the base path than at the dish. To claim with any kind of pride that I punched out the pitcher would be like having pride in entering puberty. I struck out "the pitcher" and got Dave Roberts to ground out to end it.

The next inning, Zito and I switched roles as I came to bat. I threw right-handed but I hit left-handed. Back when I was a kid, when my dad thought I was going to be a left-handed power hitter, he told me that lefty was the way to go since it would put me closer to first base. Unfortunately for him, I was slow, which really wasn't that bad, I guess, since I couldn't hit either. Saying I couldn't hit is actually a nice way of putting it; I was an embarrassment at the plate. Over the years, as my pitching kept me afloat in the game, teammates handy with the lumber would pepper me with their guaranteed hitting fixes on how to stand, swing, step, and track. Looking back now, I wonder if they were just messing with me as I never became comfortable at the plate, let alone consistent, and I swung like I was trying to pull-start a lawn mower. In six years of minor league ball, I'd never recorded a hit. My batting average was a career .000. I was as out as out could get, and I hadn't even stepped in the box yet.

Since pitchers know that no one expects them to do anything productive at the plate, some of them treat a two out swing-away situation like free pulls on a slot machine. They swing as hard as they can and hope for the best. After all, who cares if they strike out? That's what they're supposed to do. I, however, entered that box with one goal: not to embarrass myself.

There is some kind of etiquette about tapping the catcher's shin guards when you come to bat the first time. I wasn't sure exactly what I was supposed to do. I wanted to look cool, but I think I just kind of poked him with my bat head. "Take it easy on me," I said. "It's my first time."

The catcher said nothing. I swallowed. Zito wound.

Usually, the first pitch from one pitcher to another in a swing-away situation is a fastball, sometimes referred to as the courtesy fastball in case you're the type of pitcher who feels like swinging and usually ending the at bat on the first pitch. After that, it's all breaking stuff because ESPN highlights look better when the strikeout total next to your name is higher.

I took the first pitch. Courtesy or not, it's remarkably easy to lay off pitches when you know you can't hit any of them. That doesn't mean they can't hit you, though. Lefty on lefty is scary as hell. Zito's arm angle had me edging farther and farther away from the plate on each pitch, but when Zito uncorked that huge hook of his, I bailed out completely. I thought for sure it was going to decapitate me, but when I opened my eyes and looked to the catcher, the pitch was caught just out of the zone for a ball. I was certain I would see his hook again after my reaction, but it didn't come. Zito fell behind on me, and then, as fate would have it, he walked me.

I completely blanked. I was not prepared for this contingency. I stared stupidly at the umpire because ball four did not compute. It had been years since I'd been on first base, and I had no idea what to do there. Out of instinct, I actually took a step toward the dugout before it registered I was going the wrong way. I tried to play my error off like I was just going to give the bat back, forgetting they had people who collected them. Then, instead of cutting my losses and heading to first, I stepped back into the box and looked dull-faced at the umpire again.

"First base is that way," said the umpire, gesturing with a tilt of his head.

"Yeah, r-right. Thank you, sir," I said. I dropped my bat and jogged awkwardly down the line.

I actually made it all the way to third base, but I didn't score. When I arrived there, the umpire asked me when was the last time I was at third base. I said I didn't know. He laughed. Then he told me which direction was home, in case I got lost again.

Back on the mound, I made it through the third inning one-two-three, earning a shot at the fourth. We were still trailing 2-0, but I felt like I was winning if only because I finally had a good inning. If I had another good inning, I might see the fifth.

The Giants had other plans, though. Kung Fu Panda roped a double off me to start the fourth. My dear friend Ishikawa struck out. Then Rich Aurilla grounded out, moving Sandoval to third. With two outs and "The Pitcher" on deck, the executive decision came for me to intentionally walk Emmanuel Burriss to get to Zito. *God bless the National League*, I thought, *where you can always rely on a pitcher to kill the momentum.*

Zito dug in, Panda led off, Bard flashed a curveball. We needed this out so no reason to gamble with a courtesy fastball. My first hook came in for a strike. My second garnered a hack from Zito that looked remarkably similar to my own. When I got the ball back, I thought of how cool it would be to tell my friends I struck out Barry Zito, a multimillionaire, with my curve.

As expected, Bard flashed two fingers for the bender. I came set. Checked the dancing Panda at third. Measured up Zito. Locked on home and hurled a hook that was meant to get me through my third scoreless inning. Zito grabbed his bat and yanked his lawn mower with all his might, squibbing the ball aloft and just over the heads of my infielders. It landed in shallow right for a hit. Panda scored to make it 3-0 Giants.

God damn you, Zito! my mind exploded. *You're ruining my life! You were supposed to strike out, this is the National fucking League!* The fans were all applauding yet laughing at the same time . . . I didn't think it was that funny.

Apparently neither did Bud. He was on the horn to the pen after Zito dinked his RBI single. Soon I could hear the crack of leather coming from the bullpen. As it was, I had a tight pitch count and a short leash. Now I was staring at the top of the order with two runners on.

Dave Roberts was up again, and I knew if I didn't get him out this time around, I would be out of the game. I was pissed off, but it was not distracting. Actually, the anger I was feeling helped me tune out the overwhelming fear of failure I'd been operating under since I'd shown up. I was pissed at everyone and everything, and as long as it had a hold of me, the ramifications of what could go wrong on my next pitch didn't seem to affect me. I wound and pitched at Roberts in attack mode, and, for my effort, he yielded a ground out to get me out of my jam.

Soon after we were off the field, and I was cooling off, Balsley informed me that Cha Seung Baek would be batting in my place. I was offended by that. Not that I wasn't going to get to pitch another inning, and not that they didn't ask me how I felt, but because they had the audacity to take me out of the lineup when I had a 1,000 on-base percentage.

After the game, reporters surrounded me asking what my debut felt like. I didn't know what to say other than the clichéd stuff about dreams coming true. This is what every athlete says after they make their debut, and I now understood why. It's way too complicated to explain all the emotional overload in a snappy sound bite. Saying it was a dream come true sounds way better than saying, "Between trying not to wet myself, wanting to kill Barry Zito, hoping a meteor would crush me, and forgetting where first base was, a no-decision is great!"

The reporters seemed satisfied, and so did the coaches. I wasn't called in to the office after the game to be told I was going back to Triple A. After everyone showered, ate, and left for the afternoon, I was still part of the club.

Chapter Fifty-three

Sunday was another day game. As a starter, I was expected to sit in the dugout for the contest instead of the bullpen. I didn't know anyone in the dugout aside from a few faces from Triple A, and most of those faces were position players. Since position players and pitchers usually don't have much to discuss, I kept to myself, doing my best to blend in by following the lead of the other dugout occupants. When they stood along the fence railing, I stood along the fence railing. When they sat on the bench, I sat on the bench. When they cheered, I cheered. It was like baseball's version of attending mass.

The nice thing about minor league bullpens is there aren't any coaches to monitor players' behavior—probably the main reason players act like juvenile delinquents while in it. Major league bullpens do have one coach, but most of the time he knows what bullpen life is like and doesn't obstruct its denizens from their idiosyncrasies. Dugouts are not the same. With almost four times as many coaches in the major league dugout as the minor, it's easy to speak out of place or catch someone's ear the wrong way, especially if you're a rookie who should be staying out of the way. However, the concept of learning from others by not asking questions, always being quiet and keeping your head down, seemed ironic to me. Of course, I dared not express that irony to anyone older and more experienced than myself, which in this case, was everyone. Despite being surrounded by players, it was a very lonely place. Even guys I played with in the minors, like Hamp, Bentley, Hundo, Headley, and Estes, were way more serious than I remembered, none of them keen on nonessential small talk. Maybe it was because the team was so far below .500 when I arrived to the club, or maybe it was because I was a green and didn't know the ways of the big leagues yet, but the loose, easy feel I'd always associated with baseball wasn't around. I shook the thought from my head; I would surely see it all differently in a week or two because, after all, I was just a stupid rookie.

We lost the game, dropping our record to 48 wins and 82 losses. It was our last day in San Fran, a getaway day, and everyone was in a hurry to shower, feed, and get dressed for our team flight. While the rules of life on the baseball field were constant between Triple A and the Bigs, the rules off of it were vastly different, and my initiation into them began with the words, "Get Hayhurst to do it."

I literally had my pants down when this comment was made as I was changing into my Goodwill special. I looked around to see what exactly I was supposed to be doing as I didn't want to screw up and incur the wrath that came with it. "Do what? What am I doing?" I asked.

"Beer bag," said Sean Kazmar. Sean, or "Kaz," was a former teammate of mine, and a fellow player under the representation of my agent. He was called up from Double A to play shortstop rather serendipitously, as every other shortstop in front of him for promotion got hurt. I had more time than him at every level in the minors, including signing a year ahead of him. But now that he had arrived in the Bigs before me, he was my boss.

"Do I ask the clubby for it? Is it like a princess backpack for beer or something?" I asked, thinking of the sissy pink bag guys in the pen usually got saddled with to playfully mark their low standing. I was actually excited at the thought of carrying something like that as a rite of passage.

"No, nothing like that," said Kaz. "Just get a garbage bag, make sure it's a black one so fans can't see what you're carrying, and fill it with beer and ice."

"How many beers should I get?"

"About ten to fifteen."

"What kind?"

"A good even mix."

"Are you getting one too?"

"Yeah."

"How many other guys are getting beer bags?" I asked this so I could have some kind of semblance of where I was in the pecking order. I knew I was at the bottom, that was obvious, but knowing who the other low men were could help me know who I should shadow.

"It doesn't matter who else is getting bags. Just make sure you have one so you don't look like you're not doing your job."

It turned out that the beer bag was just the beginning of big league travel experiences. Instead of taking one bus to the airport, we took two: one for the coaches and staff, and one for the players. There were seating rules for players, of course. Players with the most service time got to sit where they wanted at the expense of everyone younger than them. However, unlike the minors, where coaches rode the bus with players, older players did not sit in the back to avoid the coaches. On the big league bus, older players sat up front. This allowed them to be the first ones off the bus when it got to wherever it was going.

Everyone who was not at the top of the heap in service time trickled to the rear of the bus, picking up seats like scavengers. Rookies were expected to double up; they were also expected to wait for their veteran counterparts to find a seat they liked before sitting themselves.

I stood until everyone was seated, then took my place next to another young guy, which wouldn't have been so bad were it not for the two bloated bags of beer we had between us. We weren't safe yet, however, because when the bus started rolling, my seatmate and I were called into bartender service. The responsibility of the person carrying the beer bag is to vend the brews within it to whoever wants one. If an older guy barks out a request for a Corona, it was my job to dig through the bag and locate one for him. If I didn't have the requested beer, I had to conference with other rookies who might have one on tap. Once I found it, I played waiter, taking the brew to the person who requested it.

"Aren't you going to open that for me?" asked Hamp.

"Sorry," I said, staring down at the bottle. Considering how many people were drinking on the bus, it was ironic to discover that a bottle opener was an afterthought. I had to crack the cap by using a hook on a seat back.

"Here you go, this Bud's for you," I said, handing it to him.

"I asked for a Coors."

"Oh shit."

"Jesus, Hayhurst, you got one job to do, figure it the fuck out, rookie."

The buses drove past the airport entrance but no one seemed to care. It traveled past the exit, the rows of no-trespassing signs, and onto some obscure service entrance where normal humans would be incarcerated for even thinking of driving there. Sure enough, a security vehicle, lights pulsing, intercepted us, but not to stop us. Rather, the vehicle escorted us onto the tarmac. Gates that never opened swung wide upon our approach. We drove past planes and the passengers who boarded them. We drove past tractors pulling luggage and fuel tanks. Jets took off beside us and still we drove, out to a lone plane parked in an obscure area I never knew airports had until today.

When the bus came to a stop, I watched the other rookies. None of them stood. Heads down, they minded their own business until every veteran leisurely rose and exited. Some of those veterans yakked away as they went, expensive cell phones pressed against expensive sunglasses crowning expensive haircuts, all of it wrapped up in expensive suits that screamed seven-figure contracts. Others sprang up with headphones cast around their necks, bumping out tunes as they drained the last of their rookie-fetched beers, stuffing the empty bottles in the crevices of the bus seats, and exited, designer luggage trolling behind them.

Next, we rookies stood. We grabbed our battered luggage and hoisted up our assigned garbage bags full of ice and beer, then followed after our lords and masters. Stepping off the bus, we formed the tail of players lining up in front of the plane. A security screening task force met us at the steps of our jet, where we were cordially asked to sit down in chairs set up specifically for us outside the plane, and kick our feet up so we might be comfortably wanded. When it was my turn, I set my travel bag down to be casually searched, then placed my twenty-pound bag of ice-cold beer next to it. I expected it to be confiscated, and me possibly arrested; after all, you can't board a commercial plane anywhere in the country with a container housing more liquid than a shot of espresso. The security force paid no mind to the beer or the puddle forming beneath it, however, and asked me to please flip my belt buckle over, wished me good day, then released me to the plane.

My God, what a glorious thing it was. Polished wood trim, cavernous leather seats, and beautiful stewardesses—I'd never been on such a nice form of transportation in my life. Just inside the cabin's entrance was a veritable buffet of food laid out for our fancy. Players mulled over plates of crab legs, quesadillas, fruit, cheese, nuts, chips, cookies, sandwiches, gum, peanut butter and jelly, vegetable plates and dips, pretzels, crackers, little meats stuck with toothpicks, trays of cold cuts, and even plastic cups of wine—both red and white. I couldn't believe my eyes. Truly, it was ambrosia, for we traveled like gods. Of course, I dared not touch any of it with my defiled rookie hands, lest I be cast out of the plane into some dark, cold place where there was much weeping and gnashing of crab leg–deprived teeth. I'd probably be stuffed in the luggage compartment or strapped to the wing.

I pressed down the aisle of the plane with no idea where I was headed, and when I arrived in the back, I was promptly commanded to turn around and retreat to another area, "where rookies belong." No one bothered to tell me where exactly that area was, but before I could locate it, I was stopped and ordered to fetch a fruit plate for one of the veterans, grab a Coors Light for another, and make sure the other rookies I passed during my quest were obediently doing their jobs with equal euphoric gratitude.

A stewardess asked me if she could take my bag of beer, which I had been dragging with me since entering, dribbling water up and down the aisle. After I found a Coors Light, I allowed her, yet when she grabbed the plastic garbage bag my hand instinctively clamped hold. Was I allowed to let her take the bag? Would I be breaking some unsaid rule if I did not? That garbage bag of beer was my sacred responsibility after all. It was my cross to bear, and I did so with pride. She assured me it was okay, I wasn't the first person she'd taken a beer bag from, and wrenched it from my white knuckles saying, "We'll take care of it from here." Then she stopped, and in an apologetic tone, said, "Unless you plan on drinking it all yourself." Was it common for big leaguers to bring garbage bags of beer on a plane? Well, yes, I guess it was since two other rookies brought bags as well and this stewardess was no beer bag virgin. But drink it all ourselves? I gave her the bag immediately before someone older could command me to start chugging.

Done playing waiter, I stood awkwardly in the aisle, wondering where in the hell I was allowed to sit. Of course, no one wanted a seatmate, even though the seats on this plane were larger, more comfortable, and possessing more legroom than those found in the elitist realms of first-class commercial cabins. In fact, they were so nice a player could sit next to another and hardly notice his presence unless he was sitting at one of the chairs built around tables where, presently, poker was flourishing with hundred-dollar bills and stacks of colored chips. I would have sat in the bathroom or simply stood the entire time if Bentley had not offered me a seat next to him.

Bentley sat in the back, from where I had just been just ejected, one seat in front of Trevor Hoffman, the lord of the Padres himself. Jilly, who I was warned could be naked at any moment, was also there, and across from Bentley was right-handed boy wonder and consummate media darling Jake Peavy. It was hallowed ground and my rookie instincts screamed out to run, but Bentley offered and I dared not refuse him. A month ago, Bentley was in Triple A with me. We spent our time throwing peanut M&M's at people in the beer garden. Now I was a rookie while he was just another god in the pantheon.

The cabin doors closed. Hoffman plugged in a traveling Bose speaker system and connected it to his iPod. Soon, the back of the plane was a concert hall. Classic rock banged away as Hoffman slouched leisurely, observing the actions of his team when not scrolling through his exhaustive music collection.

A new stewardess came and asked everyone in my area if they wanted drinks for takeoff. She hit all the veterans, then looked to me.

"And for you, sir? Anything to drink?"

I blanked. A simple question like that and I blanked. I could feel that sense of hyperawareness strike me again. The pause while I searched for words stretched painfully long, and I could feel the eyes of all the big names surrounding me, piercing me, waiting to hear what I would request. Ironically, I could say anything I wanted, the plane was stocked with a cornucopia of beverages, but every decision seemed to carry a chain of events and assumptions connected to rookie behavior. I felt as if I hadn't earned the right to ask or do anything, and yet by being there I had earned the right to ask and do anything I wanted.

"I'm fine, thank you," I forced out.

"I'll have red wine," Bentley said. "You should have some too,

Dirk. You like red wine, right?" He said it in that anybody-who's-anybody-drinks-red-wine kind of way.

I hate red wine. "Yeah, I love it." I beamed.

"He'll have some red wine, too," Bentley said. Then, turning back to me, "I don't think there is anything better than a nice glass of red wine after a game to help you relax."

"Totally," I said. *Yes, there is nothing like a nice flight in a luxury jet stuffed with crab legs, on-demand bottle service, and $500 poker buy-ins to make a guy fresh out of poverty feel relaxed. I'm right at home now that I have that glass of red wine.*

When the plane started moving and Hoffman switched the song blaring from his Bose mini-system to "Arms Wide Open" by Creed, an undeniable feeling of "fuck yeah" washed over me. I felt like I was really part of something when I heard it, some inner circle. *My God,* I thought, *I'm on a big league jet! I'm floating in the heavens with the rest of the gods of red-blooded children's dreams.* I stared out the window and could feel greatness take hold of me like the g-forces that threw me back in my luxury seat. I looked down upon the masses from my flying chariot's window. I was supreme among men. I was a big leaguer nervously sipping crappy red wine from a plastic cup! *Behold my greatness ye mortals, and cower!*

I had a quick vision of myself in my hometown, strutting down the street like I was in a Bee Gees video. Childhood enemies were blinded when they looked upon me; women were struck dumb, ensnared by my aura. Children ran to me, but a cop with gentle eyes and an Irish accent shooed them away saying, "Run along now, children. Mr. Hayhurst has important business to tend to. Top of the morning to you, Mr. Hayhurst." He'd tip his cap and I'd continue walking, walking right into the sunset, where dreams fluttered 'round like little butterflies.

After a few minutes of daydreaming, I turned back to the plane, where my butterflies fried and exploded on a naked Jilly. While I was frolicking among my manifest greatness, he had stripped down, jammed one of the tiny airplane pillows onto his head, and tied a blanket around his neck like a cape. He looked like a naked bishop with a can of Bud Light as a scepter.

"You gotta take this fucking game serious, boys! Take this shit serious!" he declared. Then, up and down the aisle he ran, bellowing, "This is a serious fucking game and you have to have a serious approach. I'm tired of all this fucking around. We're better than this!" He put a leg up on the armrest of one of the other rookies' chairs so that his bagpipe was dangling ominously before said rookie's face. "I'm just tired of us dicking around. We are better than this, and I believe that! Lotta season left, boys, but we have to fucking want it!" He did a bit of dynamic stretching as he spoke, creating a swinging motion, which, in turn, created a rocking motion between the rookie's face and the object it was trying to avoid.

Jilly took his foot down and resumed pacing the aisles, eventually making his way back to me. Thank God I was in the window seat. "How about you, Hayhurst? You take this shit seriously?" he asked, hands on naked hips. I felt strange for retaining this detail, but his entire body was tan and shaven, and when I say entire body, I mean *entire body*.

I stared at him, my plastic cup of hardly touched red wine in hand, wearing my wrinkled suit from Goodwill that smelled like dead old people. I had just carried a garbage bag full of beer past federal agents and witnessed a grown man wearing a blanket as a cape nearly tea bag another man. I said the only thing I could think of: "Your penis is tan."

"What?"

"Oh God, I take this shit very serious, sir, *very* serious." I slammed the glass of wine.

"Good!" Jilly roared. "Good, because we don't want guys up here who are just going to fuck around."

I nodded. "No sir, no, we don't."

Chapter Fifty-four

A stewardess brought me a fresh garbage bag of beer cans after the plane landed in San Diego. Again, those with the least service time stayed seated until the vets deplaned. Upon their exit, I gathered up my stuff and followed them out and onto another set of buses that parked on the tarmac for our convenience.

The buses took us to Petco Park, the great cathedral of San Diego baseball I'd been trying to get into since I first signed my contract. I had actually been inside its hallowed walls once before, back when I was playing for the Lake Elsinore Storm. It was meant as a treat for us minor leaguers, though the experience wasn't quite the same as being a big league resident. The Storm was not permitted in the big league locker room; we changed inside an auxiliary dressing room that was smaller than some of the smallest minor league lockers. There were rules about unnecessary activity on the grass, rules about what mound to use in the bullpen, and rules concerning where we could watch the game. We were given minor league meal money for the day since, technically, it was an away game, but it didn't go far. Concessions in Petco Park were nearly ten dollars for a slice of cheese pizza and a small drink.

Even so, it was an amazing experience. The stadium was gorgeous and the crew at Petco put our names up on its gargantuan display board. The bright lights, the manicured turf, and cavernous seating, it was the genuine article, the perfect place to fantasize about what could be if everything came together. I didn't get to play on the field that day, a stroke of bad luck that left a thorn in my side for years. But—I smiled to myself as we circled the stadium—in five days I would be the genuine article as I took the mound to start against the Rockies.

The buses stopped in front of the players' and staff entrance to wait for the gates to open. There, just beyond the entrance, was a group of people: super fans. They waved at us, homemade poster board signs held over their heads, clapping and hopping up and down. They all wore Padres-logoed paraphernalia. Some, mostly the ladies, went overboard with Padres' earrings and visors with twenty or so pins stuck in the bills. There were lawn chairs next to them, indicating they'd been hanging around the place for quite some time, anxiously awaiting our return.

For some reason, I connected the size of the crowd to our win-loss record. I imagined the Yankees had larger crowds; maybe some of them were women, clad in bikinis, waving signs that said something more provocative than "Keep your chins up!"

"What the fuck is wrong with these people?" came a reply from one of the older guys on the team, staring out the window at them, smiling and waving despite his commentary. "Get a life!" he said with the same happy-to-see-you countenance on his face.

The buses pulled us into the player parking lot located under the structure of the stadium. It was full of hundred-thousand-dollar cars stocked with every luxury and amenity imaginable, including Barbie-esque girls with identity-shielding sunglasses in the driver's seats.

Our luggage, which I hadn't seen since giving it to a clubby in San Francisco, did not come with the team. Instead, it was unloaded by the Padres' clubhouse staff and brought to us. While the team waited for their bags, they went to the lockers to lounge around. I followed behind them, feeling very much the way I did when I was about to enter the lockers in San Fran.

Even if you weren't a baseball player who struggled for years in the minors with self-doubt, even if you didn't look upon reaching the big leagues as akin to entering the holy of holies, even if you'd never seen a baseball game in your life, you would, without a doubt, blurt a resounding "Wow" upon entering the Padres' clubhouse.

To start, the facility is round, like the kind of room King Arthur's round table would be located in if King Arthur had access to a hundred-million-dollar budget and stylish leather couches. The lockers formed the outer wall of the space, all of them custom-cut wood with drawers and cabinets and cubbies and plug-ins for accumulated goodies, baseball and otherwise. Mounted overhead was a ring of flat-screen Sony televisions. In all, the locker room was home to over a dozen sets facing every angle, making sure there wasn't a bad view in the house. The leather couches formed the inner circle of the place, surrounding a Padres' logo stitched into the carpet on the floor.

There were hallways on the north, south, east, and west portions of the circle. From the entrance to the locker room, the hallway directly across from me led out to the field, batting cages, and the cafeteria. The Padres had a fully stocked kitchen where I was told you could order just about anything you wanted and a clubby would make it for you. Or you could make something yourself from the vast supply of groceries in the industrial refrigerators. There were racks of chips, cookies, Cracker Jacks, and other calorie-stuffed garbage the minor league strength coach would have a conniption about if he caught us eating it. They sat on shelves for anyone to take at any time, even now, the evening after a game in another city.

The hallway to the west went to the bathroom, although the term *bathroom* didn't do it justice. The showers were marble, or some similarly expensive-looking stone. Next to the showers was a sauna, followed by a room just for pooping and reading magazines about guns, yachts, cars, and the habits of naked ladies. Finally, there was a set of sinks and mirrors surrounded by hair sprays, razors, and lotions—to make sure you looked good for the ten people standing at the gate when you left.

The hall to the west led past the coaches' offices, the clubhouse laundry space, and the weight room. What a weight room it was, too, full of the best equipment and more of those fabulous flat screens. The strength coach, that huge guy with the shaved head I saw earlier, kenneled all his powders and mixes here. There were barrels of the stuff, not to mention can after can of readymade shakes and boxes of protein bars.

I had a locker in the main room, and I spent a good deal of time looking at it, running my hands across the wood of its custom edges, feeling the fabric of my jersey hanging inside it. There was something about putting my hands on it all that made it feel more real to me. As the other guys buzzed around me, going through their post-trip routines, I walked about the place slowly, staring in awe at it all. The thing that struck me was how vast the difference was between what I knew and what I was seeing. After a career in the minors, a player comes to appreciate things as simple as Gatorade mix in the water cooler instead of water, or two choices of peanut butter for a pre-game spread. By comparison, the spartan existence of the minors made this display feel excessive to the point of absurdity. I wouldn't dare complain about it, and yet, I couldn't help but wonder how anyone could ever get used to this. How could any player say this was what he deserved? And I had only tasted the tiniest spoonful!

My thoughtful ramble came to a stop in front of the snack shelf in the cafeteria. I wanted to take one of the packs of Fig Newtons there, but I stayed my hand. I felt like I was in someone else's house and taking the Newtons would be like stealing. As I stood there, one of the other players I didn't know, who had changed out of travel clothes and into a set of street clothes, pushed past me and started wantonly grabbing items off the shelf and wedging the goodies into his computer bag until the sides bulged.

He noticed me staring pensively at the treats and said, "Go ahead, dude."

"Am I allowed?"

"Are you allowed? Jesus." He rolled his eyes and looked around to see if anyone else was hearing my talk. "You're in the damn big leagues, man. Big leaguers are allowed to eat Cracker Jacks and Fig Newtons." He pulled a few off the shelf and threw them at me. They bounced off my unready hands. I picked them up off the floor and put them all back, except for one pack of Newtons. One was enough, I decided.

"Look, you pay fifty dollars in dues a day to be here whether you eat one or twenty. Might as well get your money's worth." He grabbed another item for himself and walked out of the room. I remained, looking at the snacks for a while longer. I took one more pack of Newtons and walked out.

Our bags came shortly after our arrival. A clubhouse attendant brought mine to me, then gave me a ride on a service cart through the stadium, outside, across the street, and right up to the front of the Marriot Gaslamp Hotel, where new Padres stayed. He dropped me off in front of the hotel's doorman, who, as odd as this spectacle would have been at any other hotel, didn't bat an eye as he opened the door and bowed his head at my passing.

Much like the hotel in San Fran, the Marriot Gaslamp was stunning, and a reservation had already been made for me. While explaining all the luxuries the hotel offered, and on which floors I could find them, the lady at the front desk said the bar on the roof—known as the Sky Lounge—offered one of the best views of the ballpark anywhere—and since none of the hotel guests had to stand in line for access, I should definitely experience it. After dropping off my bags in my room, I did just that.

She was right about the view. From the edge of the rooftop bar, I could see over the Western Metal Supply building that made up the left field portion of Petco. I could see the huge banners of the great Padres icons in all their glory, including a nearly hundred-foot poster of Hoffman. I marveled at it, wondering what it must feel like for him to drive to work every day and see a building-size mural of himself on the side of a stadium. I gazed on the field, welling up with pride that I was one of the people who would say they got to play on it.

"Number Fifty-Seven!" came a voice from behind me. That was my number. I turned to see Bentley standing there with two drinks in hand. He casually made his way over to me with a big league smile stretched across his face and handed me one. "Welcome to the Sky Lounge," he said, and clinked my glass with his.

"Thanks for having me," I said.

"Enjoying your seven and seven?" he asked, referring to the seven nights in a hotel and seven nights' worth of meal money—just over a grand in cash—the Padres gave me to get settled in with.

"Very much so," I said, turning back to the view.

We stood there looking off the roof and onto the field. Bentley had been here longer than me and his seven and seven must have run out by now, which prompted me to ask him, "Are you staying here the whole time?"

"Yeah, it's cheaper than moving into an apartment since we're only here for a couple days out of the month. Besides, you can't find a lease for just a month and a half. You're committed to the hotel. Which is fine. I have an elite membership card. You should get one too"—he nudged me—"the points add up quick."

"How much is it per night?"

"I think the rates here are something like two hundred sixty dollars for a normal guest."

I choked on my drink. "Two hundred and sixty dollars?"

"Something like that." He looked to my gaping mouth and raised an eyebrow. "You're in the Show, you can afford it."

"Maybe, but that's still a lot of money."

"Not anymore." He took a sip of his drink.

"That blows me away," I said. "I mean, this off-season, I was working at a television store, and now I'm sipping a mixed drink from the top of a five-star hotel overlooking at the major league field *I* play on. I can't believe this is actually happening."

Bentley said nothing.

"Maybe I'm wrong for thinking this, but it makes me wonder why there is such a huge gap between the guys up here and the guys in the minors. I mean, if you just spread out the smallest portion of all this to the guys below it would make their lives so much easier, don't you think?"

"That's a terrible idea," said Bentley.

"Why do you say that? There is so much here."

"Because it's meant to be this way. It's a grind for a reason. The guys who can't take it don't deserve to be up here. Besides, the union fights for us to have all this. There have been guys up here who went through hell to make it like it is. It's not for just anybody."

"Maybe. I guess I've just never experienced anything like this. I know I've worked my ass to get up here, but I feel like I don't deserve all this. It's so much so fast."

"I feel like I deserve it," Bentley said, and then gulped his drink.

"Really?"

"Of course. We beat the odds; we deserve all of this. If this is what they want to give us, then take it. Don't ask questions. Besides, this here"—he waved his arms as if to claim everything around us, the field, the hotel, the bar—"this is the only level you can make an impact at. It's the only one that matters—the only one people care about. All the rest of that stuff is just practice to get here."

"But—"

"No buts." He stopped me. "This is the only league that matters. Your career in baseball starts here."

I started to speak but stopped as his words sank in. I had never thought of my life in the minors as practice. I thought of it as surviving, enduring, grinding. All of the suffering for this, now written off with one, single word. I couldn't believe he could say such a thing to me. But the more I thought about it, the more I realized he was right. The Bigs were the only level that mattered. Everything done in the minors was done to get players here. More than anyone, I knew there was no reward for those people who came close. Everything in baseball revolved around this league.

"You're here. Now you just need to focus on staying here."

"Right," I said.

He lifted his glass and clinked it against mine. "Here's to a long career in the Bigs."

Chapter Fifty-five

I came to the park early the next day. I figured, since I was young, I should probably be there before anyone else. Showing up early says you're more prepared, hungrier, and more committed than other players. It says you want to stay in the big leagues and are willing to do whatever it takes.

I knew players and staff were still formulating their opinions of me, and I wanted them to be good opinions. It might only have taken me an hour to get all my pre-game work in, but an hour would not satisfy the people who were making judgment calls about my rookie work ethic. Every player knows that any exerting activity done in excess of what is required, which has no quantifiable relationship to on-field results but is pleasing to the eye of coaches and evaluators, is called "eyewash." But, no matter how disingenuous it is, eyewash is an important part of rookie evolution. Older players expect it, and younger players freely give it because it's the only way a player can avoid getting accused of being comfortable.

This is one of baseball's greatest ironies. Young players desire nothing more than being comfortable so they might succeed, but older players detest young players who act comfortable. Not on the field, per se, but in their everyday behavior. A rookie player should always carry himself with the proper mix of terror, hunger, thankfulness, humility, confidence, and utter doubt.

Thankfully, I was in no danger of being comfortable. If anything, I felt guilty, like someone had given me a gift far too expensive for me to accept. The jet, the hotels, the money, the treatment—it was all so overwhelming it was nearly impossible for me to fake anything but utmost unworthiness. Yet, there was no way to express this sentiment except by pitching well and working hard. Like anyone who has been to the big leagues for the first time, I wanted to show I could handle the gift. I wanted to show I could be a good rookie to all who judged such things, I wanted to perform well on the field, and I wanted to be loved by my teammates.

Since I was a starter now, I had to throw mandated bullpens between my starts. I'd be facing the Rockies in a few days, and I was bound and determined to recapture the focus that got me to the Bigs—to do what everyone told me I should keep doing, which was not having hyperemotional freak-outs like the one I had in San Francisco.

Balsley and the team's bullpen catcher escorted me out to the pen before the team stretch. Since the night I talked to him on the hotel phone, I'd felt uncomfortable around Balsley. He seemed cold to me and, since he was the boss and I didn't want to piss him off, I steered clear unless he needed something from me. I thought we'd get a better feel for one another during our bullpen session. He was the big league pitching coach, after all; I wanted his approval more than anyone else's, and I would do or say anything it took to get it.

Stretched, warm, and ready to throw, I took the mound in the Padres' bullpen, told the catcher to get down, and set up low and away. I flicked my glove to announce a fastball, fired, and missed wide. The ball came back. I reset, flicked my glove again, fired, and missed, again. The ball came back. Balsley watched impassively at my side. I took a focusing breath, gave another flick, and this time threw a strike, right down the middle, belt high—the only kind of strike you're forbidden to throw.

I cringed. By this point, Abby would have said something out of nowhere about my ears not being pulled back and how it was messing up my finger extension. Balsley, however, said nothing. Instead, he walked down to the foot of the mound and looked at me. Not at my eyes like he was trying to convey a thought, but at me as a unit, like I was some piece of machinery and he wanted to see the parts move from another angle. I flicked my glove again, fired, and missed.

The silence was crushing. I shook my head and mumbled, "What the fuck is wrong with me?" *Come back to it later,* I thought. Sometimes you don't find your groove in a practice session on the first couple of tosses. Moving forward and hitting spots with your other pitches can help you get your feel back. Abby would say there is no sense in dwelling on a bad pitch when you've got other pitches that need work. I waved my glove to tell the catcher to move to the other side of the plate, then signaled for a sinker, but Balsley stopped me.

"No," he said, "stay down and away." He continued looking at me like a mechanical instrument. "No use throwing to another spot on if you can hit the one that matters most. Low and away is where you make your living; you should be able to hit it nine out of ten times at this level."

I nodded my head, consenting to his command. In fact, the catcher moved back as soon as he spoke, leaving me little option. I wouldn't dare voice my difference of opinion, of course; the big league pitching coach's word was law. I flicked my glove again, even though we all knew what I was throwing, wound and fired low and away for another miss. The ball was returned, the motion repeated, and the result the same. This went on for ten or so throws with me mixing in strikes like they were accidents. In the silence and the scrutiny, I began feeling like I had forgotten how to pitch.

I kept taking nervous glances at Balsley, but his face was stone.

He did, however, count the strikes he thought worthy, announcing them so I might hear how low the number was. When I got to ten strikes out of who knows how many, I stopped and looked at him, completely lost. I knew I was making a bad impression. Or at least I thought I was. Maybe he'd seen this before and wasn't worried about my lack of control. Maybe he knew this would happen. Maybe he knew how intimidating he was to rookies. Why wouldn't he talk to me?

In fear of suffocating in the silence, I spoke in his place. "I don't understand it," I said. "I know this sounds like a cop-out, but I'm a strike thrower. It's what I do . . . I . . ." I stopped there as Balsley turned his head away from the comment, seemingly disgusted by excuse-making.

"I believe you," he said, though I wasn't sure if he was being sarcastic. In fact, despite his softly spoken three-word reply, his face seemed to scream, *This is the big leagues, either you get the job done here, or you don't. I have no sympathy.*

I thought about the words I shared with Bentley on the roof of the hotel last night, about how this was the only place you could really make an impact. Then I thought about the type of people who made impacts up here, if I was one of them, and if they made excuses. I tried another player/coach relationship technique: an appeal to arrogance, like I did with the strength coaches back in spring training.

"I, uh, don't know how much time I'll get up here in the Show, so I want to soak up as much info as I can. Anything you see wrong, I'm all ears. You're the best coach in our system, and I obviously need to make an adjustment. I want to stay."

I regretted saying anything almost immediately. Balsley picked me apart in short order, a regular dissection on the mound. He missed nothing, factoring my stride length, my landing foot's angle in relation to my hips, the degree to which I crossed my body, and the length of my inseam compared to my torso. He even had me walk to see which way the balls of my feet struck when my foot fell. Most of the critiques focused on the mechanical, but when he was done, he told me that much of my delivery was just me compensating for me. It was like getting genetically sequenced and finding out I had more in common with poop-throwing monkeys than I did with strike-throwing big leaguers. I didn't know how I was supposed to process all the analysis, or if I even could. Balsley did confess that this point in the season wasn't the right time to work on it, which brought us back to square one: finding a way to hit the mitt low and away. The only difference now was, as I spent the rest of the bullpen time winding and missing, I could take comfort in the fact that it wasn't really my fault, what with my entire body being a grab bag of inferior products and all.

I was hoping that when the pen was over and I made it back to the locker room, I would do so with a new confidence in my ability to perform here. I wanted to believe that I could match up against the Rockies. Instead, I felt like I was an excuse maker who couldn't hit the most rudimentary of spots on account of my terrible delivery. I wanted to believe that wasn't true, but when I looked at Balsley's face, I couldn't shake the feeling I was wasting his time, and no amount of early eyewash was going to change that. This was the big leagues, after all, and not some developmental minor league practice session. What mattered here were results, period.

Chapter Fifty-six

I booked a flight to get Bonnie into San Diego the day before my start against the Rockies. It was an off day—a blessing and a curse. It was nice to have the day free to do whatever we pleased, but it also meant another day without throwing before a start. I didn't want to be rusty like I was in San Fran, and I didn't want to rearrange my hotel room so I could have another game of catch with the mattress. Instead, I left Bonnie at the hotel for about an hour and headed to the stadium by myself. One of the clubhouse crew let me in and granted me access to the batting cages, where, in the absence of a catcher, I set a ball on a batting tee and tried to knock it off from 60 feet away—my arm didn't know the difference, and the tee didn't say anything about how bad my mechanics were.

Afterward, Bonnie and I had dinner at a restaurant called Acqua Al 2. I selected the place because the night before Bonnie arrived, I had to work at this restaurant as a waiter in Adrian Gonzales's charity event. The restaurant staff, remembering me from my visit the previous night, insisted Bonnie and I eat for free. They gave us a full seven-course experience. Bonnie was very impressed by how everyone treated me like I was some big shot. I played it like it was no big deal, not speaking a word of how I busted tables for charity the previous night. I told Bonnie this was the way all big leaguers got treated, and that things were different up here in the only league that matters.

I really wanted to dazzle Bonnie, like I had been dazzled by the whole experience thus far. I bought her a dress, ordered her a massage, and the next day, the day of my start, I ordered a full room service breakfast.

We sat on my bed, eating and chatting about how things were going for me. Bonnie wanted to know where to go for the game, who to sit with, and if any of the girls she knew from the minors were present in the big leagues.

"I don't know. I know Chase's girl is here with him, but beyond that, I don't know who else is here. I barely know anyone on the team, and some of the guys I knew from Triple A I feel like I don't know up here."

"Like they've changed?"

"I don't know if they've changed, but very few of the guys are as relaxed up here, including me. And some of the guys, and this is totally my opinion because I haven't been here long enough to be sure of it, seem like they really enjoy that they're big leaguers." I ordered pancakes and I was cutting them up, not really paying attention to my words as I spoke. Instead of elaborating, I poured syrup over cuts in the grid, ensuring each piece got optimal syrup penetration.

"Of course they do," said Bonnie. "After everything you've told me about it, I can totally imagine they would." Bonnie speared some fresh fruit with her fork, more attuned to my words than I was.

"That's not what I mean. Yes, it's cool being a big leaguer, but they act like, I don't know, like it's made them more powerful, like they now have social steroids or something. They're the same people, but they're just tone-deaf or too busy to be bothered. Especially if you're unsure, nervous, or doubtful. Hell, I don't know if this even makes sense. It's hard to explain. It could just be this group of guys or the fact that we suck right now, but all the games here I just sit in silence on the bench, trying not to bother anyone.

It's nothing like Triple A, where we all talked and had a good time. Actually, the most lonely part of the day is when I'm at the park."

"You said that on the phone."

"Said what?" I took a bite.

"That you weren't talking to anyone and that it was lonely at times."

"Oh yeah." I chewed as I spoke. "It sounded pathetic then and it sounds pathetic now. This is the big leagues, I shouldn't be complaining."

"It's not pathetic. It's important to have friends wherever you're at."

"Look, I appreciate what you're saying, honey, but I'm in the big leagues. Who cares if I have a sewing circle to chitchat with, right? I should be happy I'm here." I sat my fork atop another stack of pancakes and hesitated. "But . . ."

"But what?"

"I don't know. There is something to be said for team chemistry, but . . . I don't know, Bonnie. It's early, I'm a rookie. I'll figure it out."

Bonnie stopped pressing the issue and went back to eating, as did I. After we cleared most of our plates, she said, "At least the money is great."

"Yeah, and that's a huge relief. Even if I get sent down right now, I can command minor league free agent money, which is way better than what I was making before."

"You don't think they'll send you down, though, do you?"

"This level is the most performance-driven level in all of baseball, babe. If I don't perform, anything is possible. Look at how much turnover has already happened this year. I can tell you this, if I make it into September, I'll probably stay."

"Why is that?"

"First, there is no place to send me back to come September; Triple A is done for the year. Second, the rosters expand so they don't need to worry about making space for me. They could send me home, I guess, but that doesn't make a lot of sense for them to do since September is typically when they bring up guys they want to try out."

"Is that what they're doing? Are they giving you a tryout?"

"Yes and no. I came up before September so they obviously had a role they wanted me to fill for them. Otherwise, they would have stuck me in the bullpen. But if we were in contention for something other than not losing a hundred games, they wouldn't have brought a bullpen guy into the starting rotation." I looked at Bonnie, who was doing her best to keep up with me on what all the possibilities were.

"All you need to remember is that our immediate goal is making it to September. If I can hold on long enough to be here when the rosters expand, we've got a great chance at collecting a nice payday to start our marriage with. That's why today is so important," I said. "It's my last start before September. I really need this one to go well, to show them I can handle myself up here and that they should keep me."

"You're going to do great, honey," said Bonnie, completely certain.

"I certainly feel more prepared for this one than the last one."

"Well, I don't want to do anything to distract you," said Bonnie. "We don't have to do anything special, or go anyplace. I just want you to be ready."

"I appreciate that, but we have to live this up. We're big leaguers now, right?"

"Right. I have go to the bathroom," she inserted abruptly.

"That's living large," I said as Bonnie got up and scampered into the bathroom.

"I'm sorry, honey, I've got a minor league bladder!"

Bonnie went into the bathroom, and while she was gone I ate from the unfinished bacon on her plate. Then I flipped over the bill for the room service: it was over a hundred dollars.

"Jesus Christ!" I shouted, before repeating the price of the bill out loud. "We could have eaten this same meal at Denny's for twenty—" The sound of breaking glass in the bathroom interrupted me. Suddenly Bonnie let out a screech of pain.

I stood up. "Honey, are you okay?"

"No. No, I'm not. Oh my God."

I started to the door. "Bonnie, I'm coming in, alright?"

"Be careful, there's glass."

I opened the door to the bathroom and strewn across the floor were shards of glass from a broken tumbler. Then there was blood, big half dollar–sized splats of it smeared on the tile and leading to Bonnie, sitting on the edge of the bathtub holding her foot with bloody hands.

Chapter Fifty-seven

She was pale-faced while blood oozed between her fingers. I snatched a towel from the rack and threw it down on the floor. Using it like a dry mop, I wiped the glass and some of the blood from the floor, pushing it safely out of the way and under the vanity.

I grabbed a clean towel and got down on my knees in front of Bonnie's bleeding foot. She'd cut the bottom of it, nearly an inch-long gash stretched across the arch. But the wound was deeper than it was long and bled like it went to the bone.

"Turn around and stick your foot under the tub's spout," I said, gently. Clean water turned pink as it flowed over the cut. Thankfully, there was no glass in the gash. I pulled her foot free and put the dry towel on it with as much pressure as I could without making her yelp. "Hold it down tight," I said. She grabbed hold of the towel, and I grabbed hold of her, lifting her up and carrying her into the bedroom and laying her on the bed. I went back and got some extra towels before replacing her hands with my own on the cut.

"It's not that bad," I said, though I didn't really know if it was or not. "It's a clean slice, so it's going to bleed, but holding it shut like this should stop it."

"Do you think I'll need stitches?"

"I don't know. Does it hurt much?"

"No, I can't really feel it," she said. "I was just scared of all the blood."

"I'll bet." Then I thought about her not being able to feel. I knew how long the slice was, but I didn't know how deep. "Can you feel my pressure?" I squeezed to check.

"Ouch, yes, I can feel it." She settled down and tried to act tough. "It's not that bad."

"Sure." I smiled. "Take over for me. I'm going to call the front desk." Bonnie switched hands with me. I called the lobby and had a first-aid team come up. By the time they got to the room, there was an inkblot test's amount of blood on the towel, but the bleeding around the wound had subsided. The hotel's first-aid supply was limited to gauze, Band-Aids, and creams. It would keep the bleeding stopped, but not keep the cut closed if Bonnie were to walk on it. I knew Bonnie hadn't flown all the way to San Diego to sit in the hotel room while her husband to be made his home team debut, so we needed to find a way to get her to the park without opening the wound.

I didn't know if Bonnie needed stitches, but I wouldn't be able to escort her to the hospital to find out. I had to be at the park ultra-early for my rookie eyewash time. What I needed was someone with a better read on these things than me; I needed a team trainer.

In the minors, if the children of coaches or players had a boo-boo, it wasn't uncommon for them to show up in the locker room for trainer attention. Wives, on the other hand, were a very different subject. I never saw any of them in the lockers. In fact, in all my time as a player, the words *locker room* and *wives* never entered into a sentence in a positive relationship. Asking the training crew to treat my wife seemed like a very bad idea, but today was my big day and I didn't have many options.

I felt bad for leaving Bonnie, but I had no choice. I needed the expertise of the big league training staff, but in getting it, I also needed be discreet. I didn't want anyone else, not coaches or players, to know I needed to bring my wife into the lockers to get checked out. The last thing I wanted to do was draw any unnecessary attention to myself. If this was for me, I would have gone to one of the assistant trainers I knew from my A ball days. But this was a special request, which meant I'd have to talk to the man in charge of Padre-health, Todd Hutcheson, aka "Hutch."

I was scared Hutch would chastise me for asking for special favors without so much as a week of big league time under my belt, but, as it turned out, Hutch was saintly about it. In fact, the whole training staff, once they got word of it, seemed eager to help my wife-to-be any way they could. They even formulated a plan to have Bonnie get checked out in a private room, with a separate entrance from the lockers, during the game so no one had to know she was ever there. She would be like a ghost in a sundress with a cut foot.

After I reported the instructions to Bonnie, I tried to put it all out of my mind and settle in for my start. The locker room's television arrays played continuous loops of the opposing pitcher, Aaron Cook, and hitters strolled around the place, occasionally looking up at the feed and remarking about how they hated hitting off "this fucking guy." I would have agreed with them, but I hated hitting off everyone. No doubt, Cook would slaughter me; at least he would do it from the right side instead of buckling me with towering left-handed hooks.

I watched some video of the hitters I would face, and after about a half hour of it, I'd had enough. It wasn't that I didn't think it would help, it was just that I didn't know how to apply the information. In Portland, Abby would take us down the line and give us a scouting report on the opposing team. The notes were hardly comprehensive, but they provided what we needed to know. Up here, a player could drown in information if he didn't know how to apply it. The only thing I knew was that once the game started and the lights hit me and the cameras zoomed in, it would take everything I had not to hit critical mass. The less complicated I could make things, the better.

About forty-five minutes before game time, I headed out to the pen to start warming up. Fans gushed into the park as pre-game sounds echoed into the far reaches of the stadium. Autograph hunters, dazzling light boards, concession callers. The machine was starting up again. I tried my best to tune it out, but it was still difficult as the magnitude of what it meant for the rest of my life washed over me.

Doing my best not to look at Balsley when I missed a spot, I brought my arm to a game-ready boil in the centerfield pen. I thought of the catcher's glove as a ball parked on a tee. I tried to convince myself I was alone, simply trying to hit targets like in the batting cage the previous day. I tried to convince myself there were no fans behind me, no tennis court–sized display boards advertising gift shop goodies, no relievers standing outside the pen, waiting for me to finish, and no wife hobbling along on one bleeding foot, trying to get to a place where she could watch the game. But the more I tried to tune it out, the more I tuned it in.

"Alright, let's do it," I said to anyone who cared, grabbed a towel and a water bottle, and made my way out of the pen. The reliever crew waiting just beyond the pen's gate met me with a shower of fist pounds, high fives, butt smacks, and "Go get 'ems." With their blessing, I walked across the outfield as majestically as I could.

The light boards flashed lineups and the announcer's booming voice read the batting orders. When I hit right field, the voice declared, to the elation of the home team fans, "And now the starting lineup for your San Diego Padres!"

The voice embellished the names with rolling Rs and stressed syllables, making everyone seem to have heroic proportions. Then, as the voice got to the end of the lineup, I knew my name was coming. My catcher, Nick Hundley, and Balsley entered the dugout, but I stayed outside on the grass. I had endured six years for the dream of hearing my name spoken over the loudspeaker at Petco. I did not want to miss this moment.

"And pitching, number fifty-seven, Dirk Haaaay-hurrrrst!"

The crowd let out a meek cheer reflecting my obscurity. I didn't care. It was my name being announced as the pitcher in Petco Park. Nothing could ruin this moment. I cast my eyes to the display board to see my name flashing in bright, dream-come-true lights, but, according to the big screen, "Dick Hayhurst" was pitching for the Padres. I turned around to see if anyone in the dugout noticed. They were too focused on game preparation to care about something as routine as a roster announcement. I shot a glare back at the board. Dick Hayhurst. Dick *motherfucking* Hayhurst? I've been in the organization for how long, and on the day of my debut they misspell my name into a phallic synonym? You've got to be kidding me.

Chapter Fifty-eight

The display board goof was a sign of things to come.

Though Bud Black was the kindest person to me upon my arrival in the Show, he was not shy about telling me to be more efficient. It took me nearly fifty pitches to get through the first two innings, and the only reason Bud was talking to me about being more efficient and not screaming at me was because I'd somehow managed to put up zeros. I guess I should have been thankful that, before becoming a manager, Bud was a pitcher himself. He knew what it meant to be a starter who pissed his pitch count away. When he told me to clean things up, he did so like all he wanted me to do was go out there, relax, and let those bastards dribble the ball to my infielders so I could get us through five innings.

I took his sage advice and promptly gave up four runs in the third.

Walks always catch up to you. Either they eat up your pitch count or come around to score, but they bite you in the ass one way or another. In my case, it was both. I walked three guys in three innings, one in each. I managed to dodge the damage of the first two, but, in the third, I walked Matt Holliday and tested my luck. With the pressure on and two bases occupied, I channeled the calming, soothing, *let the ball find its way to the glove of your fielders* voice of my manager, and I served up a curveball that Garrett Atkins crushed into the glove of a fan in the left field stands.

It's amazing what a single swing of the bat can do. Atkins's swing didn't just change the score, it changed September's paycheck chances, big league service time, scouting reports, player reviews, and contract opportunities—and all of it was in my head as he trotted around me. Why couldn't I tune it out? So many thoughts at once, like a densely compacted bomb of negativity went off in my brain as soon as leather struck wood. Even the act of thinking about it for the few seconds that I did made me feel guilty since any coach in the world would tell me such thoughts had no business on a baseball field.

Where was Bonnie? I wondered. Was she inside the stadium right now, or getting her foot tended to? Hopefully she was not present to see me, for she of all people could surely see through the scowl I wore to mask my thoughts and discern the wreckage beneath. I didn't want her to see this; I didn't want anyone to see this, but the only way out was forward, through the fire. It's a terrible conclusion that every starter must come to terms with at some point in his career, the realization that the damage is done, and the best you can hope for is finishing your outing by not adding to it.

I put my glove up indicating I wanted a fresh ball from the umpire, but he didn't toss me one until Atkins crossed home plate. I guess this was done so I didn't throw it at Atkins or something. The thought hadn't crossed my mind, what with all the extraneous crap currently populating it, but now it seemed like a therapeutic exercise worth trying. Instead, I attempted to channel my frustrations into effective pitching, like I did after things got hot in San Francisco. I failed. I walked one more hitter in the third inning before getting out, bringing my total walks for the game up to four. I was a bust, and after only four innings, I was removed from the game.

* * *

Jersey off, sweat soaking my undershirt and matting my hair, I sat at my locker staring into the abyss. I didn't see the custom woodwork, my shiny big league name tag, or any of the other luxury things that had stunned me when I first arrived five days ago. I saw failure, unvarnished failure that was surely broadcast in HD all around the country. I'd put myself in line for the loss as I burned through nearly one hundred pitches in four innings.

The outing played over and over in my head like a pre-game video loop. Unlike my start against the Giants, this performance didn't have a nervous rookie excuse to hide behind. This was the outing of a poor pitcher. In fact, to those wondering if my borderline success against the Giants was luck or blooming skill, this start would be the retroactive lens through which it was interpreted. It was like having two bad outings rolled into one and, with the adrenaline leaving my system and no batters to occupy my attention, I was tearing myself apart over it, completely uninterrupted.

A hand fell on my back as I sat, swirling down the spiral at my locker. It was one of the trainers. They had brought Bonnie down to the training room following my removal from the game. They patched her up enough so she could watch me pitch, and promised to finish their work when I finished mine. They were going to have her checked out by a doctor, and they thought I might like to tag along.

I lumbered into the training room, dragging the ball and chain of my fresh big league failure behind me. Bonnie was waiting for me in one of the private examination rooms of the main training room with her foot soaking in a container of warm water and iodine. When I walked into the room, she reacted to me as if I was the one injured. There were members of the team around so she didn't blubber over me, but it was easy to see that she wanted to.

"Are you alright?" we asked in unison.

"I'm okay," we both responded.

She was okay, and her injury was being well tended to. I, however, was lying as much for her sake as my own pride. I didn't want the guys around me to think I was weak.

"I've got to get some ice on my arm," I said to her. "Then I'll come back in and join you."

"Okay, honey. I'll be here."

The training staff wrapped my arm up in ice, one bag on my elbow and one on my shoulder. After they finished, I went back into the little examination room with Bonnie. When the door clicked shut, my guard went down, exposing the broken man behind the shield. I let my head fall back against the wall. Bonnie didn't say anything, knowing that when I'm in a wounded state she would have to choose her words carefully.

"Well, I had my chance and I blew it," I began.

"No, you didn't . . ." She stopped to consider her words for a moment. Then, realizing pat statements were not going to cut it, she offered, "I'm sorry. I'm sorry it was a bad outing." She put her hand on mine.

"Me too," I said. "My body just wouldn't cooperate. I couldn't throw strikes." I looked desperately to Bonnie. "I don't understand why I'm not getting the ball over the plate like I always have."

"I don't know either, honey."

"It's like I just lost it." My head went back to the wall.

"You haven't lost it."

"It sure feels that way."

"Look at me," she said, but I didn't. "Look at me. You haven't lost it. You can't think that way." She tried to pull my face around to hers, but I resisted.

I couldn't look at Bonnie. I knew where I was, and how I was expected to behave. Of all the things I dreamed of doing in a major league locker room, crying on the shoulder of my fiancée was not one of them. She wasn't supposed to be here, and I was starting to think I wasn't supposed to be here either.

"When it falls apart out there, it's like you're in free fall with no chute. You know you're falling and you can't stop it. It took a lot to make that feeling come out of me in Triple A, but here, if I fall behind on a batter I'm immediately rattled. It's like I can feel what everyone is thinking. I'm hoping I can get outs and this is the one level where I need to *know* I can get them." I mocked myself with my own laughter. "Jesus, I'm in the Bigs and hoping."

"It was just one outing, babe."

"But my career starts here," I said.

"That's not true. You've been playing for a long time. You've had a lot of success."

"Those words don't apply when the outing in question is the one that decides your future. Do you think this is going to help us stay up here through September? I don't think so."

"You're under a lot of pressure and you're expanding this into a bigger thing than it needs to be." She said it all very controlled, trying to cool me off.

"Bonnie, it doesn't get any bigger than this!"

"You're not a starter," she offered.

"I don't need your excuses," I said. "I need to pitch better. A player can't complain about his opportunity, he can only make the most of it."

The handle of the door latch turned along with the sound of a knock. In walked one of the team physicians. He introduced himself, and I responded chipper and cheery, like the entire day had been full of nothing but rainbows. "Thank you so much for seeing her."

The doctor said it was nothing, that he was happy to do so. He checked Bonnie's foot, cleaned it, and then patched it. Convinced she was in good hands, I stepped out to take off my ice bags. While assisting me in unraveling my arm from the wraps that held the ice on, one of the trainers asked me if I was worried about Bonnie while I pitched, if it was distracting.

I knew there was nothing I could do to change my outing, no way to go back in time and fix it. However, if there was a way to paint it in a different color, a way to convince those making decisions that this disaster wasn't entirely my fault, maybe this disaster wouldn't look so bad after all. Maybe Bonnie cutting her foot was a blessing in disguise. If I told the trainers I couldn't focus knowing my fiancée was hobbling around on a sliced-up foot, maybe the powers that be would show me mercy. I had an excuse, all I had to do was take it and run with it.

"It wasn't the best thing to have happen on a start day," I said, wadding up the wrap and shedding the ice. "She's my fiancée, after all. I mean, she is the most important thing in the world to me."

Chapter Fifty-nine

I got called into Buddy Black's office the next morning, I didn't need my agent or a pitching coach to tell me why. I hadn't gotten the job done, and now my worst fears were coming to fruition. At least, after I shut the door behind me, Buddy told me he would make the execution quick.

"Have a seat, this won't take long," said Buddy.

I sat as instructed and stared nobly back at Buddy like a man about to be shot for taking part in a revolution.

"CY is coming off the DL, which means he's going to slide back into your spot in the rotation."

I nodded, all the while thinking, *Bless you, Bud Black, for not telling me I sucked, but simply saying my time was up.* I braced myself for the real words, as they were surely next to come.

"So, that means we are going to slide you into the pen, back into a role you know."

"The bullpen?" I asked, trying not to show my surprise.

"Yeah. We probably won't use you for a day or two because of the innings you had yesterday, but you never know."

"Of course," I said, still quite stunned.

"Alright, that's it. You'll be in the pen tonight."

"Thanks, Skipper." Buddy nodded at me, indicating that I was both welcome and free to go.

*   *   *

My first taste of the bullpen happened well before the start of the night's game, when I was introduced to my new responsibilities as youngest guy in the pen: the Candy Bag.

Typically bullpen bags come in the form of what is commonly referred to as the pink princess backpack, complete with, but not limited to, frolicking Disney princesses, Dora the Explorer, Barbie, or any other pack embossed with colors and imagery that could induce a screaming fit from a six-year-old girl if Mommy doesn't buy it for her. These packs are considered high fashion in the world of rookie embarrassment, and though many rookies say they hate wearing the pack because "It's gay," they really love it. They are secretly proud because it symbolizes, in a humorous and fun way, that they are now part of the fold.

The Padres, however, did not have a princess backpack. No Jasmine, no Belle, not even Pocahontas. Instead, we had a standard-issue navy ball bag modified for candy by an insert that read CANDY. I was let down by it. Without the fun of being the princess pack player, I was just a mule responsible for candy transport.

The guy who carried the bag before me was also in charge of training me on proper candy bag operation. Hamp, the bag's previous owner, took me to the dugout supply room and showed me how it worked.

"Guys love these," he said, cramming pouches of pumpkin seeds into the open bag. "And make sure you get some of these too." He grabbed some pouches of sunflower seeds in varying flavors. "Guys are going through a real barbeque kick lately, but a little while ago everyone wanted Ranch. You need to pay attention to their eating habits so you have what they want." He grabbed a few other pouches and wedged them into the bag.

"Why don't I just put some of everything in the bag?"

"There is not enough room."

"Why not just get a bigger bag?"

"Welcome to the big leagues," said Hamp, deflecting the question.

He did have a lot of stuff in the bag. When he was done getting seeds, he pulled separate Ziploc plastic bags from the mother ship candy bag revealing all the goodies stashed within. There was a unique bag for chocolate, brightly colored sugary treats, seeds, and hard candies. Then Hamp pulled out a bag that had cans of dip, lighters, and packs of cigarettes.

The cigarettes caught me off guard. I knew chewing tobacco was as much a staple of the game as peanuts or Cracker Jacks, but smoking it? That didn't seem right. I envisioned running to the mound, then having to take a breather around second base because of an emphysemic coughing fit.

"Do I have to stock those?" I asked, pointing toward the cigarettes.

"No, you just need to make sure you have this chew." He pulled a box of chew off the stock shelf, took out a few of the pouches, and stuffed them into the candy bag. "You might also want to pick up a lighter now and again," he said.

I looked around the stock room for lighters. There were none.

"Where do I get the lighters from?" I asked.

"You buy them."

"I have to buy stuff for the bag?"

"Yeah. Guys who do the best candy bag pick up stuff. You know, they take pride in it." He looked at me like he was handing me the keys to my first car and expected me to wash it and tune it or something. I wondered if he knew how hard that would be for me since there were no princesses on the bag.

"Some of the stuff you'll have to buy," he continued, "like this." He pulled out a sleeve of Winterfresh gum. "This is Hoffman's favorite. He chews a pack of it a game. You'll have to pick that up. Other stuff you can steal from other locker rooms. Not every locker room we play in stocks the same candy, so keep your eyes peeled for new stuff."

"Sample the local cuisine, so to speak," I said.

"Yeah, and eat what they got too," he said.

"So that's it? Hoffman eats Winterfresh, don't overpack, and make sure to raid the opposing pantries?"

"No, then there's this side of it." Hamp opened up a side compartment on the bag to reveal the other, more important side of the candy bag. He pulled out single-serving containers of Advil, Tylenol, Excedrin, Pain-Off, and various other pills from decongestants to antacids. There were tubes of nasal clearing hot creams for sore muscles, rubber gloves so players could rub in said creams without fear of lighting their delicate hands on fire, and cough drops for when their emphysema flared up.

Then the real supplies came out: various goops and stick 'ems that some morally sensitive fans would call the use of cheating, while we in the business simply called having an edge. There was good old-fashioned pine tar, the granddaddy of all baseball grip agents that always seemed to leak and cake on everything it came into contact with no matter how well it was sealed. We had a tube of Firm Grip, a scientifically engineered knockoff of pine tar, except when you worked it into your fingers, the harder you pressed the more grip you got. Firm Grip is also a lot easier to apply to those tight spots, like belt loops, hat bills, and the creases of your mitt without making a complete mess of yourself—that, and it doesn't make your fingers smell like a pine tree.

There was shaving cream, specifically the gel stuff, which, when rubbed into the hands, makes the fingers slightly more tacky without turning them into flypaper-like pine tar or Firm Grip does. The effect of shaving cream doesn't last as long as the other two, and you can't store a dollop of it on your person in some secret place while pitching, but it should get you through an inning if applied right.

Finally, there was Coppertone Sunscreen. When rubbed into the skin and mixed with sweat and rosin, this stuff actually forms an SPF-40-caliber Fixodent, which a crafty pitcher can mix on the fly. A touch to the wrist slightly below the mitt for some screen, a wipe of the back of the neck for some sweat, a pat of the rosin bag for the third component, and you'll have enough tack to make the ball hang from your fingertips. Everyone has their preferred method of adding a grip to a ball, but which one a pitcher chooses depends on his personal feel. My job, aside from providing tasty treats, was to make sure everyone had their respective edge ready and accounted for. It was a major responsibility, a sacred trust, and something that would, as Hamp said, "piss everyone off if you don't do it right."

"I got it." I saluted him.

Hamp pushed the bag into my arms. "That's it, bro. We meet at the steps and go out to the pen as a group. Heath usually leads us."

"We go as a group, huh?"

"Yeah, of course. It shows unity."

Chapter Sixty

I put the bag down in an area close to where Hoffman would sit. Then, I took all the bags inside the main bag that were full of candy and goodies and set them around the main bag. I left the illegal substances in the main bag since they would be in plain view of fans if I didn't. Finally, I took out Hoffman's sacred pack of Winterfresh, peeled back the top of the package to make easy access to the sticks inside, then set it delicately on top of the closed main bag like a golden star on top of a tiny tree of bullpen treats. I was proud of the arrangement, like some interior decorator. However, as soon as I stepped away, the rest of the relievers ransacked my arrangement and left the bags scattered, knocking Hoffman's gum from its throne.

More than anything, I wanted the arrangement to impress Hoffman. I wanted him to see that I was a good rookie and a good steward of junk food. I went back to the pile of bags and tidied things up, replacing the gum to its perch just before Hoffman's arrival.

The other relievers greeted him by throwing handfuls of sunflower seeds at him, laughing as the seeds showered over him and plinked off the coffee cup he was carrying. I dared not throw any at him, but I did watch his every move, the ease of his stride, the firmness of his gaze. All my life I'd wanted to play on the same team as him, and now, I was. I was in his bullpen. Maybe I'd even pitch in a game that he would come into to save? It was one of those big league moments that left me spinning, wondering if this was really happening.

He arrived at my candy bag. I bit my bottom lip in anticipation of him being impressed by the well-arranged, expertly organized display of calories. He stared hard at the bag, holding his coffee in his left hand. *Was this the best candy-bagging he'd ever seen? Was he going to congratulate me?*

"What the hell is this?" he shouted. Then he picked up some of the bags and emptied their contents on the floor. "What's all this other crap?" he shouted and started kicking the items across the bullpen floor. "How hard is it to do this job? Who the hell packed this?" He tossed the main bag across the pen where it bounced on the floor and came to a rest near my feet.

Everyone in the pen turned their heads and looked down at me. I couldn't breathe I was so terrified. I managed to get my shaking down long enough to claim responsibility. "I did it," I said.

"Gum, seeds, it's not that hard." He kicked another bag, spraying more goodies around the floor. "Now pick it up!" he commanded.

"I'm sorry, I'm so sorry," I said, leaping from my seat like a slave motivated by fear of death. I grabbed the main bag and threw candy into it so vigorously that I missed the bag completely, throwing the candy back on the floor. When I cursed myself and went to retrieve my misses, a collective laughter broke out among the pen. I looked up to see that everyone, including Hoffman was laughing.

"Stop, stop," said Hoffman. "I'm just kidding."

Everyone had grins on their faces—everyone except me.

"You're fine, kid. We're just playing with you. Here, I'll help you," said Hoffman, helping me corral some of the candy.

"The look on your face was priceless," said one of the guys in the pen. Some of the other guys threw seeds on me as I stood, still in shock.

"I thought he was going to shit himself," said another.

"You understand, when I saw that you unwrapped my gum, I had to do it." Hoffman shrugged as he handed me some of the contents he booted. "No one has ever done that before."

"But, but, you're sure you're okay with my bag?"

"It's fine," said Hoffman. "It's great."

"Okay," I said as another handful of seeds rained down on me.

A few innings later, Bonnie came by with her camera out. I noticed her waving at me, discreetly at first. When I didn't respond, she started calling my number. I hopped up and shushed her and came over to the railing to see what she wanted.

"Can you pose for me, so I can get some shots of you?"

I turned around to see if I'd drawn any attention from the other guys on the team. "Honey, it's my first day out here. I don't want to do anything stupid."

"Are you allowed to take pictures?"

"I guess, but if I'm posing for them I'll never hear the end of it."

"Well, don't pose, just act natural."

I stood there tense and rigid as she focused the camera on me.

"Smile."

"Just take the picture," I said.

"You'll be happy I took these when you're done this season."

One of the older guys came up from the underground bunker section of the pen to stand next to me. I spun around and nodded to him, windmilling my arm around to make it look like I was stretching out and not getting my picture taken by my fiancée. When he passed, I turned back to face Bonnie, who was holding the camera up, trained on me.

"What are you doing now?"

"I'm videoing, for my parents. Tell them 'Hi.' They'll love it."

"Hi, Mr. and Mrs. St. John," I whispered.

"I don't think they'll be able to hear that over the crowd noise."

"*Himisterandmissesstjohn!*" I snapped. "Okay, that's enough. Put the camera away, please."

"Okay, okay." She smiled and put the camera back into her purse. "I'm glad you're back out here doing what you know." As she spoke, other fans had walked over to investigate why I was so close to the fence. With the crowd around, eating and pointing at me, I felt like I was some animal at a really expensive and well-lit zoo.

"Yeah." I kept shifting around uncomfortably.

"Fifty-Seven! Can I have your autograph?"

"I can't sign during the game."

"Will you get Hoffman to come over here for me?"

"Kid, I can't even get Hoffman to come over here for me."

"Will you try?"

"No."

"Honey, do you have to work out after the game or anything?" Bonnie asked.

"I don't think so. Just meet me at the family lounge."

"How do I get to the wives' lounge?" asked one of the fans.

"Jesus, Hay, get her number and take her out to dinner. We got a game going on over here."

"Isn't that Hamp?" asked Bonnie. "He knows we're engaged, right?"

I turned back to Hamp and smiled and put my hand up and gave him the one-more-minute gesture. "Babe, I have to go. I'll see you at the wives' lounge, okay?"

"Okay. I love you."

"I . . ." I shifted uneasily, looking at all the faces around me. "*Iloveyoutoo.* Now I'll see you after."

Chapter Sixty-one

Because of my start, I had a few days off to soak up life in the pen. I watched Hoffman the most, when he was out there, that is. He was a creature of routine. He showed up at the same time every game, ate the same gum, sat in the same place, and left during the same innings to go into the training room, where he did more preparation for a potential close situation. When he was around, everyone seemed better behaved, like a teacher was in the classroom.

The thing about older players is they have so much clout in the social structure of the game that younger players fear to disturb their rituals. They tend to give them wide berths, and assume they have discovered some special recipe for success. This, combined with my rookie status, made me fearful of talking to Hoffman, even though there was no other person in the organization I wanted to talk to more than him. From time to time, I tried to work up the courage to sit down next to him, but I had no idea what to say.

When Hoffman left the pen, I realized how quiet it was. Hamp sat at the end of it, flicking seeds into the audience. Bentley went down into the bullpen's private bunker and smoked with some of the other guys. Heath sat next to the pen's coach, Akerfelds, and talked about the game. Other guys stretched and wandered, but there was very little chatter. It was a serious place and, like in the dugout, I sat at the end of the bench, keeping my mouth shut lest I somehow disrupt the focus.

When I did talk, my words always seemed to be sifted through a filter of, "Why is this rookie talking?" and, "Does he say things worthy of the big leagues?" Looking at myself through someone else's eyes had become a habit. In fact, asking questions about how I was supposed to behave was usually my main lead in to any conversation since it was the one thing everyone seemed to have an opinion on. I discovered that almost everything I did was being watched: how I handled myself around the locker room, body language during the game, reactions to comments. I guess I knew stuff like this was monitored, veterans in Triple A did it on occasion, but how intensified it was up here startled me. Furthermore, all the information was conflicting. Some of the older guys liked rookies who carried themselves with confidence; others thought that a confident swagger screamed "comfortable." Some wanted rookies to shut up and stay out of the way while others wanted rookies to be proactive in the learning process. Oddly, if you got caught pleasing one veteran in plain view of another, you ran the risk of being labeled defiant. It was almost as if no matter what you did, you ran the risk of making an enemy since everyone thought of themselves as special and to be obeyed.

The one thing that was universally accepted by veterans was good play. Performing well earned you privileges socially. This, too, was something found in the minors but intensified in the big leagues. However, since I had not performed well, I had no privileges. I found myself wanting to pitch if only to gain a chance to break free of the cone of silence I was in. In the meantime, I did my best to walk the social tightrope of being a rookie in the big leagues, balancing the opinions that veterans had on how I should behave, no matter how conflicting.

After our home stand, we headed to LA to play the Dodgers. Since it was only a two-hour drive, those of us not driving expensive, customized cars went by bus. As the team bus pulled out, so did Bonnie, leaving for home again. I was actually glad she was heading back. It was hard for me to focus on her and keep track of all the things I was supposed to be doing now that I was in the Show. With all the work I was doing to keep up rookie pretenses and appeasing the veterans, chaperoning her was becoming a distraction.

The hotel in Los Angeles was by far the best hotel I'd ever stayed in in my life. My room had twin, marble walk-in showers; a hot tub; a king-size bed with down pillows; and a sitting room with three couches and a solid oak desk. If this was my room, I couldn't imagine what Hoffman or Peavy stayed in. I actually wondered if someone on the team found out about my room, whether they would be upset because a rookie got such a nice one.

The Dodgers' ballpark, on the other hand, was a dump. The insides of the place were in dire need of renovating. The locker room was cramped and training room small. I think the clubhouse staff knew this because their service was amazing, as if to make up for the subpar facilities. They provided everything imaginable, from an unlimited supply of Dodger dogs to a computer geek who could turn your laptop into a mobile entertainment center. However, as good as they were, there was nothing they could do to make up for the Dodger fans.

Some fan bases are more aggressive than others. It's well known that Phillies fans are some of the meanest on earth. The Bronx houses that typical New York bravado, and Boston has a good reputation for verbally punishing anyone who dares challenge their Sox. But the fans at LA were nothing to scoff at. From the minute they started filing in for batting practice until the completion of the game, they were on us.

"Hey Fifty-Seven, nice career numbers. Whose dick did you suck to get up here?"

"Hey, Hayhurst, I hope you pitch tonight so we can get an easy win."

"Hayhurst, give me a ball, you fucking douche."

"Hey, Hayhurst, I got your Dodger dog right here!"

The Dodgers' pen, situated in right field, was exposed to fans above us on both the left and the right. Since the Dodgers were in contention for the play-offs, the seats were stuffed with Dodger blue. Fans yelled down at us from above, screaming how we sucked. When we tuned them out, bags of trash came sailing down on top of us. Then cups of beer were dumped over, sending us to find cover in the pen's tiny bunker. Fights intermittently broke out in the stadium—it was actually more fun to watch the police haul away fans who were duking it out than it was to watch the game, since when the police stepped in to keep the peace, they got showered with beer from the upper levels too.

We got beat the first game. Maddux, formerly of the Padres, used his powers against us to best Chris Young, my replacement. The Dodger fans made sure to rub it in as we walked off the field. Then, after they told us how bad we were, they asked us for balls. When we said no, they went back to telling us we sucked.

When I came into the locker room the next day, I noticed there were a few new nameplates above lockers. It was September now, and some familiar faces had been called up to join us. Frenchy, Anto, Luke, Chip, and Kip had all come up. Kip, Frenchy, and Anto walked into the locker room with the same dumbstruck expression I had when I was in their shoes, while Luke and Chip slipped back into a more tried-and-true routine. I was happy to see them all, more happy than I could possibly express through congratulation. It was almost as if I wanted to hold hands with them and run off giggling to some remote corner and say, "Oh my gosh, I missed you so much." Instead, when the coast was clear, I whispered inquiries about how they were doing.

"I didn't expect this to happen," said Frenchy. "I can't believe it."

"Neither did I," I said. "I still can't."

"Hey man, don't let me do anything stupid," said Frenchy.

"I don't know if I can help you there, I don't know what I'm doing most of the time myself. We lose a lot and I think guys are a little edgy because of it. Just keep your head down. That's what I do."

"Right," said Frenchy.

"What about me?" asked Anto.

"I don't know, dude. The position players seem pretty easygoing, I guess."

"Yeah, you pitchers are like a bunch of princesses. You guys love drama."

"Save it, Anto," said Frenchy.

"He may actually be right," I said.

"Told you," said Anto.

"But most of them are the same guys from Portland," Frenchy pointed out.

"Yes and no," I said. "They're the same people, but they act different now. Some of them act real arrogant for some reason."

"Why?"

"I don't know. Which reminds me, get used to the phrase, 'Welcome to the big leagues'."

I went on to tell them about the beer bag, the trick bus they were forbidden to ride, the eyewash expectations, and the coaches who were approachable and the ones who weren't. "Beyond that, just try to blend in."

They both bobbed their heads up and down and went off to get suited up.

Moments later, I greeted Chip and Luke. "Welcome back."

"Thanks, bro. Good to be back," said Chip.

"So, status report," said Luke.

"I like the paychecks, I like the plane rides, and I like the hotels. I'm just trying to prove I can stick."

"It's tough," said Luke. "That's why sticking is always talked about with such reverence."

"Yeah, but I'm back in the pen now, back doing what I know."

"You know what they say about rationalizing," said Luke, implying I'd have to follow through.

"Yeah, well, I don't think it's a stretch to say I wasn't ready to start, right?"

"It was a great opportunity, though," Chip said.

"I've still got opportunities left. Besides, now that I've got Luke up here to throw to, I'll be way more successful. And I got you here to advise me. The dream team is assembled once more, I can't fail!"

Chapter Sixty-two

I don't know how the idea got in my head, but as I sat in the pen during the second game, monitoring the bags of candy to make sure of perfect alignment, I started to envision what it would mean for me if I was the team's Dodger killer. Sure, I stunk against the Giants and the Rockies, but who were they anyway? The Dodgers were like the West Coast's version of the Yankees this year. They were running away with the NL West. If I could shut them down, maybe I could redeem myself. What if I turned out to be awesome against the powerhouse teams? I began to rationalize how ridiculous it was for them to even have me try and start after spending all year relieving. I was out of my element in the rotation, but a good relief outing against these superstars might get me back on the road to vindication.

I got a chance to prove my theory nearly as soon as I'd thought it up. In the bottom of the fourth inning, Baek was getting beat up and the call came for me to bail him out. I avoided raining trash and beer long enough to get hot. Time was called, Bud was out of the dugout, he gestured to the pen, the umpire turned and pointed, the gate opened, and out I sprinted, Dirk Hayhurst, Dodger killer.

I hit the game mound with a man on first and third. Bud handed me the game ball and the fielders dispersed. One out, that was all I needed.

Russell Martin stepped in. What did I know about him other than he was a catcher and French-Canadian? Nothing. But I didn't need to know anything; he was just another out to the Dodger killer.

Martin and I locked horns and soon I'd worked him into a payoff pitch scenario. With Baek's runs still on, I decided to go with my quickstep. Since that day in the batting cage so many months ago, I'd started using it in situations where I needed a little something extra to throw a batter off my trail. It was part of my bag of tricks now, and I'd gotten quite a few outs with it in key situations. This was one of them: James Loney on first, Andre Ethier on third, and an all-star catcher at the plate—shutting down this inning would look great on my résumé.

I came set, held, held, held, and then, the jabbing daggerlike step that had caught so many hitters off guard in Portland. I hurled a fastball and, with an equally quick stroke, Martin's bat slashed it into shallow left for a single that scored Ethier.

That wasn't supposed to happen; that *never* happened! I could feel the despair part of me starting to creep in but I fought it off. The ball wasn't hit *that* well, I told myself. I could still get out of this without too much damage. I could still be the Dodger killer. And besides, that was Baek's run, not mine. He shouldn't have let them on in the first place. This was about me.

Casey Blake stepped in next and I got him to pop out on an inside fastball to end the inning. I congratulated myself on getting out of an inning with minimal damage, and not giving up any of my own runs. The Dodger crowd yelled at me as I entered the dugout, but I ignored them. I had to keep my focus, keep my positive attitude up because I was probably going out for the next inning. I took my hat off, set my glove down, and grabbed a towel, all the while facing the bench. When I finally turned to face the field again, there was Balsley, boring a hole in me with his glare.

"What the fuck was that?" he said with the most emotion I'd heard from him since my arrival.

I didn't know what he was referring to. I thought about my

pitch selection and what I'd thrown Blake to make him pop out. My clueless face did all the talking.

"That gimmick bullshit may work down in the minors but it doesn't fly here."

"The quickstep? I wanted to throw off his timing," I stammered.

"If you can't locate, it doesn't matter what you do to his timing. You fucked around and left that pitch up. I don't ever want to see you do that shit again. This is the fucking big leagues. If you want to do that shit you can go back to Triple A. Do you understand me?"

"I . . . I . . . I'm sorry," was all I could think to say.

"You're sorry?" he scoffed. "Say that to Baek, they're his runs." His stare was too firm for me to match, and I dropped my head.

"You're done. Bentley's got the next inning. Get the fuck out of here."

The rest of my night was spent in silence. Balsley's chewing of my ass was loud and public enough to widen the cone of silence around me, even to my freshly promoted friends. After the game, Bonnie called me three or four times as I sat in my posh hotel room, thinking about the event. I'd been roughed up pretty good during my short career as a big leaguer, but nothing stung quite as bad as Balsley's comments. I wondered if his words were by design, if he was testing me, or if he just plain hated me. I was starting to hate him, but such a hate was fruitless since he was the big league coach while I was just me.

Bonnie's name and number showed up again on my phone's caller ID, but I did not answer. I didn't want to talk to her about it. I didn't want to relive it and listen to her make excuses for me. When the phone stopped ringing, I checked the message she left. "Glad you had a good outing tonight!" she said cheerily. "I'll bet you're pumped to be succeeding out of the pen! I told you you would. Have fun tonight, big leaguer, I lov—" That was all I listened to before I deleted the message and closed the phone.

Chapter Sixty-three

A week passed. I stopped answering my phone as much as I used to. Since I got called up, people had been coming out of the woodwork to tell me they'd been following my career since it started, even if I didn't know about it until now. They'd ask leading questions like, "It must feel awesome to be up there?" and, "I can't imagine what you must feel like every day?" I used to enjoy taking the calls, but now, knowing what they wanted to hear me say was so different from what I felt, I stopped picking up. Even Bonnie's voice was beginning to grate on me. Our conversations were much shorter and one-sided with my answers coming in empty yes's and no's.

Since my outing against the Dodgers, Dirk Hayhurst, the mighty Dodger killer, had only pitched once—against the Dodgers again, ironically, this time at home. I recorded a single strikeout, my first clean outing of the year. I felt good about it, if only slightly, and I did my best to fan that positive feeling into something I could stand on, even if it was only one batter.

The day after the outing, Anto, Frenchy, and I stood next to each other on the dugout fencing, waiting for team stretch to start, talking about our time in the big leagues up to this point. More rookies had come aboard, including waiver pickups, and some of the crew from the Double A team, like Mike Ekstrom and Drew

Macias. They were all joining a team that was playing for nothing, and while this lack of direction didn't matter to any of the new faces when viewed through the lens of finally reaching the Bigs and the paycheck it granted, when the euphoria wore off, the reality of playing for a team whose only goal was not losing one hundred games before the season's end set in. The basement dwelling had taken its toll on the older players, who, in turn, took out their frustration on the younger ones.

There were a lot of egos so big in the big leagues, it was a good thing the stadiums were so massive and cavernous or there would be no way they'd fit in the parks. They'd habitually analyzed why the team was losing, declaring their reasoning like sermons to us rookies who had no choice but to act as their captive audience. Everything they did or said was expected to be revered because it was done and said in the big leagues, the billion-dollar industry that had generated the very history we'd tried all our lives to be a part of. It was becoming obvious that just because certain players were more successful and recognizable didn't mean they were good teammates, communicators, or people. Yet, as it had always been, it was pointless to bring that part of the baseball life into the equation because, after all, they were gods, and we were nothing because we'd done nothing valuable on a team that could do nothing valuable.

It ate me up inside. I'd never felt more weak and pathetic in my whole career. I felt like a whiner, and maybe I was, but the experience was painful in a way I couldn't overcome. My days now consisted of watching over my shoulder and never-ending sycophancy in between embarrassing myself on national television.

"I have no idea how I am supposed to act at this point," said Frenchy. "It's like if I pitch bad and I look upset about it, I get yelled at because this is the big leagues and I'm supposed to be happy. Then, if I pitch good, and I'm happy about it, I get yelled at because I'm happy and the team is losing and I shouldn't be carrying myself around the locker room like I'm 'the man' while the

team is losing. Yesterday, I sat on the couch and got yelled at because I didn't have enough time to sit on the couch yet. Today I
got yelled at for acting timid when I'm a starter and I should be a
team leader." He held his hands out wide as if lost, then tucked
them in quickly in fear that someone might yell at him about it.

"I got a hit in my first at bat and the hitting coach told me I'll
never hit up here with the swing I have, after I just got a hit," said
Anto. "Day one in the Bigs and I'm already getting overhauled. I
don't friggin' understand it. Now I feel like I don't know what I
should do at the friggin' plate 'cause I don't want to piss the hitting coach off."

"Yesterday," continued an exasperated Frenchy, "someone
asked me if I was going to watch videotape and I said no, because
I was nervous and already overthinking myself and didn't want
anything else swimming in my head. The veteran asked me if I
thought I was too good to learn something. I said no, of course
not, so I go in and start watching video to make him happy, video
I'm not even paying attention to, and then, one of the older guys
comes in and throws me out for getting in his way!"

"That's friggin' hilarious," said Anto.

"No, it's not," pleaded Frenchy. "Everyone thinks I'm arrogant
now and I didn't do anything. They all evaluate my body language
and my actions, and then they think they can tell me how to act
when they don't know me at all." Frenchy turned to Anto. "Besides, what's wrong with what got you here?"

"I don't know. But he's the big league hitting coach. I'm going
to do what he tells me."

I could relate to everything and yet it meant nothing. There
was one truth that trumped it all and I repeated, "Yeah, it's strange.
It sucks, but this is the only league that matters. If we can't find a
way to get it done, we don't belong here," I said vacantly.

"Fine," said Frenchy. "If I get my ass kicked out there, *then* I
don't belong here. But not because some asshole has more time
than me and says I'm not acting like he thinks I should."

"If that's the case, I don't belong here," I said. "In case you haven't noticed, I'm better at kissing ass and handling the candy bag then I am at pitching."

"Come on, man, you belong. You pitched the hell out of it in triple A."

"That doesn't matter anymore. This isn't Triple A. It's all about what you do up here. It's always been about that."

"Well, you had a good outing last night."

"I faced one batter."

"Dude, stop, you're going to figure it out. You have to stay positive."

"Jesus, you want me to leave so you two can make out?" asked Anto.

"The difference between me and you guys," I said to Anto and Frenchy, "is that you're prospects and they want you here. This is an audition for me, and I'm blowing it. It's like a test to see if I'm the real deal and so far I've failed it. And don't tell me to do whatever I did to get myself here, because it's impossible to do the same things you did in Triple A up here. Everything is different."

"Remember how many times you've had to hold my hand when I felt bad these last two years?" asked Frenchy. "Well, I'm not going to let you bail on yourself now. Plenty of time left to make up for it. You've done good out of the pen. String a few more together and you'll be fine."

"If you two start kissing," Anto said, shaking his head, "I'm going to vomit right here. I got a weak stomach."

Chapter Sixty-four

I got the call again that night. It was getting easier to manage the big league stadium factor now that I'd made a few trips to the mound. I wasn't comfortable by any stretch, but I did make it through the eighth inning without much trouble, which gave me some confidence that I was improving. I felt like I'd found my command again. I felt like I'd remembered my delivery. Maybe it was calmer nerves. Maybe it was Frenchy's pep talk. Whatever it was, I didn't dwell on the issue. After punching out the next two hitters in the following inning, I got back on the mound ready to face Andre Ethier and finish my first real appearance as Dirk Hayhurst, San Diego Padre.

I knew what Ethier was capable of, the year he was having, and, most importantly, who was on deck behind him. It's funny how so many threads of life can intersect on a baseball field. In this forgettable game, one where the home team cheered more for the Dodgers than their Padres, one that I was allowed to pitch in because we were losing by a jagged number, so much of my life hung in the balance. Baseball revolves around what a player is able to repeat: throwing balls or strikes, getting hits or making outs, wins and losses, success and failure. I finally had a chance to repeat success. I could finally tune out the crowd long enough to hear my teammates cheering. I could even hear Balsley, a voice I would never be able to tune out, telling me to keep it up.

Pumping in strikes like the Dirk of old, I got Ethier to swing at a hook. I aimed it for the bottom of the zone, a plate topper that would look like a fat, juicy strike leaving my hand but fall deceptively short of hittable. When done right, bats are drawn to it like a tractor beam and Ethier's bat was no exception. He made contact with the top tenth of the ball, enough to send it sputtering on the ground between Adrian Gonzales at first and myself.

It was a "tweener," a groundball so slow and awkwardly placed it commits both the pitcher and the first baseman. I chased the ball, but, realizing I wouldn't get to it in time, broke off and headed toward the bag ready to take Adrian's throw. Ethier was right behind me, bolting down the line, unwilling to concede the at bat as a failure. Adrian, unwilling to concede it as a success, scooped and flicked the ball to me in stride. I stuck out my glove while breaking down to hit the bag, and in the rumbling of my footsteps and Ethier's, I lost the ball for a split second. It deflected off my mitt, hit the dirt, and Ethier crossed the bag safe.

There was a collective groan from the audience, which only served to punctuate the one in my soul. I'd worked on that play roughly a million times in my life. It was a play that pitchers made so many times they universally hated practicing it for its monotony. It's the one play coaches tell us we will never get beat by because we work too hard to make sure we don't . . . and I just did. Now, as a punishment for my crime of poor coordination, I would have to face Manny Ramirez.

I returned to the mound with the weight of my own self-loathing fresh upon my shoulders while one of baseball's all-time great sluggers, not to mention one of this season's hottest, strode to the plate with the carefree bounce the world had come to know him for. His pants were so baggy he looked like one of MC Hammer's backup dancers. In fact, the way his uniform billowed around him, he looked more like a gray trash bag with dreadlocks and a Dodgers' cap than a uniformed player. This was all part of his charm, and the roar of his fans nearly blew me off the mound. They kept chanting his name, screaming how much they loved him while tugging at shirts that bore his name—some even wore fake dreadlocks in imitation.

I stared him down from my elevated position. I told myself he was nobody special, that he was just another player. I told myself to not be intimidated by his legacy, or his horde of screaming worshipers. I told myself he was a clown, that he made the game look bad with all his antics, and that I would put him in his place by getting him out quickly and quietly. Then, as I watched the third pitch of the at bat sail over the right field fence, I told myself I hated the game of baseball, the big leagues, and Manny Ramirez.

Chapter Sixty-five

My cell phone rang, waking me up. I rolled over in my king-size bed at the Gaslamp Marriott and fumbled for the ringing, buzzing nuisance without taking my head out from under the pillow. When I finally grabbed hold of the phone, it stopped ringing and the line was dead. I sighed heavily and sank back into my mattress.

It was nearly noon and my head hurt. After I came out of the game last night, I went into the lockers to sulk. I didn't bother icing or doing rehab exercises; I just sat there in my own hell. A couple of the guys on the team patted me on the back and told me Manny had done that to a lot of pitchers in his career, but it was no consolation. It wasn't the home run, it was the play before the home run, and the outings before that. It was the slow but steady slipping shut of my window of opportunity in the Bigs. It was me constantly finding a way to blow it. I couldn't be further from the Dirk who turned down the All-Star game if I tried.

Jilly and Hoffman bought spread for us that night. I didn't understand why they needed to buy us food since post-game big league spreads were like gourmet meals, but I couldn't complain about what they bought. They had the crew from a local restaurant come in to our locker room and cook steaks, chicken, lobster, crab, fish—even a full sushi bar where we could order as much of any kind of sushi we wanted. As awesome as it was, I continued brooding through the experience.

That was when a couple of veteran guys insisted that I drown my sorrows with them in sake. After obediently guzzling shot after shot, the short walk back to the hotel became a long and winding one.

The missed calls section of my phone revealed my mother was the wake-up caller. She knew I was usually in bed till noon during the season, so whatever she was calling about must have been important. She'd left a message, but I decided to skip it and just call her back. She answered immediately and wasted no time in breaking the good news.

"I saw you on SportsCenter last night!"

"What?"

"You were on television. You made the ESPN highlight reel. Haven't you watched it yet? Oh no, you probably haven't because of the time change."

"What did they show?" I sat up, my voice grave.

"The home run to Manny. They showed it over and over again. I can't remember what number it was for him, but they kept saying it. He hit it good too. What did you throw him?"

"Oh fuck me," I said, and slammed back into the pillows.

"What's wrong?"

"What do you mean 'what's wrong?' I gave up a bomb to Manny fucking Ramirez and it's all over SportsCenter, that's what. Jesus, Mom, isn't it obvious?"

"Well, no, I thought you'd be happy. You always talked about wanting to make it on SportsCenter. Now you can say you have."

"I didn't want it to happen like this!"

She stuttered at what to say next, and I thought for a second she might have understood where I was coming from, but then her voice changed as if she'd stumbled on to some final truth. "I think you're looking at this the wrong way, Dirk. Think of how many people would love to say they gave up a home run to Manny."

"Just stop talking."

"What? Why? Everyone here was excited. All my friends have been watching ESPN since you got called up, and when they saw you, it was like a party around the neighborhood."

"Shut up, Mom."

"Don't tell me to shut up, I'm your mother."

"Shut up, Mom!" I screamed at her.

She did shut up, and in her silence I lay on the bed staring at the ceiling. I was close enough to the elevators that I could hear them whirring up and down through the building. I could hear traffic bustling along the street. And faintly, ever so faintly, I could hear the sound of people I'd never even met from all around the country awing over what a blast Manny hit off me.

"My head hurts," I said.

"Why?"

" 'Cause I'm dehydrated, 'cause I'm tired, 'cause the words coming out of your mouth make it hurt."

"Well, I'm sorry to bother you, Mr. Big Leaguer."

"What did you just call me?"

"Mr. Big Leaguer," she said again. "You know, your brother might be a drunk, but at least I can talk to him."

"Oh, for the love of God, now I'm the bad guy? This isn't a conversation. This is you missing the point of something, like you always do, and instead of asking where you messed up, you're mad at me for not going along with it."

"You just can't enjoy the moment so you take it out on me."

"This isn't a party, this is my job. When I don't get the results I need, this is what happens, Mom: nationally televised embarrassment. Every time I go out there the stakes are at their highest. I'm playing to keep my dream job, and every time I blow it I run the risk of losing it forever."

"Well, I'm not embarrassed," said Mom.

"You're not the one out there getting your ass kicked."

"It's just a home run, Dirk. You've given up plenty of them."

"I really hate you sometimes, you know that?"

"He said he hates me, Sam," she said, shouting over her shoulder. Then, back to me, "Your father says you're not bending over when you pitch. He says it's the same problem you always had back in high school."

"Tell him I said to mind his own fucking business and go smoke another cigarette."

"He said you should mind your own business, Sam," my mother repeated. Then, back to me again, "Your father said he's not the one giving up homers to Manny."

"Tell him I said to go—"

"You tell him," interrupted my mom. "If you two want to be nasty, you can be nasty together."

"I don't want to talk to Dad," I said.

"Why not?"

"I don't want to talk to anyone! I want to forget about this whole thing."

"Well, you can't, it's always going to be around. You just have to get over it."

"I know that, Mom! Don't you think I know that? Do you think this is my first time playing this game?"

"Geez-Louise, does Bonnie know you're like this when you pitch bad?"

"What?" Her citation of Bonnie took me off guard.

"Does Bonnie know what kind of person you turn into when you pitch bad?"

"I don't turn into any *kind* of person when I pitch bad."

"Oh yes, you do," she said with a laugh. "Oh Lord, do you ever."

"No, I don't! I turn into this person when I talk to you."

"Well, they say boys treat their wives like they treat their mothers."

If you were outside my room's window, you would have seen me throw my pillow against the glass and scream at it like I was insane.

"Calm down," said my mother. "I was just calling to tell you I was proud."

I buried my head in my hand, breathing heavily. "Okay, Mom,"

I said, collecting myself, "you saw me on SportsCenter. You're proud. I validate that. Are you happy now? Can I get off the phone now?"

"Your car got crushed by a tree last night."

"What?" I balked at the abrupt change of subject.

"Yes, we had a huge windstorm last night and it toppled a tree onto your car. The car looks like a bun around a tree-shaped hot dog. It's ruined."

"You're serious?"

"Yes, Dirk, I'm serious. It's totaled. You're going to have to find another car when you get back."

"What the . . . How?" I pulled the phone from my face and looked at it as if it were some direct line to hell. "Mom, what made you think now was the time to tell me that?"

"Well, I thought it would help you take your mind off last's night's outing."

"Oh yes, great plan, I've completely forgotten about it. Thank you so much."

"You're welcome."

I hung up.

Chapter Sixty-six

Aside from Peavy, our starters weren't going very deep into games. This meant the bullpen was getting a lot of action, even for an NL team. When the pen's red alert phone rang, many of the guys sarcastically whimpered. Some even pretended to cry, turning away with mock grief before forming finger guns with their catching hands and shooting their throwing arms like Old Yeller being put down behind the barn. This abundance of opportunity wouldn't have been a bad thing if I were even the slightest bit confident I wouldn't get my ass kicked when I came into the game.

When I got on the mound, things went berserk. I couldn't repeat my delivery or consistently hit a spot. What I could do was dwell on my many problems as I had an abundance of time to kill, sitting in my silent corner of the pen, waiting for the season to end. I mapped out everything that could go wrong in any given situation, and while other guys pretended to cringe when the pen's phone rang, I wasn't faking it.

After the Dodgers series at home, San Francisco came to town. I managed to stay out of the mess until the last game of the series when I was called in to extra innings. I entered as the long man, and would pitch as long as I could, or until the tie was broken.

I gave up two runs without recording an out, was pulled, and got the loss.

My confidence was shot. It took everything I had to convince myself I could hack it in the big leagues, that if I had my good stuff, I wouldn't be going through this. I rationalized, coached, recited, and even flat-out lied to myself to keep from going under. What I knew about myself as a baseball player was starting to slip away, and I was hanging on by teammate life support.

"It sucks, bro. I know you're down, but if nothing else, remember the paychecks," said Chip, with a punctuating head nod. "Just think how happy you and your queen are going to be knowing you don't have to worry about moving back in with your folks. Think of the new car you gonna buy with cash."

"I don't want to think of it that way. There's something wrong with being in the big leagues and just grinding out ass-kickings for checks."

"It sucks," said Luke. "You don't play well here and people think you're stealing checks, but so what? Take the money. It's basically what everyone else is doing up here right now. The season was over for a lot of these guys weeks ago. Most of them are worried about their contract status, arbitration, if they're going to have a job next year, and who's going to own the team. Don't read too far into this—it's a mess."

"That's easy for you to say, you don't have an ERA of 10."

"So do a lot of other guys. Everyone is pitching like shit right now. Don't let it rattle you."

"I'm better than this, though," I said. "You know that, you know I'm better than this, right?" They looked at me like I was some strung-out junkie.

Chip and Luke nodded their heads slowly, just like Frenchy nodded his head, and Anto his, and everyone else I cornered to talk about my insecurities with.

At first I let the insecurity come sparingly, testing the waters for compliments and pick-me-ups, but now I was letting them flow, bending conversations to my troubles and dumping my fears on anyone who would listen.

There is a threshold in baseball you only discover when things are going bad, the one your teammates have for enduring the venting of your frustrations. Every player goes through rough patches, and from time to time, every player needs to express their feelings about those rough patches to a teammate who was there and understands. But teammates tire of listening to other teammates whine extremely fast. This is when a player finds out his true friends. Chip, Anto, Luke, Frenchy: they were some of the truest friends I'd ever had in baseball, but even they had their limits.

Limits or not, I just couldn't stop myself. I had pushed everyone else out of my world, dubbing them all incapable of understanding what I was living through. This was an elite world, for elite people. I couldn't talk to Bonnie about my frustrations because she was incessantly positive, always telling me I was going to do better, always trying to discount the glaring negatives. I felt like I was one of her clients and not her husband-to-be. Then there were my parents, who still thought advising me like I was pitching in high school was reasonable nine years after graduating. My friends were too busy fawning over what it must be like to be in my shoes to empathize with my frustrations. Fans had no clue, the pitching coach had no stomach for weakness, and I'd be better off leaping from the top of the Gaslamp's rooftop bar than tell the veterans I wasn't enjoying my time in the Bigs. The only people I had left to talk to were those in similar situations, and the more I spoke to them about my problems, the less respect they had for me.

"Maybe I should ask Balsley if I can do some extra pen work? Maybe that would help me find what I've lost?"

"Not a good idea," said Luke.

"Why not? It might help me."

"It might, but you weren't doing that when you showed up here, so starting a new routine with two weeks of the season left will just make it look like you're grasping at loose ends. I'm telling you, just keep your head down and ride it out."

"It sounds like you don't want me to succeed, man," I said.

"Why would you say that, of course I want you to," said Luke.

"Then why would you advise me not to try and get better?"

Luke looked at Chip for help on the issue. Chip just looked away.

"That's not what I'm saying. I'm saying, people here are evaluating and it's obvious this group is overanalyzing character traits. I think it would make good sense just to ride it out and not draw any more attention to yourself. Maybe if you roll a few good outings together you could ask for some extra work, but . . ."

"But what?" I asked.

"But I don't think now is the time."

I didn't like Luke's answer. "If you were hitting bad, would you take extra cuts?"

"Yeah, but that's what hitters do."

"Then why can't pitchers? Why can't I?"

"I don't think Balsley likes . . . It's late in the year . . ." He shrugged. "Hey, man, you do what you need to do. I'm just telling you what I think."

I looked at him with skeptical eyes, with something very much like anger or resentment welling up inside me. Then I relaxed and thought about his words. We weren't competing against each other, after all. Maybe if Frenchy had said something like this, I would have more reason to doubt, but Luke was a catcher; he wouldn't do me dirty.

"Maybe you're right," I said.

"Yeah, man. We're all in the same boat. I need a few hits," said Luke.

"Lord, you know I could use a few," said Chip.

"You roll up some good outings, you won't even think about extra pitching," said Luke.

"Yeah," I laughed anxiously, "yeah, you're probably right."

Chapter Sixty-seven

We flew to Denver to take on the Rockies, where we would lose two of three, after already losing three of four against the Giants. I made it into one game, the second, and, ironically, managed a perfect one, two, three inning in a game we were losing by eight runs. I contributed my sudden success to the handful of change I tossed into the meditation pond next to the waterfall in the visitors' bullpen.

After game three, our getaway game with the Rockies, when the rookies got back into the locker room we discovered all our clothes were gone. Our suits, pants, and anything that could be considered street clothes aside from our socks and shoes had been removed. Hanging in their stead were little orange and white outfits, the same commonly found on Hooters girls.

Our rookie hazing began now.

It was our last cross-country trip of the year, and while all the players with a year or better of service time wore their normal suits, those of us with less were to be stuffed into Hooters costumes. It was a real wrestling match to get the outfits on. The tight orange spandex was not flattering to the bumps and bulges of the male body. To make the event less pornographic, we tried to wear underwear beneath the sheer, revealing fabric. However, our boxers and briefs proved larger than the tights, and we had to roll them up to make them fit. The extra fabric immediately shot up ass cracks and bunched up in various undercarriage hairs, resulting in a never-ending display of wedge-picking and ball-adjusting.

"How they gonna give me a small, bro? You see this ass, you think this fits into a small anything? Come on, man," said Chip, wrestling his tights on like a walrus squeezing into a tutu.

"I don't have any matching socks to wear with this," I said, looking down at how stupid my long black dress socks and dress shoes looked with orange Hooters shorts.

"You're dressed like a slutty waitress and you're worrying about your socks and shoes choice? What the hell is wrong with you?" asked Chip.

"I don't know. It just doesn't look right," I said, shrugging.

"Having a bulge in the front of these shorts doesn't look right. The socks are fine."

"Where am I going to put my ID?" I asked, though no answer came.

"I think I should wear my cup," said someone from the other side of the room, which quickly received the response of, "Get over yourself, dude, it's not that big."

Heath Bell wandered around the locker room taking pictures of us all doing our darnedest to keep our manhood in short shorts. He snapped more pics as we struggled to get our Hooters tank tops on. When we finally got everything on, and everything tucked in, we were ushered out to the field for a very special team picture.

The grounds crew stopped what they were doing to watch us come on to the field, laughing hysterically at us. Stadium staff and cleaning crews halted to stare at us, pulling out camera phones to immortalize their good fortune.

"Okay, ladies, smile for the camera," said Heath as he continued documenting.

And we did smile. We smiled and laughed because, as embarrassing as it was, it was also a rite of passage. It was like getting your degree, a moment when everyone acknowledged that we'd made it to the big leagues. There were fifteen rookies in total. Sixteen if you counted Justin Hatcher, the first-year bullpen catcher. We threw arms over each other's shoulders and smiled big for the camera. We formed the nastiest, most undesirable pack of Hooters girls that ever walked the face of the earth, and we were as proud as hell about it.

When the on field pictures stopped and our new marching orders were given, we goosed each other off the field. I thought we'd go get on our plane now, but Hoffman and Jilly had other plans. "I think it's time we bought these girls a couple of drinks."

Across the parking lot from the stadium was a restaurant known as the Chophouse. It was a bar-and-grill type of place, though we were only interested in the bar portion. With veterans on all sides of us, we were herded across the parking lot and up the steps of the Chophouse.

When we entered the place, food dropped out of mouths. Sixteen cross-dressers ambled into the joint, picking and tugging as they came. We were directed to the bar, where Jilly slapped down money and ordered a round of Patrón tequila shots. The bartender had to have the manager step in to help him mix up a batch for us. Ladies came up to have their pictures taken with us—some grabbed our butts and tried to stuff one-dollar bills down our orange shorts. The shots were distributed, clinked in a toast to our honor, then downed. Then more shots came, were clinked, and downed, Then more came. I had never drunk so much so fast, and by the time we picked and tugged our way out, I was working hard to keep a straight line back to the team buses.

We still had to get a beer bag. Still had to go through security check, survive the five-hour plane ride, and check in to the hotel in Washington. I called Bonnie from the parked plane and told her I loved her over and over again. I told her other things too, but I couldn't remember them. I think she told me she hoped I didn't do anything too stupid. I remember taking offense to that and telling her I was on a plane with a bunch of responsible adults and nothing stupid could happen. Then I told her I had to get off because one of the guys was falling out of his outfit and the other guys were trying to hit his exposed parts with ice cubes and I wanted to try.

That plane flight was one of the most liberating experiences I'd had since I'd been on the team. I don't know if it was because booze kept showing up in front of me or if it was because guys kept doing stupid and entertaining stuff, but we all had a good time. It was one of the first times I could stop thinking about my status as a rookie player and just enjoy the experience.

When the plane touched down in Washington, Hoffman turned the song blaring on his iPod speaker system to "My Way" by Frank Sinatra. I sang along to it for a verse or two before I turned to Frenchy sitting next to me and said, "You remember those transvestites in Salt Lake?"

"Yeah," said Frenchy.

"I wonder if they got started like this?"

Chapter Sixty-eight

I was sober by the time the team made it to the Ritz in downtown DC, but I wished I was still drunk. If I was, I wouldn't have remembered the feeling of being stared at by the staff and occupants of a five-star hotel, pulling bunched orange spandex from my ass while searching for where I'd stashed my credit card.

The next day was an off day. Bonnie got into town that night. She'd driven six hours after work to see me, overjoyed that I was on her side of the country again. I was happy to see her again since the rookie hazing had me feeling better about my life for the moment. We grabbed dinner in the hotel's pricey, over-the-top restaurant, then lounged in the posh hotel room eating snacks from the mini-fridge.

"I have a little something for you," said Bonnie. I was lying on the bed when she spoke.

"Oh, will I like it?" I asked, naughtily.

"Oh, you are going to love it," she said. She pulled out a Victoria's Secret bag from her luggage and set it down on the bed in front of me. I started to imagine what type of provocative outfit might be inside the bag.

"You like animal print, don't you?" she asked.

I squinted at her. I'd never really pegged her for the safari-in-the-bedroom type. "Depends if I'm the predator or the prey," I said.

"You're the prey." She giggled.

"I think I *am* going to like this."

"Okay, then you take it out of the bag."

I smiled slyly at Bonnie as I tugged the bag along. Still looking at her, I reached into the bag and felt fur. Then, my expression changed. I pulled out the item in the bag to reveal a homemade stuffed animal with purple spots, a long neck, and antlers.

"Is this a—"

"A Garfoose!" Bonnie finished. She was so excited for me to see it.

"Oh my gosh." I stared at the stuffed animal for a second. It was just like I had imagined it to be.

"Do you like it?"

I looked at Bonnie. "Do I like it? I love it! It's great!"

"I'm so glad, it took me forever to make it."

"Honey, it's amazing." I made the stuffed Garfoose dance on the bed. *"Nom, nom, nom."* I pretended to make the Garfoose bite her leg. "It's not what I had in mind when I saw the Victoria's Secret bag, but it's still fantastic."

"I made it for you because I knew you were having a rough time up here and I wanted you to feel better. Sometimes you need something around that can breathe fire on the other team, right?"

"This"—I held the Garfoose up—"this is just fantastic. Come here, gorgeous." I reached out and tugged her over to me for a kiss.

"I can't believe we're going to be married in two weeks," she said.

"I know, and there's only nine more games until the season's over," I said with a sigh of relief.

"You can survive until then, right?"

"Absolutely. With this guy to protect me, I can survive anything."

The hotel phone rang on the nightstand next to us, interrupting our fun. I picked it up, cradling the Garfoose in my arms as I put the receiver to my head.

"Hello?" I pushed the Garfoose's face toward the receiver as if it was going to do the talking, while Bonnie giggled at me.

"Dirk? It's Darren Balsley."

I put the toy down, along with my smile. "Hey. How's it going?" I asked dryly.

"Peavy's wife is expecting to give birth today or tomorrow, so he's going home to be with her for the delivery. You're going to pick up his start tomorrow, okay?"

"Uh, sure, of course," I said.

"So just come to the ballpark like you're on the starting routine again."

"Okay," I said.

"Have a good night, then."

"You too."

He hung up.

"What was that about?" asked Bonnie.

"I have to pick up tomorrow's start because Peavy had to leave town on account of his wife is giving birth."

"Oh." She noticed my anxious expression. "Is this a good thing?"

"Yeah," I said, though my voice lacked commitment. "Yeah, starting is always a good thing."

"Are you sure?"

"Yeah," I said again, preoccupied with what was ahead of me.

"Well, great." She picked up the Garfoose toy and made it play bite me on the side of my face. "You'll get this start to show them what you've learned since your last one."

"Yeah," I said, pushing the toy away. "Yeah, what I've learned."

"This is a bonus," she said.

"A bonus," I repeated. I lay back on the bed and Bonnie laid her head down across my chest. "Just a bonus. No pressure."

Chapter Sixty-nine

I stuck a final fastball into Hundo's mitt, then announced I was warm and good to go. I'd done my best to retain the scouting report regarding the Nationals' hitters and was running through mock scenarios with Hundo as we finished our warm-up sequence in the pen. The Nationals were probably the weakest lineup we'd faced to date. So weak I couldn't help but think that maybe all of the struggles I'd gone through to this point were some kind of trial, and today, against the worst team in baseball, I could turn it all around.

As I walked in from the pen with my complimentary bottle of water and towel, I did not search the stands for Bonnie. I told her the night before that once the game came around I would be all business. I told her this again when we went out for lunch. I told her a third time when I left to come to the park early. I told her as many times as the game came into my mind between the time I got the call and the moment I hit the field. I did it because each time I said the words, it was like I was telling myself that I would not be distracted. I would be like a stone, unshakable, and come game time, I would have everything in order to ensure success.

Things got heavy fast. Despite all the mental preparation, focus, and desire to vindicate myself, I walked the first batter of the game and watched him come around and score while I ran the pitch count up scuffling for outs. Once again my fastball refused to obey me, and emotions were quick to follow. Then came those familiar questions: *What is wrong with me? Why does this keep happening?*

I managed to escape the first inning with only one earned run. While my guys hit, I battled the fear that this outing would become what all the other outings had. I recycled all my best clichés: *One pitch at a time, one hitter at a time. Don't let this inning influence the next. Don't get down on yourself. This is your opportunity—embrace it. Forget the failures of the past. Forget the failures of the past. Forget the failures of the past.* It was all for nothing. When I went back out for the second inning, I yielded another walk and run, throwing nearly thirty pitches in the process.

"You're going to have to be more efficient," said Balsley when I came back in before the start of the third.

"I'm trying. I don't understand why I can't hit the mitt."

"I don't understand either," said Balsley. "But you still have to compete. You need to make an adjustment. You're nearly fifty pitches into the game and it's the third inning. You have to find a way to get it done."

I tried, Lord, did I ever. The third inning went one, two, three, and, for a moment, I actually believed I'd turned the corner. Then, in the fourth inning, I returned to form and handed out a double, a single, and a walk before getting pulled.

I sat on the bench with my head up, eyes aimed at the field though I was not there. I was in the place you go when you've completely given up on yourself. When I took long enough to look at the scoreboard, the lights didn't seem brighter to me anymore. The fans didn't seem louder, and the field wasn't bigger. Everything was so normal now. Everything was as it should be. And that was when it hit me, the most horrible part of the whole thing: no matter how hard I focused, no matter how undistracted I was, failing was normal for me.

I retreated into the clubhouse after this realization. When I arrived at my locker, the frustration I'd been holding back finally reached the tipping point, and I unleashed the pure, raging emotion I'd been trying to hide. I kicked the chair over and beat my glove against the wall before throwing it across the room. I pulled down my jerseys and threw them into a pile so I couldn't see the name on the back. I scattered my hats and flung my big league equipment bag at the trash can. Then, when I ran out of things to launch, I grabbed the sides of my locker and tried to tear them apart; tear the whole goddamn stadium down.

After a time, I sank down to the floor where I sat in mental agony over what a disaster I was. Eventually, defeated yet again, I righted my chair and collected my things. I labored to take my jersey off, as if each action required tremendous strength. When I finished, I sat in front of my locker like my dad would sit at the kitchen table when the world was a dark and dying place.

I sat with my head down until my cell phone rattled from inside the locker's wreckage. It was Bonnie texting me to tell me I'd done a good job, and that she was proud of me. I shook my head at her message, I started laughing at it at first, and then I started screaming angrily at the phone, "What the fuck are you proud of? I was fucking horrible!" I threw the phone back into the rear of the locker. Then I picked up one of the jersey pieces and pressed it over my mouth to muffle my shouts of "I hate this fucking game!" I pulled out another jersey piece and shrouded my head with it, trying to hide from the outside world, from myself. But no matter how tight I pulled my cowl, there was no hiding from the fact I'd spent my entire life trying to get to this place just to crash and burn when it mattered most.

Balsley came in during a break between innings. By the time he arrived I'd wrapped myself in ice and my frustration had calmed to the more manageable level of controlled despair and needy paranoia. I don't think Balsley's intention was to talk with me at the moment, but I didn't give him a choice.

"I don't understand why I'm not throwing strikes," I said to him, over and over again. "I know I'm better than this. I know you haven't seen the best of me. I don't understand why I'm not—"

"You know, Dirk. I don't know either," he said with a cold sigh of irritation. "Honestly, all I can tell you is there are some guys who can put it all together when they cross those white lines here, and some guys who can't. You're probably just one of the guys who can't." Then he shrugged and walked back to the game.

After he said that, there was no reason for me to ever speak to him again. There was no reason for me to even be there. I didn't care about the service time, the money, or the experience. He might as well have said to me, "You're a lost cause." In fact, he should have just shot me, because after he said those things, my life in baseball was over.

Chapter Seventy

I cast a long angry shadow as I walked Bonnie back to the hotel room. She met me after the game along with some of my other friends. They all wanted to share these sickening pleasantries about how awesome it was to see me pitch in a big league game, but I wanted none of it. I wanted them all to be quiet like they had been before when I was nothing but a career minor leaguer.

They asked for signed baseballs; not from me, of course, but a Hoffman or Peavy—for a friend of a friend. They reminded me that it was easy for me to get these things, since, after all, I told them about how I was around such big names every day, how it was all so normal for me. They asked if I could leave tickets, if I could get them a discount on merchandise, if I could call their aspiring nephews. They asked me to do all the things I promised I would do should I ever make it to the big leagues, and I wanted to scream at them for it. But, as they lifted food and drink in celebration of my coming wedding, my good health, and my *flourishing* baseball career, I could do nothing but sit bitterly under the thunderstorm that had been following me since my exit from the field.

It followed me into the hotel, up the elevator, and down the hallway with Bonnie. My words to her came out like short claps of thunder, and my eyes shot to her like lightning when her words displeased me. Unfortunately for her, sitting by and doing nothing while her husband-to-be was in such a state was not something she could abide, and so she sailed her ship right into the eye of the storm.

"I'm sorry you didn't pitch good today, honey. I know it's bothering you, but I still love you, and so do your friends."

"Great," I sneered.

"It was just a bonus outing." She took my hand. "It doesn't change the paycheck or the money we made. And you made it to the big leagues, like you always dreamed. No one can ever take that away." She started rubbing my arm but I jerked it from her and broke free of her hand.

"Eight more days, honey, you can do—"

"Stop it!" I shouted at her. "Stop it, stop it, stop it!"

Bonnie looked at me, startled.

"You just don't get it, do you? All this repetitive positive crap you keep spouting at me doesn't change a thing."

"I know we can't change the outcome of the game, but it—"

"It's not the game I'm talking about. It's the whole fucking experience, Bonnie. This whole thing has been a disaster."

"I don't understand."

"Of course you don't. No one ever understands. No one understands what it's like to do this." I threw my hands up in disgust. "You know what it was like for me sitting at that dinner table tonight, listening to all my so-called friends tell me how great it must be to be up here? Listening to them tell you how lucky you are to marry a big leaguer? All they know is what the media has showed them, they don't see the other side, this side. They don't see the failure, the paranoia, the doubt—and they don't want to see it! They don't want to hear people talk about it, and they don't want signed balls from people who create it. They only want the dream part.

"And you know, I don't want to see it either, but I don't have a choice. I'm living it. My dream has turned into a nightmare, and the worst part is I can't tell anyone about it without looking like a whiner, ungrateful, scared, or pathetic."

"You can talk to me about it." She took a step toward me but I backed away.

"And what are you going to tell me, darling?"

"That I love you, and that it's okay."

"Great!" I scoffed. "And that will fix everything, won't it?"

"I'm sorry," she said softly under my booming anger.

"Why?" My eyes flashed at her again. "Why are you sorry? Or are you just apologizing because you feel like you have to because I'm upset? Nothing you can do is going to fix this."

"I'm sorry I can't help you."

"I'm used to it," I said, and I jammed my key card into the door of our suite. The room disgusted me. The upscale furniture, and the expensive linens; the turndown service that had soft jazz playing on the clock radio and slippers at the foot of the bed. I hated all of it. I went over and turned the smooth music off and kicked the slippers away. "My parents never could, why should you be any different? This is on me. It's always been on me."

"I don't like you saying that. I don't like you saying I can't play a role in your pain. I'm going to be your wife."

"Yeah, well, there are a lot of things out there people don't like and they just have to deal with them. This is one of the things you're just going to have to deal with."

"Why would you say that? This is not something you have to deal with alone."

"Oh, it isn't, huh? Let me ask you something. Is it your name in the box score? Is it you that's out there in front of all those people getting mercy claps when you finally throw a strike? Is it you fielding questions on national television about why you stunk? Is it you being told you're probably one of the guys who can't get the fucking job done at this level?"

"No. But it hurts me when I see you hurt. I feel the pain right along with you."

"I doubt that." I shook my head at her.

"Why?" she pleaded.

"Because this isn't your life!" I roared. I stood up from the bed and bore down on her, slamming my finger into my chest as I spoke. "This is my life. I've spent all of it trying to get here, Bonnie. My entire life! All the sacrificing and scrounging and working shit jobs. Starving myself in college to cut weight, sleepless trips on buses, paychecks that put me in line for handouts—all of it done to get me to this point just so I could fall apart when it finally happened! You have no idea what that feels like! What it feels like to know your life's ambition is a waste!"

Bonnie dropped her head and sat down across the room from me. I stood, swollen with my own anger, my chest heaving up and down as I breathed in the air-conditioned room and exhaled the steam of my frustration. After a few minutes of silence and strained eye contact, I started pacing around. "You know who they brought me up here to replace?" I asked rhetorically. "Greg Maddux. Greg fucking Maddux, a first ballot hall of famer and one of my heroes. He'll always be remembered for the amazing things he did in this game. You know what I'll be remembered for?" Bonnie did not answer me. "The candy bag, if anything at all."

"You said it doesn't matter if you're remembered for anything up here. You said you just wanted to cash in."

"It matters. Everything up here matters. It defines my whole career's worth. I *had* a chance to make it something really valuable and I've ruined it. The sky was the limit and I couldn't get off the ground."

Bonnie's face cringed at my pain. She walked over to the bed where I'd sat down, cupping my face in my hands. She put a hand on my back and started rubbing.

"I know it's hard right now, but you really should think about all the positives you had in this career. You had a great season in Triple A, we made enough to get off to a great start in our marriage, and your dad is doing better."

True or not, her words just made it worse. I didn't want to hear about what had happened before this point. This point was all that mattered. "How can you not see that?" I asked, aloud as if I'd spoken everything going through my head.

"See what?"

"You're analyzing me, aren't you?" I pulled away from her.

"What?" Her face twisted in confusion.

"Is this part of your therapy method? Relentlessly trying to push me toward something good? Forgetting about the truth of the situation just because it's uncomfortable?"

"No, I'm trying to steer you back toward all the good you've done."

"No offense, Bonnie, but I've got news for you: this isn't some Share Day performance. This isn't a time for me to get up onstage and perform and if I do bad everyone claps anyways. This is a kill or be killed business. What happens here will define the rest of my life. Spare me your patronizing self-help method. There is no song you can sing me that is going to fix this."

Bonnie face started to turn pink, and tears welled up in her eyes. "Our lives," was all she said, as the drops started streaming down her face, "the rest of *our lives*."

"Right, sorry, my mistake. *Our lives*," I repeated sarcastically.

I got up and walked over to the mini-fridge in search of something to drink. As I rustled through my choices of small bottles, I did not see the frown on Bonnie's face flatten out, or her eyes narrow. She passed a hand across her wet face.

"I'm sorry you've lost your ability to enjoy the other things that make your life what it is," she said, her voice choppy from hyperventilation.

"Spare me," I said.

"No, I won't. You wanna hear a song?" she asked, coming to her feet. I looked up at her from my crouched position at the fridge.

"How about this one," she continued. "How about a song about how I don't care how much you make up here, or how much fame you collect, or how long this lasts, because if it means this is the person you'll be while it happens, I will never love you. Never," she said. Then, to make sure the point was perfectly clear, she added, "Dallas."

I stood up, towering over her shaking little frame. I opened my mouth to fire back, but it was she who spoke first. "You're not the only one who's sacrificed for this opportunity, you know. I understand that most of the people around you don't have a fucking clue what it's like to feel the way you do right now and never will. But I swear to you that if you lump me in with that group, if you lock me out, then this relationship is over. I didn't get into this with you because I thought you'd make me rich, or because I wanted to be some big league wife. I got into this because of you, when you were sleeping on your grandmother's floor and driving some shitty import. I was happier where we started than where we're at now." When she finished, her persistence broke and she collapsed on the bed sobbing.

Watching her cry made me feel disgusting. I didn't think I could feel any worse about myself as a person until I saw her there on the bed, afraid to turn her tear-filled eyes on me, the man who claimed to love her. I looked down at my hands, a bottle of vodka in one and fruit juice in the other. My God, what was I becoming, and why did it take the weeping frame of my fiancée to make me ask this question? I fell back against the wall, overwhelmed by my own repulsiveness. I dropped the bottles, then slowly, like a withering plant, I descended to the floor, sliding down the wall to my knees, where I belonged.

Chapter Seventy-one

"I'm so sorry," I said, again, now laying my head on hers. "I can't believe I said those things." We were huddled in the corner of the room in a blanket now. It's funny what part of a finely appointed room feels safe and comfortable when your heart is torn up.

"It's alright," she offered.

"No, it's not. I should never talk to you like that," I said. "There is nothing so important in my life that it can justify me hurting you the way I did. I'm sorry."

She smiled at me for the first time all night. Her face was still red from emotion, but she'd stopped crying a while ago, shortly after I crawled to her feet, begging for her forgiveness.

I shed tears as well, though mine came from different reasons than hers. Mine came from the clear realization of what life in the big leagues had done to me, and to those around me. I'd lost my confidence, my patience, and nearly my fiancée in the desperate struggle to get to and excel in the place I'd always dreamed of being. I was hurting the people I cared about as a way of getting even with what was hurting me. Bonnie would say I was misdirecting emotions, but she didn't have to. She only had to call me Dallas for me to see that in just a month's worth of time I had turned into what I despised most about this game.

"I don't want to do this anymore," I said.

"I don't want to fight anymore either," said Bonnie.

I kissed her head. "But I'm afraid I'll keep acting like this unless I learn how to deal with all the pressure up here. I suppose it would be a lot easier if I showed I had the talent."

"What was that line you said to me about how doing well just covers up the opportunity for you to get better?" asked Bonnie, citing the great baseball excuse for failure. "Maybe it's more than an excuse?"

"Yeah, maybe," I said, dropping my head, disgusted with myself.

Bonnie measured her words before continuing. "I don't want you to think I'm being positive just to be positive, but you definitely have the talent to do this with no excuses or rationalizing."

"Maybe," I said. "But pitching is not all you do up here. The scrutiny, the unspoken rules, the expectations, the egos. Obviously I can't handle it all. Look at how I've treated you. Look at how I treat myself." I nodded to the open refrigerator and the bottles of booze on the floor. "If it was just what happened on the field, that would be one thing. But it's not. This isn't just a game up here, it's a way of life, and I don't think I'm cut out for it. In fact"—I looked away from her, embarrassed by what I was about to say—"I don't think I like it here."

"I understand," said Bonnie.

"I don't. It's the big leagues," I said.

"Honey, not everything we dream of is as great as we think it's going to be when we finally realize it. Your experiences and emotions are relevant regardless of how worshiped this league is or isn't because they are yours."

"Thanks for saying that."

"Of course. And yes, that was me analyzing you."

"I guess your therapy isn't so bad after all."

"It's not all songs and positive repetition, you know."

"I'm sorry I insulted your profession. I really respect what you do. I just . . ." The words trailed away. After a few moments, I began again. "When you get the paychecks I've been getting lately . . .

When you're in front of thousands of fans and surrounded by guys watching every little thing you do like it's life or death, you start to think you're so important, and everything else is somehow not." I turned to Bonnie with a defeated look on my face. "I don't like who I am up here," I finished.

"I'm not fond of it either. Not just because of today, but because since you've got here, you've been on edge. Even before you got here, back when you were close to getting called up, you started turning into this obsessed person."

"I was so hungry for this to happen because of all I've"—I caught myself—"because of all we've sacrificed. I wanted us to have a good start. I wanted us to never struggle like my parents. I wanted our marriage to be a dream. But then, it wasn't enough. I wanted to be powerful. I wanted to be respected. I wanted to matter."

"Why do you think those things will make our life together better?" Bonnie searched my face. "Why do you need them so badly? What do they really give you besides some false sense of security? And what if struggling a little is what makes us the most happy? Some of the most fun we've had has been planning our wedding on a tight budget. You bring out a creative side of me I never knew I had. Our wedding is going to be awesome, and completely us because of the circumstances we've had to work through to pull it off. I'm proud of that," she declared.

"Me too," I said.

"We did it, we're a good team."

"I agree."

"And I still want to share my life with you," she added.

"Are you sure?" I asked.

"Absolutely."

"Even after how I acted?"

"I'm not marrying you because you're perfect, and I'm certainly not marrying you because the world loves your job. I'm marrying you because you're you and you're perfect for me. I'll fight to keep you, even if *you* are the enemy." She smiled at me, and rubbed my back. "But if you still feel guilty, I will allow you to apologize to me again in the form of a dessert from room service."

"You sure the big leagues aren't rubbing off on you a little?" I asked, reaching for the menu on the table across from us.

"Maybe a little," she said, smiling.

I handed her the menu, but before I relinquished it to her, I asked, "Would you still love me if I quit?"

"Of course, honey."

"We've made a good chunk of money this year. We've made a lot more out of baseball than most. I got to the Bigs, I've experienced my dream. I'll always get to say I made it here. I doubt anyone would ever understand it, but . . ."

"But what?"

"After Balsley said what he did to me tonight, after this whole failed experience, I feel like I don't even know what I'm playing for."

"Are you telling me this because you honestly are thinking about quitting and you want my approval, or because this has been so hard on you?"

"I don't know. My confidence is definitely shot. Maybe that's why Balsley said what he did, to give me a gut check. Well, it worked. I'm wondering what my purpose in baseball is now that I'm looking at it from the top and the bottom at the same time."

Bonnie sat with the menu on her lap and weighed her words carefully. "I don't know," she said. "That's a question only you can answer."

Chapter Seventy-two

Bonnie left at the end of the Washington series. It was more of a *see you soon* than a good-bye since, in a week, I'd be coming home myself. In two weeks we'd be married, and off on our honeymoon and a new life together. However, before that would happen, I had one more week to get through as a Padre.

After the series, the team made its long trek back across the country for our final games of the season. We went to LA, then back to Petco, where we'd finish up against the Pirates. At this point, it didn't matter who we played, where we played them, or if I played at all. I didn't care anymore. I'd lost nearly all desire for baseball, the few last remaining bits dying when I watched Bonnie wipe tears into a homemade stuffed animal.

I quit working out. No more heading into the weight room to do a forty-five-minute eyewash routine. No more showing up seven hours early to sit at my locker and fake dedication. No more sycophantic veteran worship. I didn't care what anyone thought of me, save maybe Hoffman, whom I'd been too chicken to talk to since my arrival. The way I saw it, I had a 9 ERA, I already knew I didn't belong here, so I might as well enjoy the time I had left the best way I knew how—sitting at my locker in my underwear, eating Fig Newtons and throwing the wrappers on the floor for the clubhouse elves to collect.

I asked for extra equipment I didn't need just so I could stock-pile free stuff. I even started hoarding big league baseballs, filling my computer bag with them and smuggling them from the stadium. These pleasures felt good, for a little while, but they faded fast. Even writing down the experiences of getting to the Show didn't seem to help me make sense of it all. I just could not shake the feeling that I was not supposed to be here.

The incredible irony that I should have this dilemma while sitting in a major league locker room was not lost on me. However, its lack of logic in no way diminished the empty feeling I had recently developed for the game. Naturally, as instructed by all my player friends, I thought of the money. But then I began thinking that whether it was money, Newtons, clothes, cars, or houses, having all the pleasures the big leagues could throw my way would eventually fade, and then what?

There was the fame factor. How many people would love to be me, to be standing on a major league mound, the center of the world's attention? But would there always be a crowd to brag to, and did those people really care about me, or just the ideal of wearing my jersey? The issue with fame, even moderate amounts of it, is that people feel like they have the right to rate your worth. And, as I'd learned from being around players I had yet to prove my worth to, when everyone thinks you're worthless it's pretty hard to disagree.

I decided that the will to compete was the reason I should keep going, and that to quit would be in direct defiance of that rule. But, frankly, getting your ass repeatedly kicked is no fun, especially when you have no hope of it stopping.

Team stretches came and went. Many of the other rookies took things seriously since they felt they still had something to prove. Not me, I stretched and shagged batting practice off in some distant land. I couldn't be further away from Petco, floating in a world where the sun was not powered by major league dreams, stats, and historical significance. Where no children came running up for my autograph and no gentle-eyed Irish cop tipped his hat at me. Standing out there, thinking about it all, I had to wonder if I had ever done anything significant outside a baseball field, or if it was all for nothing.

I had been sent back to the pen, and during the night's game, I sat in my corner of the pen, silent like usual. Relievers buzzed around me, eating their candy, flicking their seeds, and smoking their cigarettes. Hoffman came out around his usual time and sat in his customary spot. I watched him, like I always did, wondering what it must be like to be in his shoes knowing that all of his time in the Show had purpose and meaning. Then, something dawned on me; the season would be over in two days and I'd spent most of my time afraid to speak to the one man on this team I wanted to be around more than any other. Why not talk to him, I decided; after all, I had nothing left to lose.

I got up from my corner of bench and slunk down to his. I nodded to him, as I arrived, then took a seat next to him.

"What's up, kid?" he asked, noting my departure from standard routine.

"Hey, Hoffy. I don't mean to bother you, but I may not be up here again and I want to be able to say I actually spoke with you for more than a few seconds."

"Um, okay." Hoffman smirked at my formal explanation. "What's on your mind?"

"I know people ask you about your changeup all the time, and your routine, and your focus, and I could ask about that too. But I've been watching you ever since I got up here, and it's easy to see that your hands are massive, which makes your grip unique, and your routine is flawless, which is why your focus is unshakable. I'm not going to waste your time with questions I already know the answer to."

As I finished, I realized, from the way Hoffman seemed to be fighting back the urge to fall asleep, instead of wasting his time with questions I could ask, I was doing it by explaining ones I wouldn't ask.

I quickly cleared my throat. "You've done so much up here. So much I'll never do. But I'd like to know, outside of baseball, what is the one thing you are most proud of?"

Hoffman sat up straight and shifted his gaze from the field to me. For a second, I thought I'd asked him something too big or personal for a rookie to ask a vet.

"I'm sorry," I said. "You don't have to answer that. I'll leave you be."

"No. It's a good question," he said, his face still tight with thought.

"Really?"

"Yeah, I've never really thought about it." He gave me an amused glance. "You're a bit of a deep guy, aren't you?"

"I, uh, I've been accused of that before, yes."

"Let me think for a second," he said.

Hoffman contemplated and then looked back to me. "My family," he said. "My kids. I feel like I've been a good husband and father, and that I've raised my kids well."

I nodded my head at his noble answer, though I was quite certain my approval was the last thing he needed.

"Is that why you play, for your family?"

His head started moving up and down again. "I'd say so. The life I've been able to give them. I'm proud knowing that I've protected them from hardship by what I've been able to do on the field."

I nodded along. I wouldn't dare disagree with him, but I didn't have kids, or a wife just yet. I also didn't have millions of dollars, bids to the All-Star game, or a house-size banner of myself hanging outside the stadium like he did. I could understand his response, but I couldn't yet relate, and at the risk of saying something over the line, I asked him what I had to know. "Have you always felt that way?" I asked.

"What do you mean?"

"Have you always done this for your family?"

"Well, when you're young, this game is about you. It's about your dream and what you want to do with it. But as you age, the reason you play stops being so much about you, and starts becoming more about what you care about. You dream about baseball when you're a boy, but you realize it when you're a man. A lot changes along the way. This place can provide for you, but there are bigger things out there than you. That's what you have to keep in mind when you play. If you don't, you'll never survive up here."

I let the wisdom of his words settle on me. Hoffman added nothing to them. Instead, he continued to watch the events on the field like some old sentinel at his post.

I looked out across the field with him. I'd spent so many days in ballparks and bullpens, and yet my time was only a fraction of Hoffman's. My time around the game would probably end sooner than Hoffman's as well, and with less fanfare. But when it did, legend or failure, we would both go back to being men, to lives that baseball had provided for, or destroyed. Such was our lot.

"Are you ever afraid out there?" I asked.

Hoffman furrowed his brow. "Yeah."

"Really?"

"I worry that I'll let my team down, sure," he said.

"Ever worry you'll do more than that?"

A long fly ball was struck out to the warming track. The buzz of the crowd surged with the flight of the ball and ended in a splash of applause when the ball landed in Jilly's glove. The inning was over, and so, it seemed, was my conversation with Hoffman.

"I know how you're feeling." He smiled, standing up. "And I wish I could give you all the answers, kid, but I can't. Some things you'll have to experience for yourself to really know the answer to. We'll talk more later." He slapped me on my shoulder, then made his way out of the pen, walking across the field under a hail of autograph requests and pleas for his attention. He did not stop, though; determined, purposeful, like everything else he did, he disappeared into the dugout, back to his middle-innings routine that helped make him who he was today, leaving me to digest his words in the social silence of my rookie life in the bullpen.

Hoffman closed the game that night. He warmed up, perfect and precise and focused like a fearless man who would trust his life to his delivery. When his foot hit centerfield, the deep, unmistakable bell of AC/DC's "Hells Bells," the song that had heralded Hoffman's arrival in the game for years, rang through the stadium. Fans stood instantly, screaming for the Padre who owned number 51 and the most saves in baseball. Light boards flashed, "It's Trevor Time!" and the house-size display in left field ran clips of his legend, reminding all that they were watching history in the making.

I was glued to the railing. If there was one major league dream that turned out exactly as I expected it to, it was this one. I'd seen it all before, of course, on television and in person, but it never got old. It was just one of those sights that reminded you of why you pushed so hard. And there, watching Hoffman from centerfield, I realized that everyone has their reasons to play. Some are shallow and base, and some are as deep and rich as the history of the game itself. There is the pursuit of Hall of Fame numbers, and the desperation to simply be counted at the bottom of a list somewhere. There are paychecks, toys, families, and God himself. But whatever those reasons are, to work they have to be able to change, to evolve, just like we do.

Leaning on that rail, watching Hoffman make someone look stupid on his changeup while the crowd roared, I decided that whatever reasons I came up with for playing would be good ones because they were my reasons, and, even in this league, my reasons were the only ones that truly mattered.

Chapter Seventy-three

"I appreciate you taking the time to talk with me, and all your other advice about players and how we're viewed and family, and everything else," I said to Hoffman as he stretched his name across some baseballs I planned to use as groomsmen gifts.

The last game had ended, the season was over, and everyone was rushing to catch flights home. I'd probably get taken off the forty-man roster within the week. I'd probably never talk to Hoffman again after today since his contract negotiations weren't going as planned with the big club. I couldn't imagine him closing for anyone else, but baseball was full of things I didn't understand, even when looking at it from the top down. Welcome to the big leagues.

"My pleasure," said Hoffman. "You're interesting to talk to. You're definitely deeper than your average guy."

"Thanks, I think."

"And hey, you're still going to do a lot of great stuff on this field," he said. "But, personally, I think the best part of you is what's off the field."

I'm not sure if I blushed when he said that part, but I wouldn't be surprised if I did.

"Good luck with that book you're writing," said Hoffman.

"Oh, thanks. And good luck with everything you're up to."

"Thanks, kid. Enjoy your off-season, and congrats on your marriage."

I shook his hand after he gave me the last ball back, not as a boy star struck by a baseball hero, but as a friend. Then, after packing my own bags, I said my farewells to Chip and Luke, Frenchy and Anto. I tipped the clubbies, wished all the coaches I had words for good-bye, took one final pack of Fig Newtons, then wheeled my bags to the door of the Padres' locker room and stopped. *I might never be here again,* I thought. I took one last big breath of big league Padres air, exhaled, and then walked away.

It was a long plane flight back, but when I got off the jet, there was a little brown-eyed girl waiting for me.

"Welcome home," she said, taking my hand.

"It's good to be back," I said, lacing my fingers in hers. "So where to, Grandma's house?"

"No," she said. "Never again. From now on, the only woman you'll ever come home to is me."

The night before the wedding, I sat in the apartment that would be our first home. My groomsmen came over for a few hours to keep me company in my last moments as a bachelor. They apologized for not throwing me a bachelor party. I forgave them, explaining that the big league club threw one for me already. When they asked for juicy details, I described the sultry curves of the Hooters girls in attendance, the flowing tequila, and the X-rated party on our private jet. Then I told them it was best they didn't try to re-create the scene—they agreed wholeheartedly.

As an alternative to their party planning services, I enlisted them as carpenters and mechanics. The apartment was full of boxes of unassembled Ikea furniture, including the box containing my new bed frame. If I was going to get the apartment assembled in time to carry my wife across the threshold to more than stacks of Swedish furniture boxes, I needed their help.

After our assembly work, we stayed up late listening to music, talking about life and love and baseball while splitting a six-pack. Slowly but surely, the apartment started to come together. Then, when everything was assembled except the bed—which I felt I had the sacred duty of doing myself—my groomsmen slapped me on the ass and told me to enjoy my last night as a single.

Since I'd come home from the season, everything had been moving at warp speed. Each day leading up to the Big One was rife with one issue or another. There were the rehearsal dinner, showers, trips to furniture stores, arguments about seating arrangements, lease signings, final decoration choices, registry checks, shuttling family from the airport . . . I almost found myself wanting to go back to baseball again.

When the door clicked shut and the groomsmen left, it was just me in the apartment. Things finally started to slow down, and I had time to think about what was going to happen in less than twenty-four hours. Things I'd known were coming for months now took on a new, terrifying shape. Like mountains on the horizon unworthy of my immediate attention, they had snuck up on me so slowly I didn't realize they were here until they were just outside my window, blotting out the sun with their gargantuan size. *Holy shit*, it hit me, I was about to get married! I was going to be responsible for another human being for the rest of my life! I was going to have to be completely naked in front of a girl! I was not prepared for this!

I flung open the door, but my groomsmen were already gone. I was alone. The walls began to close in on me. The apartment was no longer "our first place," it was now a prison with Ikea furniture barricading me in. The unhung picture frames, the quilt from Bonnie's grandmother, the plastic tubs full of unpacked clothes. This was it, this was how my run as a swinging single was going to end. No fireworks, no autobiographical documentary, not even a girl jumping out of a cake with tassels on her boobs. It was just me, foreign cardboard, an empty six-pack, and a place for the washer and dryer to get hooked up.

I needed to talk to someone, but not Bonnie—that was forbidden. The only real option I had was my parents, and though a conversation with them at this point could do more to talk me out of getting married than talk me into it, I decided to risk it.

"Hello?" my dad answered. I heard the sound of late night television in the background, then its departure at the striking of the MUTE button.

"Hey, Dad," I said.

"What are you doing up?" he asked.

"I can't sleep."

"Nervous?"

"I guess. I don't know. I wonder if I'm doing the right thing. I mean, I just got back from baseball, I haven't had any time to really think about how much my life has changed, and now I'm getting married and it's going to change again."

"Little late to be thinking about this now, ain't it?"

"Yeah, I know it is."

"Sounds like cold feet."

"I don't know. Maybe more like confused feet."

"What are you confused about? You love this girl, don't you?"

"I do. But the rest of my life is a long time."

"Yeah, it usually is."

"What if, you know, this is the wrong decision!"

"There ain't no right or wrong to it," he said.

"What if we, well, what if something happens to us like it did to you and Mom?"

"You can't be thinking like that now, Dirk."

"But I am," I said. "I can't stop thinking about that kind of stuff."

"Well"—he cleared his throat—"if things go bad, then they go bad. You'll work through 'em. But you can't always think about how bad things can go."

My dad let the phone sit idle for a moment, then he began again with a more introspective tone. "I guess I can't blame you for worrying about it. We ain't exactly the Brady Bunch. But, like

I told you, you work through it. What you have to remember is, you're not in it alone. That's the strength and weakness of marriage—you never have to go it alone."

"Never alone," I repeated.

"You don't get married for yourself, you get married because you're better together than separate. Your mom and I fight, every couple does." He chuckled to himself. "I guess we might be more passionate about it than your average couple."

"You think?" I added sarcastically.

"Well, we have a family tradition to keep up."

"I don't want to keep that tradition going," I said.

"So don't," he said, assuredly. "I'll tell you, your mom and I haven't been the best at showing you the right way to live, but we've been great at showing you the wrong way. I'd say you did pretty good at learning what not to do from us, and you don't have to worry about turning out like us because you two aren't us. You need to let that go. You need to stop being afraid of stuff that ain't yet happened and may never."

"I know," I said. "I thought I had a handle on that."

"What changed?"

"Getting my ass kicked in the big leagues. I guess I'm afraid any of my dreams can turn sour now."

"That's just baseball, Dirk."

"It was more than baseball, Dad. It was my life's pursuit."

"Well, there is always next year," said my dad.

"What if I blow this marriage like I did baseball?"

"You didn't blow it in baseball, Dirk."

"I don't think the coach up there would agree with you on that," I said.

"Oh, fuck that guy," said my dad. "I've coached for a long time and you never tell kids who are out there getting their ass kicked for your club that they don't got what it takes. Look, Dirk, we may not be great at fluffing you up with encouragement, but one thing we Hayhursts are real good at is telling other people they can shove their opinions up their fucking asses. That's what you need to do with this guy's."

"I guess," I said, smiling at my dad's enthusiasm.

"Ain't no guessing about it."

"Alright," I said. "I'll try."

"Good!" said my dad. "But that don't make your feet warmer, does it?"

"No."

"You're still afraid of marriage, aren't you?"

"Yeah."

"Well, let me tell you something about that fear. Remember when you asked me about why I never went down to the wall in the backyard to pitch no more? It's because I was afraid. I always enjoyed playing, pitching the most, but after you saw me there fumbling around on the mound, I felt embarrassed of how ridiculous I must have looked because I couldn't do it like normal anymore."

"But you were making it work," I said. "You were doing it your own way. There is nothing wrong with that."

"I know that now," he said. "But, as busted up as I was then, it's worse now. I can barely get a spoon in my hand let alone a baseball. I can't walk as good neither, let alone wind up."

"I'm sorry, Dad," I said, feeling like it was my fault.

"You ain't got to be sorry. The point is, I quit doing something I enjoyed because I was afraid I'd embarrass myself, or that I'd do it wrong, or shit, I don't know, that the world would end or something. I figure you're in the same boat now, except you're walking away from more than a lump of dirt in the backyard. You can't let some asshole with a negative opinion slow you down, or what you think the people around you are thinking of you. You gotta stop doubting yourself and do what you know how to do. And stop taking more out to that mound than you need to get the job done, for Christ's sake. You go out there with the weight of the world on your back, no wonder you ain't getting anybody out.

"Now, listen, Bonnie's a good girl for you. I told you that. You two are better together and she's going to help you. I think she already has. She comes along and all of a sudden you're in the Bigs. You couldn't get your ass out of A ball with all the other girls you dated. You need to let her help you. That's the mistake I made, Dirk. When I got hurt, I didn't want anyone's help because they didn't know what it felt like to be me. Now I've lost years of my life I ain't never going get back 'cause I wanted to figure it out alone. I hurt a lot of people acting that way." He rumbled out a deep chuckle. "There's another example for you not to follow."

I didn't say anything for a long stretch after my dad finished his point. I just sat on my floor, surrounded by a half-assembled bed. It was the first silence I shared over the phone with a family member that wasn't awkward. I could hear my dad un-mute the television in the background, but I didn't mind. He didn't tell me he had to go, but he gave me space to think nonetheless.

"Dad," I said, finally.

"What?"

"We should play catch sometime."

"Oh yeah?" he asked, skeptical.

"Yeah," I said.

"It won't be much of a catch, Dirk. If I can even get a mitt on my hand."

"We'll get it on there," I said.

"Well, even if ya do, you'd have to throw the ball right in my mitt 'cause I can't catch for shit. And, no offense, but judging from how your big league time went, I don't know if you'll be able to do that," he said.

"Funny, Dad, very funny. I'll hit your mitt, and if I don't, I'll just hit you."

"That's fine. I won't feel it anyway. That's the silver lining of nerve damage."

"I didn't know it had one."

"Not many, but you take what you can get."

"I wish I could turn off my feelings, sometimes," I said.

"No, you don't," he said. "Besides, you can't. So make the most of what you can feel and stop overanalyzing it."

"Alright," I consented. "I'll try."

"Good. So," he switched gears, "you ready for tomorrow now? Or am I going to have to hold your hand all night?"

"I'm ready," I said, smiling. "Thanks, Dad."

"Whatever," he said. "Get some sleep, tomorrow's a big day."

Chapter Seventy-four

It was a beautiful day for a wedding. The landscape of the Holden Arboretum had put on its best autumn colors in honor of the event. We wanted the whole day to feel like a party with friends plus a wedding, not a formal ceremony. There was no pomp or pretense anywhere to be found, not in the homemade center pieces, the buckets of iced IBC root beer, or the casual way my dad, wearing nothing but blue jeans and his least stained T-shirt, milled around the place talking to Bonnie's dad about which band was more significant to the era they grew up in.

So far Bonnie's and my plan was going perfectly. In fact, in light of the extensive plotting we did to map out exit strategies should either of our families have a meltdown, the smoothness with which things were running was unexpected. My mom followed Bonnie's mom around, making sure things were getting done. My brother talked with Bonnie's cousin about machines they had ripped apart and put back together. My groomsmen did their best to put up with Bonnie's Army-proud brother's promises of gutting me should I hurt her. And over it all you could hear my dad's laughter at the recitation of Bonnie's dad's favorite e-mail forwards. Families are so cute when they behave.

I stood on the bridge in the middle of the arboretum—far enough away to watch it all but not participate. There was a cone of silence around me once again, not unlike the one around me before my first start as a rookie in the Show. This was my Big Day, and everyone was giving me my space so I could get into the "I do" zone.

Peering over the railing I stared down at my reflection in the pool below. I was wearing a white tuxedo with a white vest and a white tie. I even wore white Chuck Taylors, special-ordered with the date, Oct 5th, 2008, stitched across the heel. The reflection staring back up at me was a man I didn't know a year ago. He was one with a new life built from his own two hands, and a few lucky breaks. He was a big leaguer, a minor leaguer, afraid, and coura-geous. He was a man with new reasons and new confidence.

"What you looking at?" came a soft voice from behind.

I turned to see Bonnie, walking up the bridge. She was breath-taking in her white dress. Her was hair done up and a pink daisy was tucked behind one ear. She had a pink ribbon wrapped around her waist and tied in the back like a bow, as if she were a gift that was about to be given to me.

"You," I said, staring at her. "You look amazing."

We'd hired photographers to follow us around and do casual shots so we could capture the action as it happened. Presently, they were capturing what could only be described as awe over the woman I would be doing naughty things with come nightfall.

"Do you like the dress?"

"It's perfect."

"You look good, too."

"Thanks, check out my shoes." I turned around so she could see the date-stitched backs.

"Awesome!"

Bonnie came over and kissed me. Cameras clicked to immor-talize it.

"So who are all these people?" asked Bonnie, pointing at the pack of guests watching us from afar.

"That little guy there who looks like a really excited lawn gnome, that's Don. He's one of my old high school coaches. He gets me leads on places to throw in the winter. Next to him, the guy with the thin-rimmed glasses and slicked-back hair, that's Adam, my"—I corrected myself—"*our* agent. That couple next to him, the auburn-haired lady with the warm smile standing next to the dignified gentleman wearing high-water pants, that's Dee and Steve Farber. They were my host parents one year during college summer league. And that foursome your brother is showing his knife to, they are my best men, Josh, Chad, Tim, and Lavern."

"Is that your other grandparents?" Bonnie asked, gesturing to the senior couple who just came in.

"Yep. She's much nicer than the grandma you met. Just don't get her grandma talking about religion or you'll get letters of handwritten King James scripture about why the world is going to hell for not interpreting the Bible correctly."

"Oh no," said Bonnie. "They're talking to my grandparents. My grandma is in the Church of Scientology. You have no idea how many times I've been told that I could heal myself by performing my own miracles. If they find out what the other believes—"

"I got it covered," I said, putting a hand up to stop Bonnie from worrying herself. I whistled at one of my groomsmen. He turned to face me, and I went through a series of signs, not unlike a third base coach would give to a base runner. He nodded, signaled back, and went over to the two elder couples where he cordially broke between them, asking them effusive questions about what they did during the Great Depression and so on.

"How did you do that?" Bonnie looked at me.

"I can't tell the other team my signs," I said. "It's a rule."

"But we're on the same team."

"Not yet, not for at least another half hour. I can't take any chances. I can't be too sure you're not going to back out on me."

"I'm not going anywhere. My parents spent too much on this, they'd kill me."

"Are you sure? This is your last chance to run away and pursue that no-strings-attached life as a rodeo clown you've always wanted."

"There is no place I'd rather be than here. What about you?"

"Hmmm . . ." I looked back into the reflection in the pond. "I've been thinking about that a lot. So much of my life has changed in the last few weeks. Today, things are about to change again. Big changes."

Bonnie took my arm and looked into the water with me.

"I'm not the same man I was when this season started. My reasons for doing things aren't the same. I've learned that the reason a person starts something isn't always the reason they finish it. But"—I looked into Bonnie's anxious brown eyes—"I know the reason I'm going to finish this with you. I know the reason I'm going to push confidently into the future with you. I know why I'll put you before me in happiness and behind me in danger and love you through all of life's imperfections. Because you love me, and that's all the reason I'll ever need."

Bonnie kissed me, sincere, intense, and long enough for the crowd across the way to shout, "You're not married yet!"

"But we'll be soon," said Bonnie, softly, looking only at me. "Are you ready?"

"Honey," I said, "I've been ready all season."

Bonnie and I got married at sunset on an autumn day in front of a small group of friends and family. We cut a cake we made ourselves—I decorated it, complete with two Garfooses kissing on top. We danced our first dance to Al Green's "Let's Stay Together." We kissed when toasted, I gave a speech, and my dad told me he was proud of me. Then, under a shower of rice and flower petals, we ran to Bonnie's car and drove off into a future as bright as we decided to make it.

Chapter Seventy-five

"Last night was amazing," said Bonnie, from the passenger seat, her head resting on my shoulder.

"What can I say, I'm a natural."

"This morning was amazing too." She smiled deviously and leaned over to kiss me as I drove our "Just Married" mobile south through Cincinnati toward our destination—a luxury cabin in Tennessee. The cabin was fully loaded with granite countertops, leather couches, big screens, a hot tub, a pool table, and a whole slew of other things we could use to practice our glorious new discovery of marital consummation on.

"Just think, we can start every day that way from now on, if we want."

"It beats the hell out of Folgers coffee!" said Bonnie.

"Listen to you. I've created a monster!"

"So, now that I'm a big league wife, should I get fake boobs?"

"Normally I'd jump all over a sound investment like that, but considering my less-than-inspiring debut with the big club, we may want to hold off."

"Do you think they'll release you?"

"They could do anything. Designate me, demote me, or release me. Maybe something I've never heard of. I don't know all their options, to be honest. That's why I have Adam."

"The Padres will call you before they do something, right?"

"Nope. I'm bought property. They don't have to ask for my consent. They could have released me right now and I'd be the last to know it."

"Wow."

"Yeah, but it doesn't matter," I said. "This is our time, don't worry about baseball." I reached over and took her hand. I ran my fingers over her ring. "Remember the fight my parents got into the day they first met you?"

"Yes."

"I thought you were going to dump me that day, I really did."

"It was a crazy day"—she squeezed my hand—"but it wasn't the first time I'd seen something like that. Actually, that's the day I think I really knew you were the one."

I glanced curiously at her from the corner of my eye.

"The people in my family aren't perfect, you know," she said.

I snorted in protest. I'd only ever known her parents to be model citizens.

"Yeah, I know my mom and dad seem perfect, but they've had their issues. My dad grew up very similarly to yours. He was around alcohol abuse and violence most of his young life. His parents had issues worse than yours, and he and his brother never got along very well. My mom's mom was abusive. She made my mom feel so terrible about herself it still bothers her to this day. When my parents got married, they wanted to be something different, just like you. That's what I love about you: you want to be your own person and you're willing to endure for it."

"I'm trying," I said. "But I'll never be able to separate myself from what I've come from."

"And I don't think you should try. You know, there is one thing about your family that I really admire," continued Bonnie.

"What's that?"

"They aren't afraid to say what they feel. They may not say it tactfully, but they express it. I think that's one of the reasons they are still together this day, after all they've been through, and I think it's one of the reasons our relationship will work."

I smiled, looking down the road and into the future. We were crossing the border of Cincinnati, heading into Kentucky. The Reds' stadium was disappearing into the background, along with Ohio.

"So, now that it's all said and done, am I still the best thing that's ever happened to you?" asked Bonnie.

I looked over at Bonnie, who was hanging on my response. Among all the other firsts of our married life, this was the first loaded question a husband must answer properly for the sake of his wife.

I stared at her blankly. "Ask me again in a year and I'll let you know."

She slugged me.

"My dad would be proud to see us continuing the fine tradition of family violence."

"You earned that one."

"Of course you're the best thing that's ever happened to me."

Satisfied, Bonnie put away her fists and started to bridge the center console for high-speed smooches, when my phone, sitting in one of the car's cup holders, vibrated from an incoming call. Spare change rattled like jingle bells as it shook, displaying an unknown number.

"Hello?" I answered.

"Hello, Dirk?"

"Yes, this is him."

"Hey, Dirk." He introduced himself as one of the assistant Padre GMs, someone I never knew was in the organization until today. "How are you?"

"I'm fine. I'm on my way to my honeymoon. Just got married yesterday," I said proudly. Then I looked over at Bonnie and mouthed the words, *the Padres.* Her eyes lit up.

"Congratulations!" he said. "Well, I won't take up your time then. I just wanted to call you and let you know we took you off the forty-man roster and designated you for assignment."

"Oh." I took a big breath. "What a great way to start my honeymoon," I said with a halfhearted laugh. "I guess I knew this would happen. Gotta get guys out in the big leagues if you want to stay there, huh?" Bonnie was locked on to me as I spoke. I pointed to myself then sharply pointed downward to fill her on the particulars.

"Well, we felt like you could pitch, and wanted to keep you on the Portland roster. We were hoping you would make the transaction smoothly, but you've been claimed by another team."

"What?" I slowed the car down abruptly. Bonnie white-knuckled her armrest.

"You've been acquired by the Blue Jays."

"I'm not a Padre anymore?"

"Correct. Your contract has been picked up by the Jays."

"Wh-Wh-What do I do now?"

"Someone from the Jays will call you shortly to fill you in."

"Who?"

"The person I talked to was an assistant GM, Alex Anthopoulis."

"I'm sorry, did you say Alex Bartakomous?"

"Anthopolous," he repeated. "He'll call you soon."

"Is there anything else I should do?"

"No, not that I know of."

"Okay. Um." I wasn't sure how to end the call. "Thank you?"

"Thank you, and best of luck in your career. Oh, and enjoy your honeymoon!"

The line went dead, and just like that, my time with the Padres was over. Six years of my life concluded in five minutes via cell phone chatter with a stranger on the highways of Kentucky. All the guys I'd known for so long, all the towns and the teams and the memories—all of it—over, like someone just hit the SELL button on a stock.

Stupefied, I looked over to Bonnie, who was rigid and gasping for details.

"Canada," I said, stunned. "We're going to Canada."

Epilogue

Laughter was brewing in the spring training meeting room as George Poulis, the Toronto Blue Jays big league trainer, shuffled up to the podium in the front. It was his turn on the introductions merry-go-round, and something about what he was going to say had several of the veteran guys snickering like devious school kids. I didn't know George very well yet. I didn't know anyone in the room well yet. It was only my second day with the club, and other than the Jays' affinity for Greeks, I was still getting immersed in the culture, figuring out important things like inside jokes and unexplained giggles.

Of course the guys I was sitting among looked like a ball team, just like the kind you'd find in any other spring training facility this time of year. Just like the kind I left behind in San Diego. There were a few big names, a few small names, and a few no names. We wore Majestic brand pants, tailored to fit us perfectly, complete with a few personal modifications that would assuredly get us fined if this were minor league camp. Free Phiten necklaces coiled around our necks and imbued us with their mystic powers while equally free sponsor-paid shoes of all makes and models housed our precious feet. Dip cans of every flavor were passed around like party favors, and complimentary Red Bulls were slugged with abandon. Some players brought their expensive gloves to the meeting and were still bending the newness out of them. Others talked rapidly about some embarrassing nightlife story, former teammates, or the roads that brought them here. Travis Snider, for example, talked about what he ate last night to the newly acquired former Pirate, Jose Bautista. Ricky Romero compared designer cleats with fellow pitcher Brandon League. Jessie Litsch fell all over himself as Sean Marcum ripped on Jessie Carlson. And then there was the great Roy Halladay, who sat in uninterrupted silence, content to observe.

Along the right side of the meeting room, coaches congregated with front office faces and trainers. They came in after all the players were accounted for and introduced themselves to us in an orderly fashion, stepping out of line long enough to state their names and roles. Dave Steib and Pat Henkin, two legendary Jays pitchers, were in attendance under the guise of guest coaches whom, we were told, "we should all take the opportunity to glean wisdom from." Steib, however, did his best to dispel the prestige of his presence by saying the only reason he kept coming back was the free food.

The coaching staff wore Jays windbreakers or fleece sweatshirts with Jays logos stitched in. Most had on Jays hats, with color-co-ordinated sunglasses resting atop the bill like polarized tiaras. The office personnel wore more professional attire: ties, suits, and the like. The training staff wore their customary khaki, and the meatheads, of course, sported the latest space-age workout shorts with shirts that read, INTENSITY! tucked into them.

As new as spring training for another team in another state in another league was, it all seemed familiar. It was remarkable how similarly the fraternity of baseball players indoctrinated its subjects regardless of the employer. We all spoke the same abrasive, sarcastic, ballplayer language. We all understood the inflection used to mask a compliment in a put-down. We all knew the value and place of service time. Baseball is a unique world, but once you experience it firsthand, there is no mistaking how it operates, and this group of new teammates, sitting around joking and goofing off and treating each other with the highest amount of respect a player can give to another, which is to say, no respect at all, were just like so many teammates I'd known before.

"Tell us about the grapes, George," came a heckle from an older player.

George had just finished introducing himself and his complement of trainers. He did so in an extra respectful and genuine way, which, of course, made him a prime target for us savages, who wanted nothing more than to corrupt him.

"Alright, real quick, guys," said George, getting suddenly serious. "Our goal is to keep you healthy. No lost playing time. That means we don't want guys getting sick by spreading germs. But . . ." George seemed to blush at the topic he was about to explain to us, which made the players quite happy. "I followed a player into the bathroom the other day. He went to use the toilet while I took a leak at the urinal. When I finished up, I went to wash my hands, but he"—George started shaking his head in disgust—"he just shut the stall door and walked out! He didn't wash his hands!

"So I followed him down the hallway, and he turns into the cafeteria and starts eating grapes from the fruit bowl with his bare hands! He's got"—his voice got softer, like he was going to say a bad word—"fecal matter on his hands! Now, that fecal matter is on the grapes. Sure enough, other guys come into the place and are eating his fecal matter! You know how many guys go through the cafeteria eating his fecal matter?" George let the questions hang in the air as if the notion of it should scare us like a fire-and-brimstone sermon.

"Don't eat the grapes, boys. There's shit on the grapes!" someone shouted.

"Why didn't you say something to him, George? You just let the bastard shit on our grapes?"

"It was probably Carlson," came the booming voice of BJ Ryan.

"No way, dude. That's disgusting," protested Carlson, who cringed as BJ slapped a massive paw on his shoulder and shook him like a sapling.

George seemed to shrug off the heckles and disruption. The fact that the story was known by older players suggested this was not as recent a tale as George was making it out be, and I'm sure the heckling wasn't a new thing either. It's amazing what becomes tradition for a team.

"So, you'll notice," continued George, "there are hand sanitizer stations set up all around the facility. There is no excuse not to clean your hands. So, uh, let's just be considerate of one another and we can all stay healthy this year."

George was offered a playfully mocking round of applause for his plea on public health as he walked away from the center of the room.

In George's place, a very powerful individual came to address us, and on his approach the humor subsided. Cito Gaston now stood before us, prepared to give his 2009 inaugural spring training address.

There was a podium at the front of the room that Cito gripped using both hands. He looked up at us casually but did not introduce himself—he was our manager, and that was all we really needed to know.

Cito spoke in easy, relaxed tones about how the team had talent, just as much as any of the other big name, major market, extravagantly compensated clubs we'd be going up against. He said he expected us to hold our own this season, even shine when the opportunity presented itself. He said several other things that make for good, inspirational starts to another year in the grind, but it was the words he used at the end of this talk that stuck with me the most.

"We're here for you, so if you need something extra, you let one of us know. If you want to talk about something, my door is always open, Okay? Even when it's closed, it's open."

We all nodded our heads like diligent students.

"We got a few off days this spring, and we're going to do everything we can to make sure we take them. You guys who have family coming into town and need a day to spend time with them, let me know and we'll try and work something out. I know it's important to spend time with your family during this game. When the game is over, and it's going to be for all of us, they're what you'll have left. So spend the time with them you need to, it's important. You may not see it now, but you will."

As Cito spoke, I looked around the room, scanning the faces of my new family. The Blue Jays wanted me here. In fact, they claimed me because they saw something in me when I thought everyone in baseball could care less. That, and, ironically, because Balsley gave them a glowing recommendation on my potential. Ultimately, the Jays believed I had something worth taking a chance on, and so they brought me to my first big league camp to prove it.

"We work hard here, but we also have a good time." Cito looked around the room at the faces he would construct his next team from. "I look forward to a successful season with you. That's all I have." On that, he released us, and the motley crew of would-be 2009 Blue Jays walked from the room, joking and laughing and talking about fecal matter as we went, ready for another season of chasing dreams and turning them into realities.

Because of contract language and roster changes, I couldn't make the team out of camp that year. My invite was more of an audition than a real chance, but it was one I made the most of. I pitched so well in my first big league camp invite that Cito, after calling me up in May from Triple-A Las Vegas, said to the press that he wished he could have broken camp with me on the team. It was a major league compliment from a major league legend, and I did my best to prove myself worthy of it, going on to post a 2.78 ERA in my half season of big league service time as a Jay. Sure, a half a season didn't make me an All-Star, or an icon, or get my jersey retired. But it did let me provide a home for Bonnie, buy a car for my parents, and grant me the confidence to believe that I was no longer out of my league.